Microsoft PowerPoint 97 Ex~~ Skills Roadmap

Skill Area	Required Task	
Creating Presentations	Create from a template	1
	Create from an existing presentation	1
	Delete slides	3
Adding Textual Information	Enter text in a slide and outline view	2
	Enter bulleted information	4
	Change the text alignment	5
Adding Visual Elements	Add formatting	11
	Build a graph	10
	Draw an object	14
	Rotate and fill an object	15
	Scale and size an object	15
	Add a table	13
	Add shapes	14
	Animate objects	24
	Add transitions	24
	Add an organizational chart	12
	Set custom options	10
	Check styles	14
Importing and exporting data	Add clip art	16
	Insert a Microsoft Excel chart	18
	Import text from Microsoft Word	18
	Add scanned images	16
	Add sound and movies	16
	Export an outline to Word	18
Modifying presentations	Change the sequence of a slide	7
	Find and replace text	8
	Modify the slide master	19

201 W. 103rd Street, Indianapolis, IN 46290 (317) 581-3500
Copyright© 1997 by Que® Corporation.

Microsoft PowerPoint 97 Expert User Skills Roadmap

Skill Area	Required Task	Lessons
Modifying presentations	Modify sequence in outline mode	7
	Change tabs	6
	Change fonts	6
	Change the alignment of text	6
Editing presentations	Using the spelling checker	9
	Add speaker notes	22
	Set automatic slide timing	25
Customizing presentations	Create a custom background	20
	Customize a color scheme	20
	Customize clip art and other objects	17
	Recolor and edit objects	17
	Apply a template from another presentation	21
	Add links to other slides within the presentation	26
	Hide slides	7, 26
Delivering presentations	Start a slide show from any slide	23
	Use on-screen navigation tools	23
	Generate meeting notes	27
	Incorporate meeting feedback electronically	27
	Print slides in a variety of formats	29
	Print color presentations	29
	Export to overhead	29
	Export to 35mm slides	29
	Deliver through Presentation Conferencing	28
	Save a presentation to use on another computer	23
	Save a presentation to deliver over the Internet	30

Microsoft Office
User Specialist:

PowerPoint 97
Exam Guide

By Jane Calabria and Dorothy Burke

A Division of Macmillan Computer Publishing
201 West 103rd Street   Indianapolis, IN 46290 USA

Certified Microsoft Office User:
PowerPoint 97 Exam Guide

©1997 Que Corporation

Library of Congress Catalog Card Number: 97-80542

International Standard Book Number: 0-7897-1289-x

99 98 97   8 7 6 5 4 3 2 1

Interpretation of the printing code: The rightmost double-digit number is the year of the book's first printing; the rightmost single-digit number is the number of the book's printing. For example, a printing code of 97-1 shows that this copy of the book was printed during the first printing of the book in 1997.

Printed in the United States of America

Publisher
David Dwyer

Executive Editors
Mary Foote
Brad Koch

Director of Editorial Services
Carla Hall

Managing Editor
Thomas Hayes

Acquisitions Editor
Nancy Maragioglio

Development Editor
Kezia Endsley

Technical Editor
Michael D. Wykoff

Production Editor
Brian Sweany

Book Designer
Glenn Larsen

Cover Designer
Dan Armstrong

Production Supervisor
Andrew Stone

Production Team
Jack Belbot
Brad Lenser
Chris Livengood

Indexer
Tim Tate

About the Authors

Jane Calabria has authored or contributed to no fewer than 12 Que books, which include *Microsoft Windows 95 6 in 1*, *Microsoft Works 6 in 1*, and *Professional Developers Guide to Domino 4.5*. She has been an independent consultant since 1990 and used her first computer in 1981—a hand-held 16K Radio Shack special. She became hooked on that little computer when, within a week, she was teaching herself Basic and writing programs. Since 1992 she has been training, consulting, and developing applications. Jane teaches Windows, Windows NT, a variety of databases, desktop applications, electronic mail, and the Internet. As consultants and trainers, Jane and her husband, Rob Kirkland, write about, teach and conduct seminars nationally on operating systems and Lotus Notes. Jane is heard weekly in the Philadelphia area on KYW News Radio 1060 AM, giving reports on computing and computer news as "JC on PCs." Her reports are also found on AOL. She can be reached at **74754.3360@compuserve.com**.

Dorothy Burke started her professional life as a technical magazine editor. She has been an independent consultant and trainer for many years. She has contributed to several Que books, including *Special Edition, Using PowerPoint, Microsoft Windows NT Workstation 4.0 6 in 1*, and *Ten Minute Guide to Lotus Notes Mail 4.5*. As a trainer, Dorothy teaches desktop publishing, operating systems, spreadsheets, and word processing and graphics programs, as well as Lotus Notes and Domino. As a consultant, Dorothy works with Lotus Notes and Domino, developing applications. Dorothy can be reached at **70161.364@compuserve.com**.

Jane and Dorothy have teamed up successfully on several Que books. Both are certified in several products including Lotus Notes and Domino, and travel the United States teaching and consulting.

Trademarks

All terms mentioned in this book that are known to be trademarks have been appropriately capitalized. Que cannot attest to the accuracy of this information. Use of a term in this book should not be regarded as affecting the validity of any trademark or service mark.

Dedication

To Microsoft, for allowing the end user to measure and prove their valuable skills sets.

Acknowledgments

Thanks to Nancy Maragioglio for presenting this opportunity to us, and to Brad Koch for keeping us very busy this year! The Microsoft end user certification is a very exciting area for us and we are thrilled to be a part of this project.

Thanks to our dedicated crew at Macmillan Computer Publishing. A special thanks to the editorial team on this Exam Guide—Kezia Endsley, Michael Wykoff, and Brian Sweany.

Contents at a Glance

Introduction 1

1   **Creating a Presentation** 5

2   **Working with Slides in Different Views** 19

3   **Adding and Deleting Slides** 29

4   **Creating Bulleted Lists** 39

5   **Adding Text to a Slide** 49

6   **Changing the Look of Your Text** 61

7   **Rearranging Slides in a Presentation** 71

8   **Finding and Replacing Text** 79

9   **Checking Spelling** 85

10   **Adding a Graph to a Slide** 93

11   **Enhancing a Graph** 103

12   **Adding An Organizational Chart** 121

13   **Creating a Table** 131

14   **Drawing Objects on a Slide** 147

15   **Positioning and Sizing Objects** 159

16   **Adding Pictures, Sounds, and Movies** 173

17   **Editing Objects** 181

18   **Importing and Exporting Data** 191

19   **Changing a Presentation's Look** 199

20   **Working with Presentation Colors and Backgrounds** 207

21   **Creating a Template** 215

22   **Creating Speaker's Notes** 221

23   **Viewing a Slide Show** 229

24   **Transitions and Animation** 241

25   **Working with Slide Timings** 251

26   **Customizing Slide Shows** 257

27   **Taking Notes During a Slide Show** 263

28   **Presentation Conferencing** 271

29   **Printing Presentations, Notes, and Handouts** 279

30   **Using PowerPoint Presentations on the Internet** 289

Appendix A   Glossary 299

Appendix B   Student Preparation Guide 305

Index 311

Table of Contents

Introduction 1

    Who Should Use This Book 1

    Why *This* Book? 2

    How This Book Is Organized 2

    Conventions Used in This Book 3

1   Creating a Presentation 5

    Starting a New Presentation 6

        Creating Presentations with the AutoContent Wizard 7

        Creating Presentations from a Template 10

        Creating Presentations from a Blank Presentation 12

        Creating Presentations from an Existing Presentation 13

    Saving Your Presentation 14

    Review Questions 16

    Review Question Answers 16

    Practice Lab 17

        Create from a Template 17

        Create from an Existing Presentation 17

2   Working with Slides in Different Views 19

    Changing Views 20

    Moving from Slide to Slide 21

    Using the Slide Miniature Window 22

    Editing Text in a Slide and Outline View 23

        Entering and Editing Text in Outline View 23

        Changing the Text's Outline Level 24

        Moving Paragraphs in Outline View 25

        Entering and Editing Text in Slide View 25

    Review Questions 27

    Review Question Answers 27

    Practice Lab 27

        Enter Text in a Slide and Outline View 28

3   Adding and Deleting Slides **29**

Inserting a Slide 30

Adding Slides from Another Presentation 31

Creating Slides from a Document Outline 33

Selecting Slides 34

Deleting Slides 35

Cutting, Copying, and Pasting Slides 35

Review Questions 37

Review Question Answers 37

Practice Lab 37

    Delete Slides 38

4   Creating Bulleted Lists **39**

Entering Bulleted Information 40

Changing the Bullet Character 40

Promoting and Demoting Bulleted Paragraphs 42

Adjusting the Indents 43

Using the Text Anchor 44

Review Questions 46

Review Question Answers 46

Practice Lab 47

    Enter Bulleted Information 47

5   Adding Text to a Slide **49**

Creating a Text Box 50

Selecting, Deleting, Sizing, and Moving a Text Box 51

Editing Text in a Text Box 52

Changing the Text Alignment 52

Adjusting the Line Spacing 53

Using WordArt to Manipulate Text 55

Review Questions 58

Review Question Answers 58

Practice Lab 59

    Change the Text Alignment 59

6   Changing the Look of Your Text **61**

   Changing Fonts 62

      Changing Fonts from a Dialog Box 62

      Changing Fonts with the Formatting Toolbar 63

      Changing the Font Color with the Drawing Toolbar 65

   Copying Text Formats 65

   Changing Tabs 65

   Changing the Alignment of Text 67

   Review Questions 68

   Review Question Answers 68

   Practice Lab 69

      Change Fonts 69

      Change Tabs 69

      Change the Alignment of Text 69

7   Rearranging Slides in a Presentation **71**

   Changing the Sequence of a Slide 72

   Modifying Sequence in Outline Mode 73

   Hiding Slides 74

   Review Questions 76

   Review Question Answers 76

   Practice Lab 76

      Change the Sequence of a Slide 77

      Modify Sequence in Outline Mode 77

8   Finding and Replacing Text **79**

   Finding and Replacing Text 80

      Finding Text 80

      Replacing Text 81

   Review Questions 83

   Review Question Answers 83

   Practice Lab 83

      Find and Replace Text 83

9 Checking Spelling **85**

Using the Spelling Checker 86

    Checking as You Type 86

    Checking the Entire Presentation 86

Using AutoCorrect 88

Review Questions 90

Review Question Answers 90

Practice Lab 91

    Using the Spelling Checker 91

10 Adding a Graph to a Slide **93**

Building a Graph 94

Editing the Datasheet 96

Changing the Data Series 98

Changing the Chart Type 98

Setting Custom Options—Applying Custom Chart Types 100

Review Questions 101

Review Question Answers 101

Practice Lab 102

    Build a Graph 102

11 Enhancing a Graph **103**

What Can You Add to a Chart? 104

Displaying the Chart in Microsoft Graph 105

Parts of a Chart 105

Adding Titles 106

Adding Formatting 107

    Formatting Text on a Chart 107

    Formatting the Axes 109

    Adding Borders and Shading to Your Chart 112

    Placing the Legend 112

    Setting the Gridline Style 113

    Changing the Look of 3-D Charts 114

    Choosing Colors and Patterns 115

Exploding (Cutting) a Pie Slice 116

Adding Data Labels 116

Using a Data Table 117

Review Questions 119

Review Question Answers 119

Practice Lab 120

    Add Formatting 120

12   Adding an Organizational Chart 121

Creating an Organizational Chart 122

Editing an Organizational Chart 124

    Selecting One or More Levels 125

    Moving and Deleting Boxes 125

    Selecting a Chart Style 126

    Formatting the Text 126

    Changing the Look of Boxes and Lines 127

Review Questions 128

Review Question Answers 128

Practice Lab 128

    Add an Organizational Chart 128

13   Creating a Table 131

Adding a Table 132

Working in a Table 133

Revising a Table 134

    Deleting and Inserting Cells, Rows, and Columns 135

    Moving or Copying Columns and Rows 136

Adding Borders and Shading to a Table 137

Automatic Table Formatting 139

Rotating Text in a Table 140

Modifying Table Structure 140

    Changing Column Width 141

    Changing Row Height 142

    Merging and Splitting Cells 144

Review Questions 145

Review Question Answers 145

Practice Lab 146

    Add a Table 146

14   Drawing Objects on a Slide 147

PowerPoint's Drawing Tools 148

Drawing an Object 150

Adding Shapes 150

Adding Text to an Object 151

Tips for Working with Objects 153

Checking Styles 153

Review Questions 156

Review Question Answers 156

Practice Lab 156

    Add Shapes 157

    Draw an Object 157

    Check Styles 157

15   Positioning and Sizing Objects 159

Selecting Objects 160

Working with Layers of Objects 161

Grouping and Ungrouping Objects 162

Cutting, Copying, and Pasting Objects 162

Duplicating and Aligning Objects 163

Scaling and Sizing Objects 164

Rotating and Filling Objects 165

    Rotating an Object 165

    Filling an Object 166

Selecting Line Attributes 168

Cropping a Picture 169

Review Questions 171

Review Question Answers 171

Practice Lab 171

    Rotate and Fill an Object 172

    Scale and Size an Object 172

16   Adding Pictures, Sounds, and Movies 173

Introducing the Clip Gallery 174

Adding Clip Art 175

Adding Scanned Images 175

Adding Sounds and Movies 176

Making Movies and Sounds Play Automatically 177

Review Questions 179

Review Question Answers 179

Practice Lab 179

    Add Clip Art 180

    Add Scanned Images 180

    Add Sound and Movies 180

17   Editing Objects 181

Recoloring and Editing Objects 182

    Creating and Editing Freeform Objects 182

    Recoloring Objects 184

Customizing Clip Art and Other Objects 185

Review Questions 188

Review Question Answers 188

Practice Lab 189

    Recolor and Edit Objects 189

    Customize Clip Art and Other Objects 189

18   Importing and Exporting Data 191

Inserting a Microsoft Excel Chart 192

Importing Text from Microsoft Word 193

    Importing Text into a Slide 193

    Importing Text into a PowerPoint Outline 195

Exporting an Outline to Word 196

Review Questions 197

Review Question Answers 197

Practice Lab 198

    Insert a Microsoft Excel Chart 198

    Import Text from Microsoft Word 198

    Export an Outline to Word 198

19 Changing a Presentation's Look **199**

Giving Your Slides a Professional Look 200

Applying a Presentation Design Template 200

Using AutoLayouts 201

Modifying the Slide Master 202

Review Questions 204

Review Question Answers 204

Practice Lab 204

Modify the Slide Master 205

20 Working with Presentation Colors and Backgrounds **207**

Understanding Color Schemes and Backgrounds 208

Selecting a Color Scheme 208

Customizing a Color Scheme 209

Copying a Slide's Color Scheme to Another Slide 211

Creating a Custom Background 211

Review Questions 213

Review Question Answers 213

Practice Lab 214

Customize a Color Scheme 214

Create a Custom Background 214

21 Creating a Template **215**

Saving Your Presentation as a Template 216

Applying a Template from Another Presentation 217

Review Questions 219

Review Question Answers 219

Practice Lab 219

Apply a Template from Another Presentation 219

22 Creating Speaker's Notes **221**

Understanding Speaker's Notes 222

Adding Speaker's Notes 222

Changing the Size of the Slide and Text Box 223

Working with the Notes Master 224

Review Questions 226

Review Question Answers 226

Practice Lab 226

    Add Speaker's Notes 227

23 Viewing a Slide Show 229

Starting a Slide Show from Any Slide 230

Using On-Screen Navigation Tools 230

Setting Slide Show Options 232

Adding Action Buttons on Slides 234

Saving a Presentation to Use on Another Computer 236

Review Questions 238

Review Question Answers 238

Practice Lab 239

    Start a Slide Show from Any Slide 239

    Use On-Screen Navigation Tools 239

    Save a Presentation to Use on Another Computer 239

24 Transitions and Animation 241

Adding Transitions 242

Animating Objects 244

    Animating the Text on a Slide 244

    Using Custom Animation 245

    Using Other Animation Options 246

Review Questions 248

Review Question Answers 248

Practice Lab 249

    Add Transitions 249

    Animate Objects 249

25 Working with Slide Timings 251

Setting Automatic Slide Timing 252

    Setting the Slide Timings Manually 252

    Setting the Slide Timings as You Rehearse 253

Viewing Rehearsed Timings During a Slide Show 254

Review Questions 255

Review Question Answers 255

Practice Lab 256

    Set Automatic Slide Timing 256

26 Customizing Slide Shows 257

Adding Links to Other Slides Within the Presentation 258

Hiding Slides 260

Review Questions 261

Review Question Answers 261

Practice Lab 261

    Add Links to Other Slides Within the Presentation 262

    Hide Slides 262

27 Taking Notes During a Slide Show 263

Annotating Slides 264

Generating Meeting Notes 265

Incorporating Meeting Feedback Electronically 267

Review Questions 268

Review Question Answers 268

Practice Lab 269

    Generate Meeting Notes 269

    Incorporate Meeting Feedback Electronically 269

28 Presentation Conferencing 271

Delivering Through Presentation Conferencing 272

Preparing for a Presentation Conference 272

Conducting a Presentation Conference 274

Participating in a Presentation Conference 275

Review Questions 276

Review Question Answers 276

Practice Lab 277

    Delivery through Presentation Conferencing 277

29 Printing Presentations, Notes, and Handouts **279**

   Printing Color Presentations 280

   Printing Slides in a Variety of Formats 280

   Printing in Black and White 282

   Exporting to Overheads 282

   Exporting to 35mm Slides 285

   Review Questions 286

   Review Question Answers 286

   Practice Lab 287

      Print Slides in a Variety of Formats 287

      Print Color Presentations 287

      Export to Overheads 287

      Export to 35mm Slides 287

30 Using PowerPoint Presentations on the Internet **289**

   Using Web Presentation Designs 290

      Using PowerPoint's Presentation Templates for the Web....................... 291

   Adding URL Hyperlinks 292

   Saving a Presentation to Deliver over the Internet.................................... 293

   Review Questions 296

   Review Question Answers 296

   Practice Lab 296

      Save a Presentation to Deliver over the Internet 297

Appendix A   Glossary **299**

Appendix B   Student Preparation Guide **305**

   Studying for the Tests... 306

   Levels of Certification 306

   Required Tasks 306

      Expert User... 307

   Registering for the Exams.. 309

   Taking the Tests 309

Index **311**

INTRODUCTION

Congratulations on your decision to become a Certified Microsoft Office User! This is your opportunity to present to the world your qualifications as an expert user of Microsoft Office products.

The *Microsoft Office User Specialist PowerPoint 97 Exam Guide* is your ticket to certification success! Using this guide, you can review tasks that are included in your certification test and prepare yourself for the Microsoft PowerPoint 97 Expert Exam. Here you will find tutorials that step you through tasks, review questions and practice labs. All that you need to learn, study and prepare for your PowerPoint exam can be found in the *Microsoft PowerPoint 97 Exam Guide*.

Who Should Use This Book

The *Microsoft Office User Specialist PowerPoint 97 Exam Guide* is for anyone who:

▶ Wants to expand his or her PowerPoint 97 skills.

▶ Is seeking certification in Microsoft PowerPoint 97.

▶ Wants to learn or reference tasks in short, concise lessons.

▶ Is an instructor or trainer preparing groups of people for the Microsoft PowerPoint 97 Expert Exam.

Why *This* Book?

The tools and information you need to prepare for your certification tests are presented to you in a reasonable and concise method. The authors are experienced trainers and consultants, having taught computer applications, operating systems, hardware, networking, and programming classes for many years. As consultants they have worked with companies all over the country providing systems, software, and education solutions.

The *Microsoft PowerPoint 97 Exam Guide* includes tutorials, review summaries, and practice labs. Required tasks for passing the Certification exam are covered not once, but three times. Tasks are presented first in tutorial format, using Que's proven step-by-step format. Tasks are then reviewed through a series of questions (yes, the answers are provided). Finally, skills are reinforced through practice labs provided in each lesson.

How This Book Is Organized

Microsoft PowerPoint 97 Exam Guide contains:

▶ **Lessons** You can work through the book lesson by lesson, building upon your skills, or you can use the book as a quick reference when you want to perform a new task or practice for the exams. Organized by Skills Area (according to the Certified Microsoft Office User exam), each lesson first identifies the Skill Area and the Required Tasks for that Skill Area that are covered in the lesson. Each lesson contains:

   ▶ **Tutorials** Step-by-step instructions to complete Required Tasks for Skills Areas identified in the Certified Microsoft Office User exams.

   ▶ **Review Questions** Thought-provoking questions and answers built to reinforce how a task is performed and alternate methods to completing tasks.

   ▶ **Practice Labs** Exercises that apply tasks in a "real life" situation without the aid of step-by-step instruction. This is your chance to test yourself in the Required Tasks and Skills Areas.

   ▶ **Instructor Tips** Productivity or study tips, "inside" information on using PowerPoint 97, and real-life experiences from the authors/instructors help you in your quest to master PowerPoint.

   ▶ **Warnings** Tips on techniques that might give you trouble and suggestions for how to use the technique safely.

▶ **Tear Card**   The Microsoft Office User Proficiency Guidelines mapped to the contents of the book, to assist you in quickly locating Required Tasks and Skill Areas.

▶ **Students Appendix: Your Roadmap to Success!**   Information on how to prepare for exams, what to expect during the exam process, and how to sign up for an exam.

▶ **Glossary**   List of terms and definitions found throughout the book and in the software and/or exams.

▶ **Bonus CD-ROM**   The CD contains files to use with the Practice Labs as well as Instructor files that consist of PowerPoint 97 customizable presentations. Combined with the Microsoft Excel 97 PowerPoint Guide as the class handout, these slides are the perfect tool for instructor-led exam preparation.

Conventions Used in This Book

Commands, directions, and explanations in this book are presented in the clearest format possible:

▶ Titles of windows and dialog boxes are capitalized to distinguish them from regular text. For example, the Custom Conventions box refers to an onscreen box whose title bar reads "Custom Conventions".

▶ A series of menu selections that you must click will be separated by commas. For instance, Select **Start**, **Programs**, **PowerPoint** means that you click the Start button, the Programs menu choice and then the PowerPoint option.

▶ As a further help, commands you are directed to type will also be in **bold** type so you can see them clearly.

▶ You might also be directed to hold down several keys simultaneously, as in the command Press **Ctrl+F2**. The two keys that you press will be connected with the plus sign (+).

Some information is offset in sidebars to draw your attention.

 Required Tasks   Identify the Required Tasks for each Skill Area.

Instructor Tips   Provide timesaving shortcuts and workarounds and insider information on learning and applying new skills.

 Warnings   These warn you of situations that can land you in trouble.

 Term Tips   Provide concise definitions for both PowerPoint and general application technology.

Creating a Presentation

This lesson covers two of the three Required Tasks for the "Creating Presentations" Skill Area.

In this lesson, you learn the following Required Tasks for your exam:

► Create from a template

► Create from an existing presentation

For a complete list of Required Tasks for the Skill Area "Creating Presentations," refer to the User Skills Roadmap.

Starting a New Presentation

PowerPoint offers several ways to create a new presentation. Before you begin, you need to decide which method is right for you:

▶ **AutoContent Wizard** walks you through each step of creating a new presentation by asking you a series of questions about the purpose of the presentation, the style you want to use, how you want the handouts to appear, what media you're going to use to output your presentation, and so on. The resulting presentation contains sample text that you replace with your own.

▶ A **template** offers a standardized group of slides, all with a similar look and feel, with blank placeholders for you to insert text, graphs, and clip art.

▶ The **blank presentation** lets you start your presentation from scratch. It has a blank background and minimal formatting. Although you can use the blank presentation to prepare a one-page diagram or chart that won't be part of a presentation, a blank presentation is usually where you start when you want to create your own template. This method isn't recommended for beginners.

 Wizard A wizard is a feature that automates an operation and helps you perform that operation. It displays a series of dialog boxes that ask you design and content questions. You select options and type text. When you are done, the wizard creates something (in this case, a presentation) according to your instructions.

 Template A template is a set of related slide designs included with PowerPoint. When you select a template, PowerPoint applies the color scheme and general layout of the template to each slide in the presentation.

When you start PowerPoint (**Start**, **Programs**, **Microsoft PowerPoint**), the PowerPoint dialog box appears (see Figure 1.1). From this dialog box, you choose how you want to start your presentation. Choose **AutoContent Wizard**, **Template**, or **Blank Presentation** and then click **OK**.

Figure 1.1

Select the method you want to use to create your presentation.

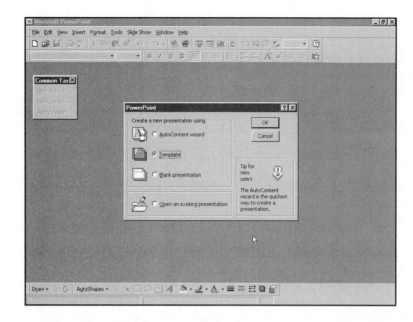

The PowerPoint dialog box appears only when you first start the program. After you close this dialog box it won't appear until the next time you start the PowerPoint program. However, if you choose **File**, **New** from the menu, you still open the New Presentation dialog box, as explained in the following sections of this lesson.

Creating Presentations with the AutoContent Wizard

Using the AutoContent Wizard, you select the type of presentation you want to create (strategy, training, reporting, conveying bad news, and so on) and PowerPoint creates an outline for the presentation. Follow these steps to use the AutoContent Wizard:

1. If you have the PowerPoint dialog box open (refer to Figure 1.1) because you've just started your PowerPoint program, select **AutoContent Wizard** and click **OK**.

    If you already have the program open and are starting a new presentation, choose **File**, **New** from the menu. The New Presentation dialog box appears. Select the **Presentations** tab (see Figure 1.2) and then double-click the **AutoContent Wizard** icon.

Figure 1.2

To start the AutoContent Wizard, select the Presentations tab and then double-click Auto-Content Wizard.

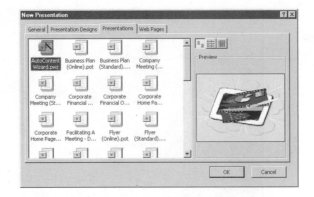

2. The AutoContent Wizard dialog box appears. Click **Next** to continue, or **Cancel** to close the dialog box without starting the presentation.

3. In this step, the AutoContent Wizard asks you to select the type of presentation you want to create (see Figure 1.3). Click one of the category buttons, such as **Corporate** or **Sales/Marketing**, that best represents the type of presentation you're planning to give. Then, select a type from the list on the right that further specifies your presentation's purpose—for example, **Financial Overview** from the **Corporate** category or **Marketing Plan** from the **Sales/Marketing** category. Click **Next** to continue (click **Back** to go back to the previous dialog box).

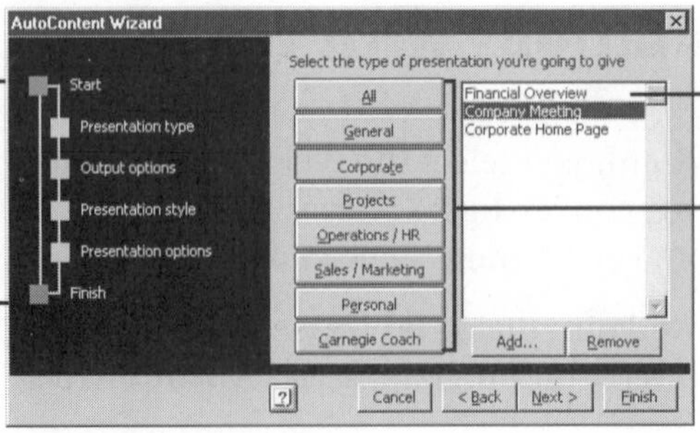

Figure 1.3

Select the category and the type of presentation you want to create.

4. Select the type of output you're planning for this presentation—in other words, how you're planning to share this information with your audience. Select **Presentations, Informal Meetings, Handouts** if the presentation will have a live narrator controlling the action; or select **Internet, Kiosk** to create a self-running presentation that doesn't require a narrator. Click **Next**.

5. If you selected **Presentations**, **Informal Meetings**, **Handouts**, the next screen asks you to select the type of output you want to use when giving the presentation (see Figure 1.4). Select **On-Screen Presentation** (projected from the computer monitor), **Black and White Overheads**, **Color Overheads**, or **35mm Slides**. You must also indicate whether you intend to print handouts to accompany the presentation by selecting **Yes** or **No**. Click **Next**.

Figure 1.4

Choose the type of output you want to use when giving your presentation.

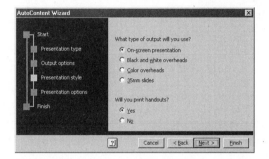

If you selected **Internet**, **Kiosk**, the next screen asks you what items you want to appear on each Web page: **Copyright Notice on Each Page**, **Date Last Updated**, and/or **E-Mail Address**. Select the items you want. If you elected to add the copyright information, you must enter the copyright information you want on each page in the box below the option. Likewise, if you chose to add the e-mail address, you must enter that address in the box below the option (see Figure 1.5). Click **Next**.

Figure 1.5

Select which items you want to appear on each Web page and then enter the copyright and e-mail address if necessary.

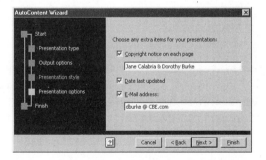

6. If you chose **Presentations**, **Informal Meetings**, **Handouts** as your output, then select what you want to appear on your title slide: **Presentation Title**, **Your Name**, and/or **Additional Information** (see Figure 1.6). Click **Next**.

Figure 1.6

Enter the information you want to appear on the title slide for your presentation.

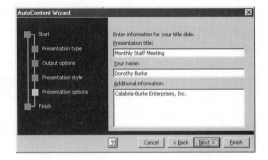

7. Now that the AutoContent Wizard has all the answers it needs to complete the presentation, click **Finish**.

  Make Sure You're Finished   As long as you haven't clicked **Finish**, you can always click **Back** to return to previous screens in the Wizard and make changes. After you click **Finish**, however, there's no turning back—you will have to work with the presentation to customize it, which takes more steps and time.

The beginnings of your presentation appear in the PowerPoint Outline view with sample text in place. To enter your own text, select the sample text and type over it. You'll learn more about the Outline view and how to enter text in your presentation in Lesson 2, "Working with Slides in Different Views."

Creating Presentations from a Template

PowerPoint offers two types of templates for creating presentations:

▶   **Presentation Templates**   These templates provide a color scheme for slides and a basic outline for slide text. Their names reflect the purpose of the presentation, such as "Communicating Bad News." The AutoContent Wizard uses these same templates when helping you prepare a presentation.

▶   **Presentation Design Templates**   These templates offer only a color scheme and a "look" for slides, such as "Dad's Tie," which has a striped-tie motif on the left side of the slide. You must provide your own content for each slide.

To start a new presentation using a template, follow these steps:

1. If you've just started the PowerPoint program, select **Template** from the PowerPoint dialog box and click **OK**. The New Presentation dialog box appears with the **Presentation Designs** tab automatically selected (see Figure 1.7).

Figure 1.7

Click a presentation design icon and see a preview of how a slide will look using that design.

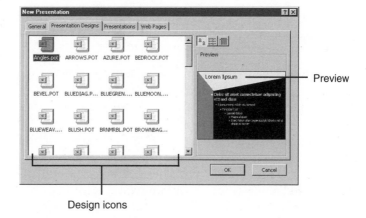

If you've been working in PowerPoint and want to start a new presentation, choose **File**, **New** from the menu. When the New Presentation dialog box appears, select the **Presentation Designs** tab (refer to Figure 1.7).

2. Select a design for your presentation by clicking the appropriate icon. A preview of the design appears on the right side of the dialog box.

 Use Sample Text to Build Presentations You might want to use sample text as a basis for your presentation. When the New Presentation dialog box is open, select the **Presentations** tab. Select the icon for the type of presentation you want to make and then click **OK**. The presentation opens in the Outline view with sample text there to help guide you in preparing the presentation. Select the sample text and type your text over it. You'll learn more about entering text in Lesson 2.

3. Click **OK**. The New Slide dialog box appears (see Figure 1.8).

Figure 1.8

Select the layout of the first slide of your presentation. Choose Blank to design your own layout.

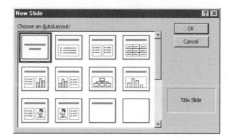

4. Each template has a set of AutoLayouts that contains predefined layouts of different types of slides—title, bulleted list, graph, organization chart, and so on. The AutoLayouts have placeholders for entering text, placing graphs, or holding clip art. Select the AutoLayout you want to use for the first slide of your presentation (it's recommended that you start with the **Title Slide** layout) and then click **OK**.

5. The first slide of your presentation appears. The slide has several boxes on it called *placeholders*. Follow the instructions and click in the text boxes to enter your text there (you'll learn more about this in Lesson 2).

Templates provide you with a unifying "look" for your presentation and give you "fill in the blanks" ease by providing predesigned pages with placeholders for you to pop in text, artwork, or charts. You don't have to be a designer to come up with a great looking presentation. Use Standard templates for presentations you want to print on paper, or as overheads or 35mm slides or for projection; and use Online templates for presentations you want to put on the Web or a kiosk.

Creating Presentations from a Blank Presentation

Starting with the blank presentation is not recommended for beginners because there is minimal formatting and no color scheme in place. However, you may need a blank background to print a few graphs for a report or signs for the bulletin board. More experienced users can work with the blank presentation to help create custom presentations or templates.

To start a blank presentation, follow these steps:

1. If you've just started the PowerPoint program, select **Blank Presentation** from the PowerPoint dialog box (refer to Figure 1.1) and click **OK**. The New Slide dialog box appears (refer to Figure 1.8).

   If you were already using PowerPoint and want to start a new presentation, choose **File**, **New** from the menu. When the New Presentation dialog box appears (refer to Figure 1.7), select the **General** tab. Then double-click the **Blank Presentation** icon. The New Slide dialog box appears, as shown in Figure 1.8.

  Quick Start   To quickly start a blank presentation, click the **New** button on the Standard toolbar. The New Slide dialog box opens.

2. Select the AutoLayout you want to use to set up your first slide and click **OK**.

In Lesson 20, "Working with Presentation Colors and Backgrounds," you learn about applying color schemes and backgrounds to your slides. You also learn about customizing the slide master. Using those skills you can create your own look. In Lesson 21, "Creating a Template," you learn to save your presentation as a template that you can use as the basis for creating other presentations.

Creating Presentations from an Existing Presentation

To use an existing presentation as the basis for a new presentation, follow these steps:

1. If you just started PowerPoint, select **Open an Existing Presentation** from the PowerPoint dialog box. Then click **OK**.

 If PowerPoint is already running, choose **File**, **Open** from the menu or click the **Open** button on the Standard toolbar.

2. The Open dialog box appears. If you need to specify a different drive or folder where you have the file stored, select the appropriate one from the **Look In** drop-down list.

3. Select the name of the file from the list or enter it in the **File Name** box.

4. Click **Open**.

5. Choose **File**, **Save As** from the menu to open the Save As dialog box (see Figure 1.9). Enter a different name in the **File Name** box and click **Save**. By doing this early, before you make any changes, you avoid accidentally saving the file with the original name and obliterating the original file.

6. Once the file is open, delete or add slides (see Lesson 3 for instructions) and replace text as needed (see Lesson 2 to learn how to enter text).

7. To save the file once it's complete or to update it as you go along, choose **File**, **Save** from the menu, press **Ctrl+S**, or click the **Save** button on the toolbar.

> **Make a Template Instead** If you keep using the same existing presentation to start new presentations, save yourself some time and save the existing presentation as a template. See Lesson 21 to learn how.

Figure 1.9

Enter a new name for the file so you don't overwrite the original presentation when you save it.

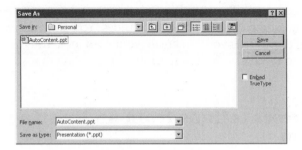

Saving Your Presentation

Soon after creating your presentation, you should save it on disk to protect the work you have done.

To save a presentation the first time, do the following:

1. Choose **File**, **Save** from the menu, or click the **Save** button on the Standard toolbar, or press **Ctrl+S**. The Save dialog box appears (see Figure 1.10).

Figure 1.10

Type the name of the presentation file in the File Name box and then click Save.

2. In the **File Name** text box, type the name you want to assign to the presentation. The name can be up to 255 characters long and can include spaces. However, file names cannot include any of the following characters: forward slash (/), backslash (\), greater than sign (>), less than sign (<), asterisk (*),question mark (?), quotation mark ("), pipe symbol (|), or colon (:). To make it easier to find the file later, make the filename short and descriptive. You don't need to add the file extension .PPT because PowerPoint automatically does that for you.

3. From the **Save In** drop-down list, select the drive or folder in which you want to store the file.

4. Click **Save**. The name of the file appears on the title bar of the presentation window.

To update the file after you've made changes, choose **File**, **Save** from the menu, or click the **Save** button on the menu, or press **Ctrl+S**.

When you're finished with the file, choose **File**, **Close** from the menu to close the file. If you haven't saved your changes, PowerPoint will ask if you want to save before closing. Select **Yes** to save the file, **No** to close without saving, or **Cancel** to close the dialog box but leave the file open.

Review Questions

1. True or False: Presentation Templates contain a basic outline to help you in developing the presentation contents.

2. True or False: The AutoContent Wizard uses templates.

3. How do you create a new presentation?

4. What is a template?

5. True or False: AutoContent Wizard walks you through each step of creating a new presentation by directing you to open existing presentations and modify them for your purposes.

Review Question Answers

1. True. Presentation Templates offer a color scheme, layout, and suggested outline. Presentation *Design* Templates offer design only. For more information, refer to "Creating Presentations from a Template."

2. True. The AutoContent Wizard walks you through each step of creating a new presentation by asking you a series of questions. The resulting presentation contains sample text in templates. For more information, refer to "Creating Presentations with the AutoContent Wizard."

3. There are three ways to create a new presentation:

   ▶ Start the AutoContent Wizard by selecting **File**, **New** from the menu. On the Presentations tab, double-click the **AutoContent Wizard** icon.

   ▶ Use a template by choosing **File**, **New** from the menu and select a template from the **Presentations Design** tab.

   ▶ Create a blank presentation by choosing **File**, **New** from the menu and selecting **Blank Presentation** from the **General** tab.

   For more information, refer to "Starting a New Presentation."

4. A template is a set of related slide designs that comes with PowerPoint. When you select a template, PowerPoint applies the color scheme and general layout of the template to each slide in the presentation. For more information, refer to "Starting a Presentation" and "Creating from a Template."

5. False. **AutoContent Wizard** walks you through each step of creating a new presentation by asking you a series of questions about the purpose of the presentation, the style you want to use, how you want the handouts to appear, and so on. For more information, refer to "Starting a New Presentation."

Practice Lab

The Microsoft Expert User Exam lists three Required Tasks for the Skill Area "Creating Presentations." Two of these tasks have been covered in this lesson. Following, you will find a practice lab for the Required Tasks covered in this lesson.

 Required Tasks   The Required Tasks covered in this lesson are Create from a Template and Create from an Existing Presentation.

Create from a Template

Using the Standard Flyer Presentation Design Template, create a flyer for an imaginary company. The flyer should contain information about the company picnic. Save the presentation as "picnic."

To see an example of a picnic presentation, open the file Lesson1a.ppt on the CD-ROM. The file Lesson1.ppt is an example of a presentation created by using the AutoContent Wizard.

Create from an Existing Presentation

Open the file Picnic.ppt you just created. Make changes to the presentation so that the flyer contains information on the company dinner to celebrate the company's million dollar sales milestone.

Working with Slides in Different Views

This lesson covers one of the three Required Tasks for the "Adding Textual Information" Skill Area.

In this lesson, you learn the following Required Task for your exam:

▶ Enter text in a Slide and Outline view

For a complete list of Required Tasks for the Skill Area "Adding Textual Information," refer to the User Skills Roadmap.

Changing Views

PowerPoint can display your presentation in five different views:

 ▶ **Slide View**   This view shows you one slide at a time. You may enter text, insert graphs or charts, add clip art, or create diagrams directly on the slide while in this view.

▶ **Outline View**   The fastest way to enter all the text for your presentation is to use the Outline view. All titles and body text entered in the Outline will automatically appear on the slides; any text entered in text placeholders in the Slide View automatically appears in the Outline. Use the Outline to organize your presentation and to change the order of slides and bullet paragraphs.

▶ **Slide Sorter View**   In this view, you see a miniature of each slide in the presentation. You may reposition, delete, or copy slides to change the order of the slides in the presentation. You also use this view to set up transitions and timing for slide shows.

▶ **Notes Page View**   Use this view to create speaker's notes for any or all of the slides in the presentation. Each page in the Notes Page view corresponds to a slide, and a picture of the slide appears at the top of the page. You add text under the slide picture that the speaker needs during the presentation.

▶ **Slide Show**   The slide show is an electronic presentation in which each slide fills the screen. Use this view when giving an on-screen presentation but also when reviewing your slides before printing or showing them.

To change from one view to another, choose **View** from the menu and then select **Slide**, **Outline**, **Slide Sorter**, **Notes Page**, or **Slide Show**. A quicker way to switch views is to click the button for the desired view at the bottom of the presentation window (see Figure 2.1).

Figure 2.1

In Outline view, double-click the Slide icon to change to Slide view of that slide.

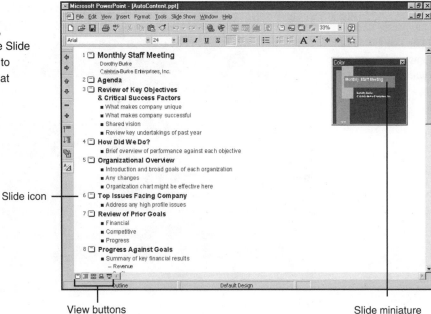

Slide icon

View buttons

Slide miniature

Moving from Slide to Slide

When you have more than one slide in your presentation, you need to go to a specific slide to work on it. How you get to that slide depends upon which view you're in at the time:

▶ In Outline view, scroll up or down to see the slide you want. Click the Slide icon to select the slide (refer to Figure 2.1), or click anywhere inside the text to edit it. To quickly jump to the Slide view of a particular slide, double-click its slide icon.

▶ In Slide view or Notes Page view, click the **Previous Slide** or **Next Slide** buttons at the bottom of the vertical scroll bar, or drag the scroll box until the desired slide number appears (see Figure 2.2), or press **Page Up** or **Page Down**.

Figure 2.2

Drag the scroll box until you see the name or number of the slide you want and then release the mouse button.

Slide number and title of slide that will appear

Previous Slide button

Next Slide button

Scroll box

▶ In Slide Sorter view, click the desired slide (a thick border indicates the selected slide). Use the scroll bar to see additional slides. To quickly see a slide in the Slide view, double-click it.

Using the Slide Miniature Window

The slide miniature window (refer to Figure 2.1) displays the currently selected slide in a small window on top of whatever view you're using.

To turn the slide miniature on or off, choose **View**, **Slide Miniature** from the menu.

In Outline view, the slide miniature shows a color version of the selected slide. In all other views, it shows an alternative version of the slide. For example, if you are currently displaying the slides on-screen in color, the slide miniature window shows them in black and white. Conversely, if the slides are displayed in black and white, the slide miniature shows them in color.

This makes the slide miniature particularly useful if you're developing a presentation for two different media—for example, an on-screen presentation in color and a black-and-white set of printouts. By checking the slide miniature, you won't inadvertently make a change in color that would be unattractive or illegible when printed in black and white.

 Color or Black and White?   To toggle between Black and White and Color views on-screen, choose **View**, **Black and White** (if you're currently viewing color) or **View**, **Color** (if you're currently viewing black and white). Or, click the **Color/Black and White** button on the Standard toolbar to toggle back and forth.

Editing Text in a Slide and Outline View

If you created a presentation using the AutoContent Wizard you already have several slides, but they may not contain the text you want to use. You need to edit that text.

If you created your presentation from a template or used a blank presentation, you have one slide on the screen to which you want to add text.

In the following sections, you'll learn to add and edit text in the Outline and Slide views. In later lessons, you'll add pictures, graphs, organizational charts, and other objects.

 Object   An object is any item on a slide, including text, graphics, and charts.

Entering and Editing Text in Outline View

Outline view (see Figure 2.3) provides the easiest way to edit all the text in the presentation, because it's all in one place.

You simply click to move the insertion point where you want it and then type in your text. Press the **Delete** key to remove characters to the right of the insertion point or the **Backspace** key to remove characters to the left of the insertion point.

To select text, hold down the left mouse button and drag the mouse pointer over the desired text to select more than one word. Double-click a word to select just that word. To select a bullet paragraph, click the bullet. Click the slide icon to select all the text on a slide.

Figure 2.3

Do your major text editing in the Outline view, where you can see most of the text in your presentation.

Outlining Toolbar

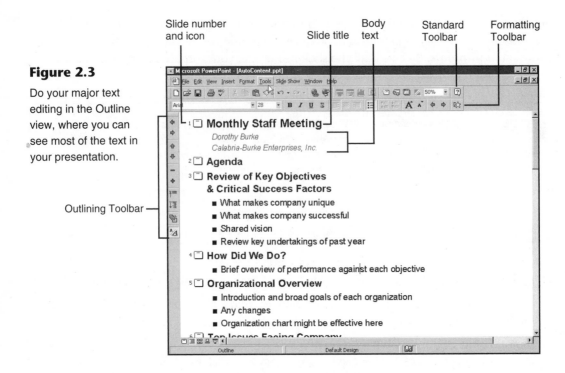

After the text is selected, press the **Delete** or **Backspace** key to remove the text or type to replace the highlighted text. To move selected text, point in the middle of the selected text and drag it to the new location, or choose **Edit**, **Cut** (or click the **Cut** button on the Standard toolbar), move your insertion point to the location where you want to put the text, and choose **Edit**, **Paste** (or click the **Paste** button on the Standard toolbar).

 Auto Word Select When you select text, PowerPoint automatically selects whole words. If you want to select individual characters, choose **Tools**, **Options** from the menu, select the **Edit** tab, deselect the **Automatic Word Selection** option, and then click **OK**. To select individual characters on a one-time basis, hold down the **Shift** key and press the left or right arrow key.

Changing the Text's Outline Level

In the Outline, the text in your presentation is organized in a multilevel outline format. The slide titles are at the top level of the outline, and the slide contents are subordinate under that. You may even have bullets that appear beneath other bullets and indented farther to the right (as "sub-topics" under a bullet point).

Changing the level of a paragraph from title down to bullet paragraph or changing from a bullet paragraph down to an indented bullet paragraph (or "sub-topic") is known as *demoting*. Moving an indented paragraph out to a bullet paragraph or moving a bullet paragraph to the left to become a title is called *promoting*. This can be done easily within the Outline view:

▶ **Demote One Level**   Click the text and then press **Tab** or click the **Demote** button on the Outlining toolbar.

▶ **Promote One Level**   Click the text and then press **Shift+Tab** or click the **Promote** button on the Outlining toolbar.

Moving Paragraphs in Outline View

As you work in Outline view, you may find that some lines of text or paragraphs need to be rearranged. There are several ways to move lines or paragraphs in Outline view:

▶ **Move a paragraph up one paragraph**   Click in the paragraph and then click the **Move Up** button on the Outlining toolbar.

▶ **Move a paragraph down one paragraph**   Click in the paragraph and then click the **Move Down** button on the Outlining toolbar.

▶ **Dragging**   Move the mouse pointer to the left of the paragraph (over the bullet or slide icon if there is one) until the mouse pointer turns into a four-headed arrow. Then hold down the left mouse button and drag up or down (be careful not to drag left or right, as that promotes or demotes the paragraph) until the horizontal line appears where you want the paragraph to go. Release the mouse button.

▶ **Cut and Paste**   Select the paragraph(s) you want to move, click the **Cut** button on the Standard toolbar, place your cursor where you want the paragraph to appear, and click the **Paste** button on the Standard toolbar.

Entering and Editing Text in Slide View

When you create a presentation by starting with a blank presentation or a template, your first slide has text placeholders where you click and add text (as you can see in the title slide in Figure 2.4). The "click here" text that appears in each placeholder shows you the text formatting and alignment that will be applied to any text you enter there, unless you make changes. (See Lesson 6, "Changing the Look of Your Text," to learn how to format the text.)

Figure 2.4

Click in a placeholder and enter your text.

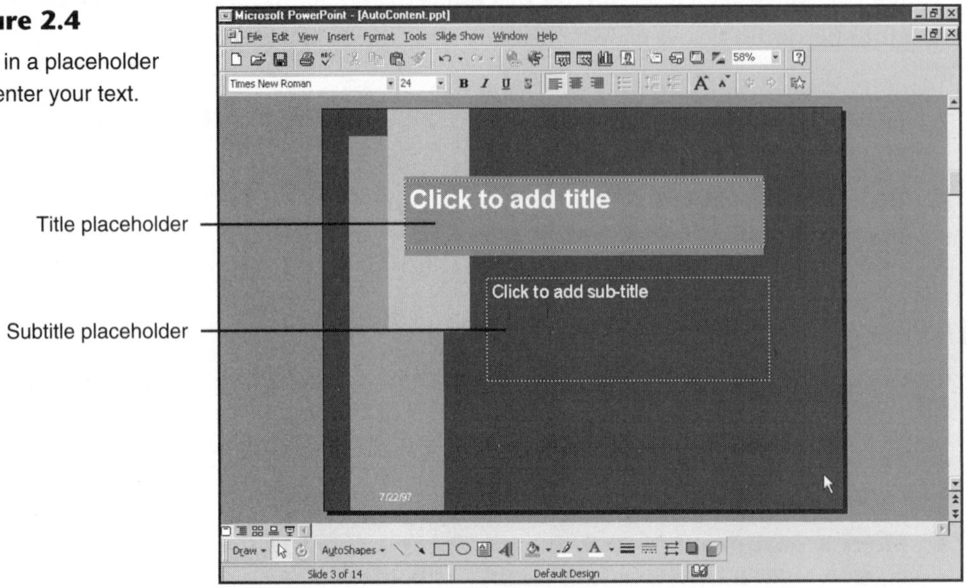

Title placeholder

Subtitle placeholder

If you started your presentation by using the AutoContent Wizard or if you're editing an existing presentation, you need to edit the sample or existing text. Click in the text box to place the insertion point where you want to add or delete text.

You move the insertion point within the text placeholder or text box by using the arrow keys or clicking where you want to place it. Press the **Delete** key to remove characters to the right of the insertion point or the **Backspace** key to remove characters to the left of the insertion point.

To select text, hold down the left mouse button and drag the mouse pointer over the desired text to select more than one word. Double-click on a word to select just that word. After the text is selected, press the **Delete** or **Backspace** key to remove the text or type to replace the highlighted text.

Review Questions

1. How do you change to Outline View?

2. How do you edit text in Outline View?

3. How do you preview the slides in black and white?

4. What are the three methods for moving paragraphs in the Outline view?

5. How do you change the level of a bullet paragraph?

Review Question Answers

1. Choose **View**, **Outline** from the menu. Alternatively, click the **Outline** view button on the bottom of the presentation window. For more information, refer to "Changing Views."

2. Switch to Outline view and use normal text editing skills to edit text. To demote or promote outline levels, use the **Tab** or **Shift+Tab** keys or click the **Demote** and **Promote** buttons on the Outlining toolbar. For more information, refer to "Entering and Editing Text in Outline View."

3. Choose **View**, **Black and White** from the menu or click the **Black and White** button on the Standard toolbar. For more information, refer to "Using the Slide Miniature Window."

4. Using the **Move Up** and **Move Down** buttons, dragging, or cut and paste. For more information, refer to "Moving Paragraphs in Outline View."

5. Select the paragraph and click the Promote or Demote buttons, or press **Tab** or **Shift+Tab**. For more information, refer to "Changing the Text's Outline Level."

Practice Lab

The Microsoft Expert User Exam lists three Required Tasks for the Skill Area "Adding Textual Information." One of these tasks has been covered in this lesson. Following, you find a practice lab for the Required Task covered in this lesson.

Required Tasks   The Required Task covered in this lesson is Enter Text in a Slide and Outline View.

Enter Text in a Slide and Outline View

Open the file Lesson2.ppt located on the CD-ROM. Practice using different views by viewing the presentation in each of the following views:

▶ Slide View

▶ Outline View

▶ Slide Sorter View

▶ Notes Page View

▶ Slide Show (To move through the slides, click your left mouse button or press the **Spacebar**. Press **Esc** to exit the Slide Show.)

In Slide View, go to Slide 8, "Revenue and Profit." Add text to indicate that the forecast for the second quarter was 500,000 and the actual sales were 450,000.

In Outline View, go to Slide 11, "Goals for Next Period" and add some goals. Go to Slide 6, "Review of Prior Goals" and demote the second and fourth bullets.

To see an example of a completed exercise, open the file Lesson2a.ppt on the CD-ROM.

3

Adding and Deleting Slides

This lesson covers one of the three Required Tasks for the "Creating Presentations" Skill Area.

In this lesson, you learn the following Required Task for your exam:

▶   Delete slides

For a complete list of Required Tasks for the Skill Area "Creating Presentations," refer to the User Skills Roadmap.

Inserting a Slide

If you started with a template or a blank presentation, you began with one slide. You need to round out your presentation with additional slides. Even if you started with the AutoContent Wizard and have several slides, you may still need to add more.

Slides can be added from the Slide, Outline, Slide Sorter, and Notes Page views. To insert a slide, follow these steps:

1. In Slide view or Notes Page view, the new slide appears after the slide you have on-screen. In Outline view, the new slide appears after the slide where you have your cursor (unless your cursor is at the beginning of the slide title, in which case it appears before that slide).

   In Slide Sorter view, the new slide appears after the selected slide. Have the appropriate slide on-screen or selected so that the new slide appears in the correct position in your presentation.

 New Slide Out of Place? If your new slide appears in the wrong order, don't panic. You can shuffle the order of the slides around in Slide Sorter view. Refer to Lesson 7, "Rearranging Slides in a Presentation," to learn how to rearrange the order of your slides.

2. Choose **Insert**, **New Slide** from the menu or click the **New Slide** button on the Standard toolbar.

3. The New Slide dialog box appears (see Figure 3.1). Select an AutoLayout for the slide—title page, bulleted list, graph, organization chart, and so on—by clicking the layout icon.

 AutoLayout Any new slides you add will have the same background coloring, title font, bullet type, and graphics as the other slides in the presentation. The template controls that. Within each template are a series of page layouts, to meet specific design needs for each slide. These page layouts, called *AutoLayouts*, structure where your text, artwork, and charts go on the slide by having placeholders for these items.

4. Click **OK**. The slide appears with the appropriate placeholders (except in Outline view). To add or edit the text, pictures, graphs, or drawings, you may find it easier to switch to Slide view to work on the new slide.

Figure 3.1

Select an AutoLayout from the New Slide dialog box.

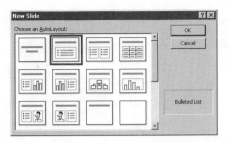

 Cloning a Slide   To create an exact replica of a slide, select the slide you want to duplicate. Then choose **Insert**, **Duplicate Slide** from the menu. The new slide is inserted after the original slide, but you can move it later (see Lesson 7 to learn about rearranging slide order).

 Create an Agenda Slide   There is a special type of slide, called a summary slide, that you can add to your presentation. It includes the titles of other slides. To add this slide you must start from Slide Sorter or Outline view and then select the slides you want to appear on your summary slide (hold down **Shift** and click each slide or each slide icon). Click the **Summary Slide** button on the Slide Sorter or Outlining toolbar. A new slide, with bulleted titles from the selected slides, appears in front of the first selected slide.

Adding Slides from Another Presentation

If you want to insert some or all of the slides from another presentation into your current presentation, follow these steps:

1. Open the presentation into which you want to insert the slides, if it's not already open.

2. Select the slide located before the position where you want to insert the slides.

3. Choose **Insert**, **Slides from Files** from the menu. The Slide Finder dialog box appears.

4. Click the **Browse** button to display the Insert Slides from Files dialog box (see Figure 3.2).

Figure 3.2

Select the drive and folder where the file is stored and then double-click the filename.

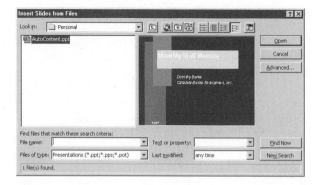

5. Select the drive and/or folder from the **Look In** drop-down list, if needed.

6. Double-click the name of the presentation that contains the slides you want to insert into the open presentation.

7. Click the **Display** button. The slides from the presentation appear in the Slide Finder window (see Figure 3.3).

Figure 3.3

Select the slides you want to add to your current presentation and then click Insert.

Click to view slides as a list with a Preview window

Scroll to see additional slides

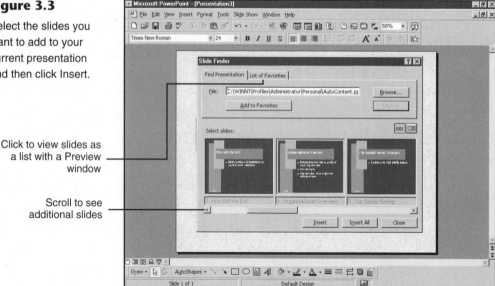

8. Click the slides you want to insert and then click the **Insert** button. If you want to insert all the slides, click the **Insert All** button.

9. When you are finished inserting slides, click the **Close** button. The inserted slides appear right after the slide that you selected in step 2. Note that they also take on the characteristics of your current template instead of looking as they did in their original presentation.

Make a Favorites List If there is a presentation that you regularly use to insert slides from, you can add it to your Favorites List by clicking the **Add to Favorites** button in the Open dialog box when you open the file. Then the next time you want to insert slides from that presentation, just click the **Look In Favorites** button in the Open dialog box and select the presentation from the list. If the **Web** toolbar is showing on your screen, click the **Favorites** button to see **Add to Favorites** and **Open Favorites** choices.

Creating Slides from a Document Outline

If you have a word processing document with outline-style headings in it, PowerPoint can pull the headings from the document and use the headings to create slides with bulleted lists.

To create slides from a document outline, follow these steps:

1. Open the presentation into which you want to insert the slides, if it's not already open.

2. Select the slide located before the position where you want to insert the slides.

3. Choose **Insert**, **Slides from Outline** from the menu. The Insert Outline dialog box appears (see Figure 3.4).

Figure 3.4

Double-click the name of the outline document file to convert the entire outline to slides and insert them into your current presentation.

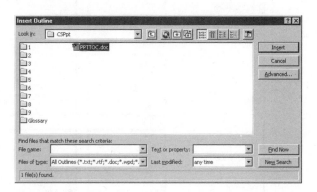

4. Select the drive and folder where the file is stored from the Look In drop-down list, if necessary.

5. Double-click the name of the document file.

6. The slides appear after the slide you selected in step 2. You will probably have to do some editing, but you won't have to create the entire presentation from scratch.

Selecting Slides

When you want to perform operations on slides—copying, cutting, deleting, moving—you must first select the slide or slides to be involved in the operation.

Follow these directions to select slides:

▶ **To select a single slide.** In the Slide and Notes Page views, the currently displayed file is the selected file. In the Slide Sorter and Outline views, click the slide to select it. A selected slide in Slide Sorter view gets a box around it. In Outline view, the slide icon and all text related to the slide are highlighted.

▶ **To select two or more neighboring slides.** In Outline view, click at the beginning of the first slide, hold down the **Shift** key, and then click the end of the last slide in the group.

▶ **To select a rectangular block of neighboring slides.** In Slide Sorter view, click and drag a "selection box" around the slides you want to select. All slides that fall within the boundaries of the selection box become selected (see Figure 3.5).

Figure 3.5

Slides do not have to be completely within the selection box to be included in the selection.

Started dragging box here

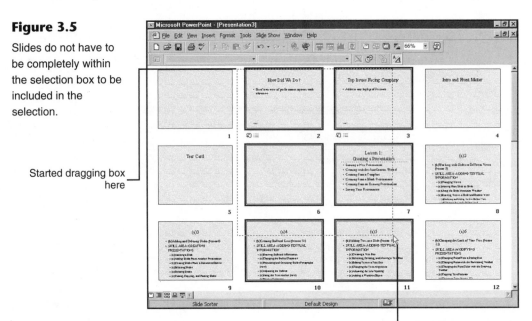

Released mouse button here

▶ **To select two or more non-neighboring slides.** In Slide Sorter view, hold down the Shift key while clicking each slide that you want to select.

Deleting Slides

You can delete slides from any of the views except the Slide Show. To delete a slide, follow these steps:

1. Display the slide you want to delete in the Slide or Notes Page view, or select the slide in the Slide Sorter or Outline view. To delete multiple slides, use the selection methods listed in the "Selecting Slides" section to select more than one slide.

2. Choose **Edit**, **Delete Slide** from the menu. When you have the slide(s) selected in the Slide Sorter or Outline view, pressing the **Delete** key also works.

 Oops! If you deleted a slide by mistake, get it back by choosing **Edit**, **Undo** from the menu, clicking the **Undo** button on the Standard toolbar, or pressing **Ctrl+Z**. You can undo several steps by doing Undo as many times as steps you want to undo. Just be aware that Undo doesn't undo every action in PowerPoint. If the menu command is grayed out, you won't be able to undo the last step.

Cutting, Copying, and Pasting Slides

The Cut, Copy, and Paste commands help you to rearrange your slides and also to copy slides to another presentation from your current presentation.

To copy or move slides, follow these instructions:

1. Change to the Slide Sorter or Outline view.

2. Select the slide(s) you want to copy or move.

 3. To copy the selected slide(s) to the Windows Clipboard, choose **Edit**, **Copy** from the menu, click the **Copy** button on the Standard toolbar, or press **Ctrl+C**.

 To move the selected slide(s) to the Windows Clipboard, choose **Edit**, **Cut** from the menu, click the **Cut** button on the Standard toolbar, or press **Ctrl+X**.

 Before You Cut or Copy If you have cut or copied something previously, make sure you paste it out before you do another cut or copy. Otherwise, you will lose whatever you cut or copied before.

4. If you want to paste the slide(s) into a different presentation, open that presentation.

5. In Slide Sorter view, select the slide after which you want to place the cut or copied slide(s). In Outline view, move the insertion point to the end of the text in the slide after which you want to insert the cut or copied slide(s). Always paste the slide(s) into the same type of view you cut or copied them from.

6. Choose **Edit**, **Paste** from the menu, click the **Paste** button on the Standard toolbar, or press **Ctrl+V**. PowerPoint inserts the cut or copied slide(s).

> **Windows Clipboard**   A temporary memory holding area for items you have cut or copied. The items remain in the Clipboard until you cut or copy another item or until you shut down your computer. They can be pasted out again and again.

Review Questions

1. How do you delete a slide?

2. How do you insert a slide in Slide Sorter view?

3. In Outline view, how do you select more than one slide?

4. True or False: Even if you have an outline for the presentation in a word processing document, you have to retype the text into PowerPoint to make the presentation.

5. When you copy slides from another presentation into your current presentation, what happens to the look of the slides?

Review Question Answers

1. There are several ways to delete a slide from a presentation. Deleting slides can be done from any view except Slide Show view. To delete a slide, display the slide in the Slide or Notes Page view, or select the slide in the Slide Sorter or Outline view. Choose **Edit**, **Delete Slide** from the menu. If you are in Slide Sorter or Outline view, you can press the **Delete** key in lieu of using the menu choices. For more information, refer to "Deleting Slides."

2. Select the slide which will be just before the new slide. Choose **Insert**, **New Slide** from the menu or click the **New Slide** button on the Standard toolbar. For more information, refer to "Inserting a Slide."

3. Click at the beginning of the first slide, hold down the **Shift** key, and click at the end of the last slide. For more information, refer to "Selecting Slides."

4. False. Choose **Insert**, **Slides from Outline** to import the text from the word processing document.

5. The slides take on the slide background, colors, fonts, and bullets from the template attached to your current presentation. For more information, refer to "Adding Slides from Another Presentation."

Practice Lab

The Microsoft Expert User Exam lists three Required Tasks for the Skill Area "Creating Presentations." This lesson covers one of the three Required Tasks. Following you find a practice lab for the Required Task covered in this lesson.

Required Tasks   The Required Task covered in this lesson is Delete Slides.

Delete Slides

Open Lesson3.ppt from the CD-ROM. In Slide Sorter view, delete Slides 8 and 10. Note what happens to the slide numbering when you do that.

To see an example of a completed exercise, open the file Lesson3.ppt on the CD-ROM.

Creating Bulleted Lists

This lesson covers one of the three Required Tasks for the "Adding Textual Information" Skill Area.

In this lesson, you learn the following Required Task for your exam:

▶ Enter bulleted information

For a complete list of Required Tasks for the Skill Area "Adding Textual Information," refer to the User Skills Roadmap.

Entering Bulleted Information

Bulleted lists are the preferred way to present information in presentations because they highlight the main points being made by the speaker. In Outline view, the bulleted list is the default style. When you press Enter after a slide title, the body content of the slide automatically appears in bullet format, unless you selected a different AutoLayout when you created the slide (see Lesson 3, "Adding and Deleting Slides," to learn about inserting slides).

If you selected the Bulleted List AutoLayout when you inserted the slide, a placeholder for bulleted text appears on the slide in Slide view. The body text placeholders in any of the AutoLayouts (Text & Chart, Chart & Text, 2 Column Text, Clip Art & Text, Text & Clip Art, Text & Object, Object & Text, and so on) automatically default to bulleted lists.

 To turn bullets on and off for any selected paragraph, click the **Bullets** button on the Formatting toolbar. Or, choose **Format**, **Bullets** from the menu or right-click the paragraph and choose **Bullet** from the pop-up menu, and then deselect the **Use a Bullet** option before clicking **OK**.

After the bullets are turned on for a paragraph, the text in that paragraph will automatically indent when it wraps to a second line. When you press **Enter** at the end of a paragraph, a bullet appears at the beginning of the next paragraph.

> **Moving a Bulleted Item**   To move a bullet item up or down in a bulleted list in either the Slide or Outline view, move your mouse pointer to the left of the bullet. When it becomes a four-headed arrow, drag up or down until you see a horizontal line appear where you want the bullet item to go. Then release the mouse button. Be careful not to drag left or right, as you may accidentally indent the bullet text.

Changing the Bullet Character

The character of the bullet depends on the template you're using for your presentation. The only way you can change the bullet character for the entire presentation is to change the slide master, as you will learn to do in Lesson 19, "Changing a Presentation's Look."

To change the bullet character for an individual bullet item or selected bulleted paragraphs, follow these instructions:

1. Switch to Slide view and select the paragraph(s) that you want to change.

2. Choose **Format**, **Bullet** from the menu or right-click the paragraph(s) and choose **Bullet** from the pop-up menu. The Bullet dialog box appears (see Figure 4.1).

Figure 4.1

Select the bullet character or symbol that you want to use for the selected paragraphs.

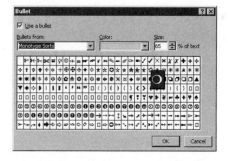

3. From the **Bullets From** drop-down list, select the character set (symbol font) that has the bullet you want. The bullets in that character set are displayed in the dialog box.

 Which character set do I select? Each character set is nothing more than a font that's installed on your computer. Some fonts are better suited for bullets than others—open several and examine the characters each one contains. Wingdings or Monotype Sorts are good choices.

4. Click the character you want to use for the bullet. PowerPoint enlarges the character when you click it, as shown in Figure 4.1.

5. The size of the bullet is relative to the text around it, so it's measured as a percentage of the text size. To change the size of the bullet, specify a percentage in the **Size** box or use the up and down arrows to select a size.

6. Select the bullet color from the **Color** drop-down list.

7. Click **OK**.

 Numbered Lists PowerPoint doesn't automatically number lists. If you need numbered paragraphs, turn off the bullets for each paragraph involved. Type a number and a period before each paragraph and then press Tab before typing the paragraph text. Try to restrict use of numbered lists to lists that must be followed sequentially; all other lists can be bulleted.

Promoting and Demoting Bulleted Paragraphs

In Outline view, text appears in a multilevel format, with the slide title being at the top level of the outline, and the slide contents subordinate under that. You may even have bullets that appear beneath other bullets and indented farther to the right (as "subtopics" under a bullet point).

To change the level of a paragraph from title down to bulleted paragraph or from a bulleted paragraph down to an indented bulleted paragraph (or "subtopic") is called *demoting*. Moving a indented paragraph out to a bulleted paragraph or a bulleted paragraph to the left to become a title is called *promoting*.

When you work with bulleted lists in Slide view, you still have a multilevel organization in which there are first-level bulleted paragraphs, and second-level bulleted paragraphs are indented beneath them. The second level bulleted text is smaller than the first level text. PowerPoint also allows third-level bullets and fourth level bullets (see Figure 4.2), although those levels are harder to read and may distract the audience.

Figure 4.2

PowerPoint enables you to create several levels of bullet paragraphs.

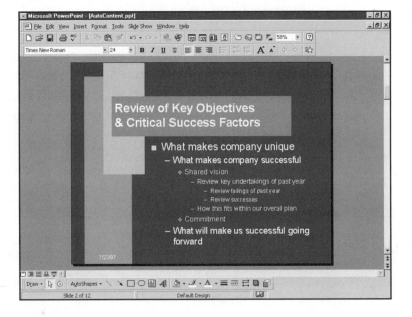

Changing the level of a bullet paragraph can be done easily:

▶ **Demote One Level**   Click the paragraph text (or select several paragraphs) and then press **Tab** or click the **Demote** button on the Outlining toolbar or the Formatting toolbar.

▶ **Promote One Level**   Click the paragraph text (or select several paragraphs) and then press **Shift+Tab** or click the **Promote** button on the Outlining toolbar or the Formatting toolbar.

Adjusting the Indents

Indents allow you to move one or more lines of a paragraph in from the left margin. You may want to adjust these indents to move text farther in from the left margin, to separate the text from the bullet character, or to further indent the second- or third-level bulleted paragraphs.

To adjust the indents of your bulleted paragraphs:

1. With the slide displayed in Slide view, select the paragraph(s) that you want to adjust.

2. If the Ruler isn't visible, choose **View**, **Ruler** from the menu.

3. Drag one of the indent markers to set the indents for the paragraph (see Figure 4.3).

    ▷ Drag the top marker to move the bullet closer to or farther from the text in the first line.

    ▷ Drag the bottom marker to move all the text closer to or farther from the bullet. The text remains lined up with the first letter of the first line.

    ▷ Drag the box below the bottom marker to move the bullet and the text closer to or farther from the left margin of the text box.

4. To turn the Ruler off, choose **View**, **Ruler** from the menu.

Figure 4.3

Drag the indent markers to set the distance of the text from the left margin.

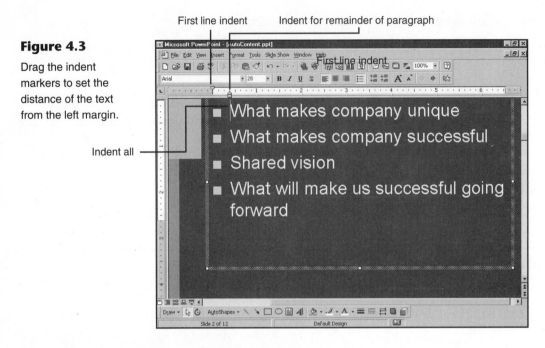

Using the Text Anchor

A few bulleted paragraphs or short bulleted paragraphs within a large text box look like they're all shoved into the top-left corner of the box.

To align your bulleted paragraphs within the text box, while still keeping the bullets aligned, follow these instructions:

1. Click in the text box to select it.

2. Choose **Format**, **AutoShape** from the menu.

3. When the Format AutoShape dialog box appears, select the **Text Box** tab (see Figure 4.4).

4. From the Text Anchor Point drop-down list, select the type of alignment you want (**Top**, **Middle**, **Bottom**, **Top Centered**, **Middle Centered**, or **Bottom Centered**).

5. Click **OK**. The text is aligned within the text box (see Figure 4.5).

Figure 4.4

Set the text anchor
type to specify how the
bullet text is aligned
within the text box.

Figure 4.5

The bulleted para-
graphs have a top-
centered text anchor.

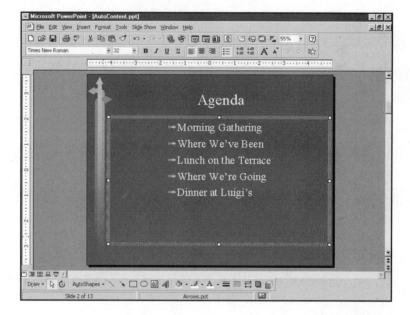

Review Questions

1. How do you turn an existing list into a bulleted list?

2. How do you change the character of a bullet?

3. How do you demote a bullet level?

4. True or False: If you select a number as the bullet style, PowerPoint automatically numbers your paragraphs.

5. How do you change the order of the bullets on a slide?

Review Question Answers

1. There are several ways to turn an existing list into a bulleted list. Highlight the list and:

   ▶ Click the **Bullets** button on the formatting toolbar.

   ▶ Choose **Format**, **Bullets** from the menu.

   ▶ Right-click the highlighted list and choose **Bullet** from the pop-up menu.

   For more information, refer to "Entering Bulleted Information."

2. Select the paragraph(s) in which you want to change the bullet character. Choose **Format**, **Bullet** from the menu or right-click the paragraph(s) and choose **Bullet** from the pop-up menu. From the Bullets From drop-down list, select the bullet you want. If desired, change the size and color of the bullet by specifying a percentage in the **Size** box, and a color in the **Color** box. Click **OK**. For more information, refer to "Changing the Bullet Character."

3. To demote one level, click the text and press the **Tab** key or click the **Demote** button on the Outlining toolbar. To promote one level use **Shift+Tab** or click the Promote button on the Outlining toolbar. For more information, refer to "Promoting and Demoting Bulleted Paragraphs."

4. False. PowerPoint doesn't automatically number paragraphs. You must number the paragraphs manually. For more information, refer to "Changing the Bullet Character."

5. In Outline or Slide view, point at the bullet in front of the paragraph you want to move and drag up or down until a horizontal line appears where you want the paragraph to go. In Outline view, select the bullet paragraph and click the **Move Up** or **Move Down** button. For more information, refer to "Entering Bulleted Information."

Practice Lab

The Microsoft Expert User Exam lists three Required Tasks for the Skill Area "Adding Textual Information." One of these tasks has been covered in this lesson. Following you will find a practice lab for the Required Task covered in this lesson.

 Required Tasks   The Required Task covered in this lesson is Enter Bulleted Information.

Enter Bulleted Information

Open Lesson4.ppt from the CD-ROM. In Slide view, go to Slide 2. Change the list on Slide 2 to a bulleted list. Change the bullets to stars. Add a bullet item after **People Love our product** that reads **80% of our sales is from repeat orders!** Demote the new line so that it is indented under the bullet item that reads **People love our product** and change the bullet character to a smiley face (☺).

LESSON 5

Adding Text to a Slide

This lesson covers one of the three Required Tasks for the "Adding Textual Information" Skill Area.

In this lesson, you learn the following Required Task for your exam:

▶ Change the text alignment

For a complete list of Required Tasks for the Skill Area "Adding Textual Information," refer to the User Skills Roadmap. Also covered in this chapter are several skills related to adding text to a slide, such as creating and modifying text boxes and adjusting line spacing.

Creating a Text Box

PowerPoint has several methods available for adding text to your presentation. In Lesson 2, "Working with Slides in Different Views," you learned how to add and edit text in the Outline view and in the text placeholders in the Slide view. There are occasions, however, when you need text outside these placeholders, such as a subtitle or note.

To add text to the slide outside of the text placeholders, you must create a text box. Like the text placeholders (which are text boxes created by the AutoLayout you selected when you created the slide), any text box can contain bulleted lists, notes, and labels for illustrations. Unlike text placeholders, you must determine the formatting of the text box as you add it to the slide.

To create a text box, follow these steps:

1. Switch to the Slide view of the slide to which you want to add the text box (or add a new slide by choosing **Insert**, **Slide** from the menu or clicking the **New Slide** button on the Standard toolbar).

2. Choose **Insert**, **Text Box** from the menu or click the **Text Box** button on the Drawing toolbar.

3. Move the mouse pointer to where you want the upper-left corner of the box to appear.

4. Hold down the left mouse button and drag the mouse pointer to the right until the box is the desired width. It doesn't matter how far you drag down vertically because a new box will always be one line high.

5. Release the mouse button. The text box appears with the insertion point in position and ready for you to enter your text (see Figure 5.1).

6. Type the text that you want to appear in the text box. The text will wrap to the next line when it reaches the right border of the box. The box will increase in depth to accommodate the additional lines of text. To start a new paragraph, press **Enter**.

7. When you are done entering text, click anywhere outside the text box. The border around the text box disappears.

Figure 5.1

The text box is ready
for you to enter text.

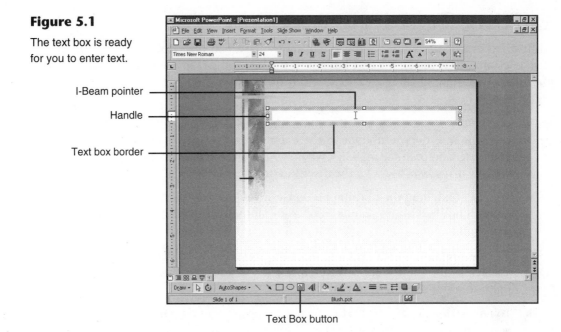

I-Beam pointer

Handle

Text box border

Text Box button

Selecting, Deleting, Sizing, and Moving a Text Box

If you go back and click anywhere inside the text box, a selection box or border appears
around the box. When you click the border, handles (small white boxes) appear around
the text box (refer to Figure 5.1). The handles indicate that the text box is selected, but
they are also used when you change the size of the box.

▶ To delete a text box, select it and then press the **Delete** key.

▶ To change the size of a selected text box, drag one of the handles. When you
point at a handle, your mouse pointer changes to a two-headed arrow that indicates which directions you can drag that handle (the corner handles can move in
all four directions). After you change the size of the text box, the text wraps automatically to fit as needed inside the box.

▶ To move a selected text box, point at the border (away from the handles) until
your mouse pointer becomes a four-headed arrow. Then click and drag the text
box to a new position (you see only the outline of the box until you release the
mouse button). If you only want to move a selected box a little bit, use the arrow
keys to "nudge" the box in the direction of the arrow.

Editing Text in a Text Box

Editing text in a text box is the same as editing text in a text placeholder (see Lesson 2). First, click anywhere inside the text box (or in the text if the box border is not visible) to place an insertion point there and then do one of the following:

▶ To insert text, click the I-beam pointer (your mouse pointer looks like an upper-case I when in a text box, as shown in Figure 5.1) where you want to insert the text. The insertion point appears there. Enter your text. If you need to move your insertion point again, click where you want to place the insertion point or use the arrow keys to move the insertion point.

▶ To select text, drag the I-beam pointer over the text you want to select. Or, double-click in the middle of a word to select that word (triple-click to select a paragraph).

▶ To delete text, select the text and press the **Delete** key. To delete individual characters, use the **Delete** or **Backspace** keys to delete single characters to the right or left of the insertion point.

▶ To replace text, select the text you want to replace and type the new text. When you start typing, PowerPoint deletes the selected text.

▶ To copy text that you want to place elsewhere in the text box (or in another text box), select the text you want to copy and choose **Edit**, **Copy** from the menu, click the **Copy** button on the Standard toolbar, press **Ctrl+C**, or right-click the text and choose **Copy** from the pop-up menu.

▶ To cut text that you want to move elsewhere in the text box (or to another text box), select the text you want to cut and choose **Edit**, **Cut** from the menu, click the **Cut** button on the Standard toolbar, press **Ctrl+X**, or right-click the text and choose **Cut** from the pop-up menu.

▶ To paste text that you've copied or cut to the Clipboard, place the insertion point where you want the text to appear and then choose **Edit**, **Paste** from the menu, click the **Paste** button on the Standard toolbar, press **Ctrl+V**, or right-click and choose **Paste** from the pop-up menu.

Changing the Text Alignment

The borders of the text box act as the margins for the text you enter. Normally, PowerPoint aligns the text to the left edge of the box and leaves the ends of the lines ragged on the right. That is because the default setting is left-aligned.

To change the alignment of the text within a text box, follow these steps:

1. Click inside the paragraph you want to align or select multiple paragraphs.

2. Choose **Format**, **Alignment** from the menu.

3. From the submenu that appears, select **Left**, **Center**, **Right**, or **Justify** (see Figure 5.2 for examples).

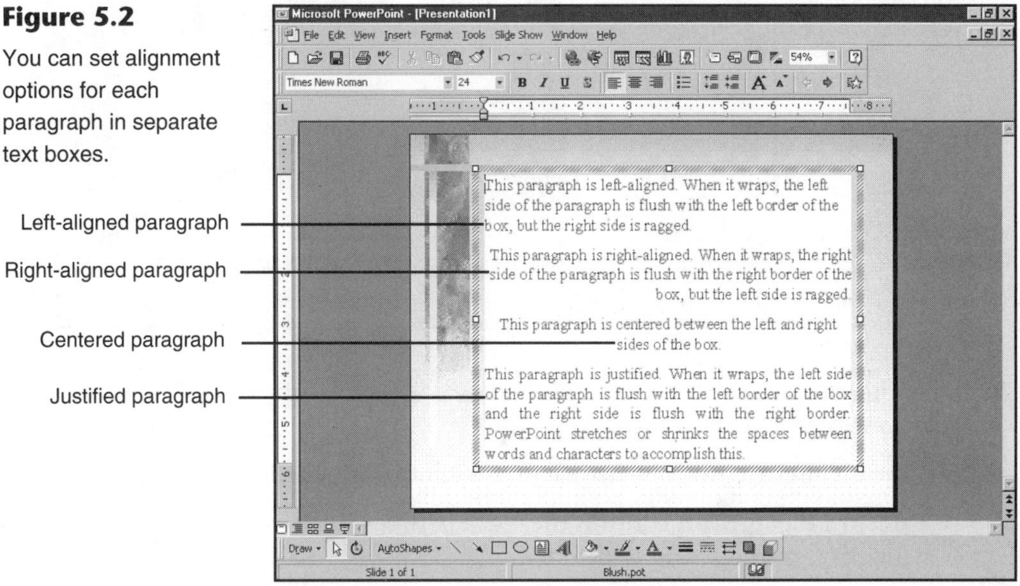

Figure 5.2

You can set alignment options for each paragraph in separate text boxes.

Left-aligned paragraph ——

Right-aligned paragraph ——

Centered paragraph ——

Justified paragraph ——

Alignment Shortcuts To quickly set the alignment of a selected paragraph, with your insertion point in the paragraph you want to change, click the **Left Alignment**, **Center Alignment** (or click the **Right Alignment** button on the Formatting toolbar). Or, use the keyboard shortcuts: **Ctrl+L** for left alignment, **Ctrl+R** for right alignment, or **Ctrl+E** for center alignment.

Adjusting the Line Spacing

When you enter text in a text box, it's automatically single-spaced. To change the line spacing of a paragraph, follow these steps:

1. Click inside the paragraph you want to change, or select all the paragraphs you want to change.

2. Choose **Format**, **Line Spacing** from the menu. The Line Spacing dialog box opens (see Figure 5.3).

Figure 5.3

When specifying the line spacing, try keeping the paragraphs single-spaced, but adding space either before or after each paragraph to separate them.

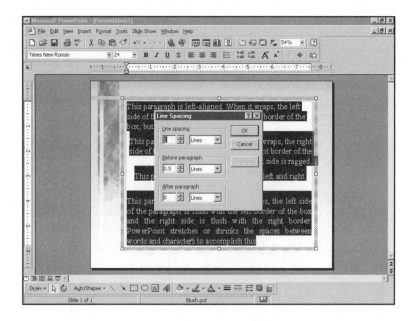

3. Enter the spacing amount in the appropriate boxes or use the up and down arrows to select the spacing you want:

   ▶ **Line Spacing** controls the space between the lines in a paragraph.

   ▶ **Before Paragraph** controls the space between a selected paragraph and the paragraph that comes before it.

   ▶ **After Paragraph** controls the space between a selected paragraph and the paragraph that comes after it.

4. Click **OK**.

 Lines or Points? The drop-down list box to the right of each setting in the Line Spacing dialog box allows you to choose either **Lines** or **Points**. A *line* is the current line height based on the font size. A *point* is a unit used to measure text; there are 72 points in an inch. If you're used to single, double, or one and a half line spacing from your word processor, stick with lines. If you understand desktop publishing, points are familiar to you. Use **Points** to specify line spacing smaller than a line (such as 6 points).

Quick Spacing Click in the paragraph for which you want to change the line spacing. Then click the **Increase Paragraph Spacing** or **Decrease Paragraph Spacing** button on the Formatting toolbar to change the spacing before the paragraph.

Using WordArt to Manipulate Text

WordArt is a separate program that's packaged with either Microsoft Office 97 or PowerPoint 97. WordArt twists your text into preset shapes (such as circular text) and then adds it to your slide as an *embedded* object. Because it's an embedded object, you move it and size it as one piece but when you want to edit the text you're going to use the tools from the Microsoft WordArt program.

To insert a WordArt object into a slide, follow these steps:

1. In Slide view, display the slide on which you want to place the WordArt object.

 2. Click the **Insert WordArt** button on the Drawing toolbar or choose **Insert**, **Picture**, **WordArt** from the menu.

3. Select the WordArt effect you want from the WordArt Gallery dialog box (see Figure 5.4). Click **OK**.

Figure 5.4

Click the example that is closest to the shape you want for your WordArt object.

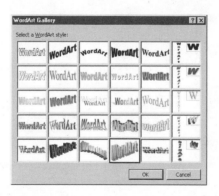

4. When the Edit WordArt Text dialog box appears (see Figure 5.5), replace "Your Text Here" with your own text. Here, it has been replaced with "Great News!"

Figure 5.5

Replace the text
sample "Your Text
Here" with your own
text, such as "Great
News!"

Font

Enter your text here

Size   Bold and Italic buttons

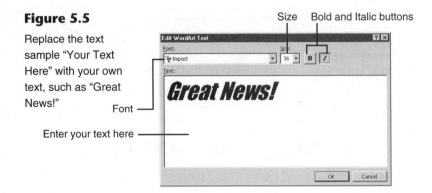

5. Choose a font from the drop-down list and choose a size. If you want bold or italic type, click the appropriate buttons. Click **OK**.

6. The WordArt appears in your document, with sizing handles around it to show it's still selected. PowerPoint also displays the WordArt toolbar (see Figure 5.6).

Figure 5.6

The WordArt object
has sizing handles,
plus a handle for
adjusting the shape.

Shaping handle

WordArt toolbar

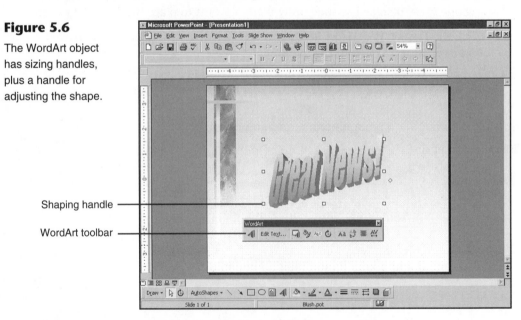

7. Use the sizing handles to change the height and width of the graphic. Use the yellow diamond handles to adjust the shape of the WordArt.

8. Use the buttons on the WordArt toolbar to modify the WordArt. (See Table 5.1 for descriptions of the WordArt tools.)

9. Deselect the WordArt by clicking somewhere else in your slide. The WordArt can then be moved and sized using the same methods as moving and sizing a text box.

Table 5.1 WordArt Toolbar Buttons

Button	Name	Description
	Insert WordArt	Inserts a new WordArt object on your slide.
Edit Text...	Edit Text	Opens the Edit WordArt Text dialog box so you can change the text of your WordArt, the font, the size, or the bold and italic styles.
	WordArt Gallery	Opens the WordArt Gallery of predefined effects.
	Format WordArt	Opens the Format WordArt dialog box where you select fill colors, position, size, and text-wrapping options.
Abc	WordArt Shape	Displays a palette of preset shapes to apply to the WordArt object.
	Free Rotate	Enables the Free Rotate tool (drag a corner of the object to set it at a new angle).
Aa	WordArt Same Letter Heights	Changes the height of the lowercase letters to match that of the uppercase letters.
Ab b	WordArt Vertical Text	Gives the text a vertical orientation.
	WordArt Alignment	Offers a set of alignment options to align the WordArt text within the boundaries of the object.
AV	WordArt Character Spacing	Changes the spacing between the letters of the WordArt text (selections range from Very Tight to Very Loose).

If you need to go back and edit the WordArt text, double-click in the middle of the WordArt and change the entry. To change the look of the WordArt, click it once to display the WordArt toolbar and then select options to modify the appearance of the object.

Review Questions

1. How do you create a text box?

2. How do you move a text box?

3. How do you change the text alignment in a text box?

4. How to you add more space between paragraphs?

5. How do you add a WordArt object to a slide?

Review Question Answers

1. In Slide view, select the slide to which you want to add the text box. Choose **Insert**, **Text Box** from the menu or click the **Text Box** button on the Drawing toolbar. Size the text box and type the text inside of the box. To start a new paragraph, press **Enter**. When you are finished, click outside the text box. For more information, refer to "Creating a Text Box."

2. Point at the border of the box (not the handles) until the mouse pointer becomes a four-headed arrow. Drag the box to a new location. Or, select the text box and then press an arrow key to move the box in the direction of the arrow. For more information, refer to "Selecting, Deleting, Sizing, and Moving a Text Box."

3. Select the text or paragraph and choose **Format**, **Alignment** from the menu. Select **Left**, **Center**, **Right**, or **Justify**. Alternatively, select the text and click one of the alignment buttons on the Formatting toolbar. For more information, refer to "Changing the Text Alignment."

4. Select the paragraph(s). Click the **Increase Paragraph Spacing** or **Decrease Paragraph Spacing** button on the Formatting toolbar. Or, choose **Format**, **Line Spacing** from the menu and specify the amount of space in the **Before Paragraph** or **After Paragraph** box. Click **OK**. For more information, refer to "Adjusting the Line Spacing."

5. When you're in the Slide view of the slide, choose **Insert**, **Picture**, **WordArt** from the menu or click the **Insert WordArt** button on the Drawing toolbar. Select a WordArt effect and click **OK**. Replace "Your Text Here" with your text and click **OK**.

Practice Lab

The Microsoft Expert User Exam lists three Required Tasks for the Skill Area "Adding Textual Information." This lesson covers one of these tasks. Following you will find a practice lab for the Required Task covered in this lesson.

 Required Tasks   The Required Task covered in this lesson is Change the Text Alignment.

Change the Text Alignment

Open Lesson5.ppt from the CD-ROM. Center-align all of the text on Slide 1. Center-align the text that appears in the green box on the balance of the slides in the presentation.

To see an example of a completed exercise, open the Lesson5a.ppt file.

LESSON 6

Changing the Look of Your Text

This lesson covers three of the seven Required Tasks for the "Modifying Presentations" Skill Area.

In this lesson, you learn the following Required Tasks for your exam:

▶ Change fonts

▶ Change tabs

▶ Change the alignment of text

For a complete list of Required Tasks for the Skill Area "Modifying Presentations," refer to the User Skills Roadmap.

Changing Fonts

A *font* is a family of characters that share the same design or typeface, such as Courier or Arial. When selecting a font, be careful to choose a readable one. Some decorative fonts, while pretty, are difficult to read when the text is longer than one or two words.

Restrict the fonts in your presentation to one or two. Using too many fonts is confusing. Instead, apply different font styles (such as bold and italic), sizes, colors, and effects (such as shadow) to emphasize or differentiate text.

Changing Fonts from a Dialog Box

Use the Font dialog box when you want to add several enhancements to your text at one time. You can select several options at once within the dialog box and then press OK once to have them take effect. Follow these steps to apply font enhancements to your text:

1. Select existing text or click where you are about to enter text to affect the font thereafter.

2. Choose **Format**, **Font** from the menu or right-click the text and select **Font** from the pop-up menu. The Font dialog box appears (see Figure 6.1).

Figure 6.1

Select the font, font style, size, color, and effects you want to apply to your text.

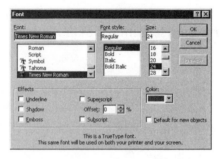

3. From the **Font** list, select the font you want to use.

4. From the **Font Style** list, select the style you want to apply to the text (choose **Regular** to remove any styles from selected text).

5. From the **Size** list, select the point size you want to apply to the text or enter a size directly into the box (even sizes that don't appear on the list, if your fonts are scalable).

 Scalable Fonts The TT next to a font name identifies the font as a TrueType font. TrueType fonts are *scalable*, which means you can set them at any point size. TrueType is a brand name, so you may have other brands of fonts installed on your computer, such as Adobe fonts. Each type of font has its own symbol in the font list. Fonts with printer icons in front are the fonts that came with your printer. Depending on your printer, these may also be scalable.

6. Under **Effects**, select any special effects that you want to apply:

   ▶ **Underline** places a single, thin underline under the text.

   ▶ **Shadow** places a duplicate of the text in a different color behind the text, just slightly offset to give the impression of a shadow.

   ▶ **Emboss** makes text appear as if it was raised off the page in relief.

   ▶ **Superscript** reduces the text in size and raises it above the baseline, as in ProductName™.

   ▶ **Subscript** reduces the text in size and places it slightly below the baseline, as in H_2O.

7. To change the color of the text, select the desired color from the **Color** drop-down list (click **More Colors** to see a larger selection).

8. If you want every new text box (not placeholders) to have these same font attributes from now on, check **Default for New Objects**.

9. Click **OK** to apply the font choices to the selected text or to the text you're about to type.

 Title and Text Placeholders   If you change the font of a title or the text in a text placeholder on an individual slide, that change only applies to that slide. To change the font for all the titles or placeholders in a presentation, you must change the slide master. See Lesson 19, "Changing a Presentation's Look," to learn how to modify the slide master.

Changing Fonts with the Formatting Toolbar

The Formatting toolbar contains several tools for changing the font, size, and style of text.

To change the appearance of existing text, select the text and then use the appropriate tool. See Table 6.1 for a description of the tools on the Formatting toolbar.

Table 6.1   Formatting Tools

Button	Name	Description
Times New Roman	Font	Selects the font you want from the drop-down list.
14	Font Size	Selects the size you want for your font (in points) from the drop-down list.
B	Bold	Applies the bold style to your text.
I	Italic	Applies the italic style to your text.
U	Underline	Applies a single underline to the text.
S	Shadow	Adds a shadow to your text.
≡	Left Alignment	Makes your text align to the left border of the text box.
≡	Center Alignment	Aligns your text horizontally between the left and right borders of the text box.
≡	Right Alignment	Aligns the text to the right border of the text box.
⁞≡	Bullets	Adds bullets in front of the paragraph.
⇅≡	Increase Paragraph Spacing	Adds more space before the paragraph.
⇅≡	Decrease Paragraph Spacing	Decreases the space before the paragraph.
A	Increase Font Size	Increases the font size to the next higher size.
A	Decrease Font Size	Decreases the font size to the next smaller size.

Changing the Font Color with the Drawing Toolbar

The Font Color button on the Drawing toolbar enables you to change the color of selected text. To use the **Font Color** button, do the following:

1. Select the text that you want to modify.

2. Click the **Font Color** button to apply the displayed color to your text. Click the arrow next to the button to choose a different color.

3. Click the color you want to apply to the text or select **More Font Colors** to have more color choices.

Copying Text Formats

After you have the format set for some of the text in your presentation, you can pick up that formatting to apply it to other text. To copy text formats, do the following:

1. Select the text that has the format you want to use.

2. Click the **Format Painter** button on the Standard toolbar.

3. Drag the mouse pointer across the text to which you want to apply the format.

Changing Tabs

A presentation often uses tabbed columns to display information, such as the three-column list shown in Figure 6.2.

Figure 6.2

Use tabs to create a multicolumn list.

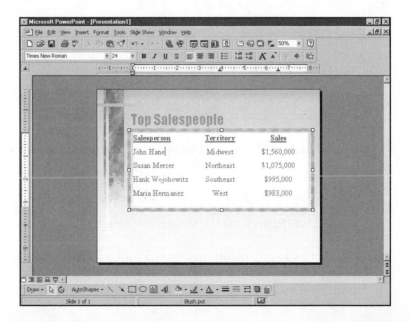

Follow these instructions to set tabs:

1. In Slide view, display the slide where you want to create the tabbed columns.

2. Create a text box for the tabbed text (refer Lesson 5, "Adding Text to a Slide," to learn how to create a text box). To set tabs inside a text box where you already have text, select the text.

3. Choose **View**, **Ruler** from the menu to display the ruler, if it isn't already showing.

4. Click the tab type selector at the left end of the ruler (see Figure 6.3). Each time you click the selector, it cycles to another tab type. Keep clicking until you see the type of tab you want to set:

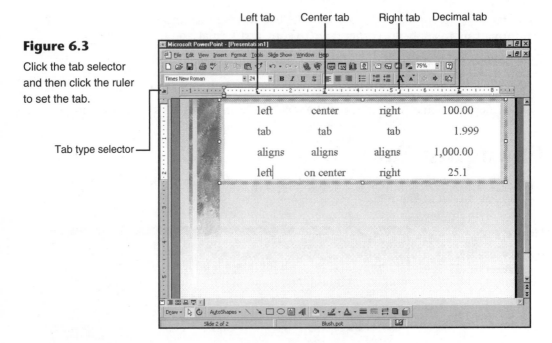

Figure 6.3

Click the tab selector and then click the ruler to set the tab.

Tab type selector

▶ **Left** tab aligns the left end of the tabbed text at the tab stop.

▶ **Right** tab aligns the right end of the tabbed text at the tab stop.

▶ **Center** tab centers the tabbed text under the tab stop.

▶ **Decimal** tab aligns the tabbed numbers by the decimal point.

5. Click in the ruler (close to the bottom border is best) to place a tab stop. If the tab stop is not exactly at the measurement where you want it, drag the stop to the desired location. To delete a tab stop, drag it off the ruler and release.

6. Repeat steps 4 and 5 for each tab stop you want to set.

7. To turn off the ruler, choose **View**, **Ruler** from the menu.

Changing the Alignment of Text

Normally, PowerPoint aligns the text to the left edge of the text box and leaves the ends of the lines ragged on the right. That is because the default alignment setting is left-aligned.

To change the alignment of the text within a text box, follow these steps:

1. Click inside the paragraph you want to align or select multiple paragraphs.

2. Choose **Format**, **Alignment** from the menu.

3. From the submenu that appears, select **Left**, **Center**, **Right**, or **Justify**.

 Alignment Shortcuts   To quickly set the alignment of a selected paragraph, click the **Left Alignment**, **Center Alignment**, or **Right Alignment** button on the Formatting toolbar. Or, use the keyboard shortcuts: **Ctrl+L** for left alignment, **Ctrl+R** for right alignment, or **Ctrl+E** for center alignment.

Review Questions

1. Explain how to change the font.

2. How do you create a multicolumn list using tab settings?

3. Describe how to change text alignment.

4. How do you set the color of text?

5. How do you copy the text format from existing text to another text selection?

Review Question Answers

1. Select existing text or click where you want to enter new text. Choose **Format**, **Font** from the menu or right-click the text and select **Font** from the pop-up menu. Select the font you want from the **Font** list. Select a style from the **Font Style** list (if applicable) and any special effects in the **Effects** list. Change the **Color** if desired and click **OK**. For more information, refer to "Changing Fonts."

2. In Slide view, display the slide you want to create multicolumns in. Create a text box for the tabbed text. Choose **View**, **Ruler** from the menu. Click the tab type selector at the left end of the ruler and select the type of tab (left tab, and so forth). Click the ruler to place a tab stop. Click to set all of the tab stops you need. For more information, refer to "Changing Tabs."

3. Click in the paragraph you want to align or select multiple paragraphs. Choose **Format**, **Alignment** from the menu and select the alignment. Alternatively, click the alignment buttons on the Formatting toolbar. For more information, refer to "Changing the Alignment of Text."

4. Select the text and click the **Font Color** button on the Drawing toolbar, or choose **Format**, **Font** from the menu, make a selection from the **Color** box, and click OK. For more information, refer to "Changing the Font Color with the Drawing Toolbar."

5. Select the text that has the format you want to copy. Click the **Format Painter** button on the Standard toolbar. Use the mouse pointer to select the text to which you want to copy the format.

Practice Lab

The Microsoft Expert User Exam lists seven Required Tasks for the Skill Area "Modifying Presentations." Three of these tasks are covered in this lesson. Following you will find a practice lab for the Required Tasks covered in this lesson.

 Required Tasks The Required Tasks covered in this lesson are Change Fonts, Change Tabs, and Change the Alignment of Text.

For this lab, open Lesson6.ppt from the CD-ROM.

Change Fonts

Change the font for the title page to Times New Roman.

Change Tabs

Insert a new blank slide after Slide 7, "Progress Against Goals." Add a text box and create a three-column look by inserting three tab stops about 1.5 inches apart. Make the spacing of the tabs even. Enter the following information:

Unit Sales for First Quarter

Item	Jan	Feb	Mar
Cordials	889.88	79.84	889.98
Bars	79.84	9.90	50.60
Ice Cream	1001	444.56	449.90

Change the Alignment of Text

Decimal-align the columns and numbers you created in the previous step.

To see an example of a completed exercise, open the file Lesson6a.ppt on the CD-ROM.

LESSON 7

Rearranging Slides in a Presentation

This lesson covers two of the seven Required Tasks for the "Modifying Presentations" Skill Area.

In this lesson you learn the following Required Tasks for your exam:

- ▶ Change the sequence of a slide
- ▶ Modify sequence in outline mode

For a complete list of Required Tasks for the Skill Area "Modifying Presentations," refer to the User Skills Roadmap.

Changing the Sequence of a Slide

The Slide Sorter view shows miniature versions of the slides in your presentation. This enables you to view many of your slides at one time. To rearrange the order of your slides, follow these steps:

1. Switch to the Slide Sorter view by choosing **View**, **Slide Sorter** from the menu or by clicking the **Slide Sorter View** button above the status bar.

2. Move the mouse pointer over the slide you want to move.

3. Hold down the left mouse button and drag over the slide before or after where you want to insert the slide. As you drag the mouse pointer, a vertical line appears showing where you are moving the slide (see Figure 7.1). If you can't see your destination as you drag, just continue dragging in the direction of the destination and the display will scroll in that direction.

Figure 7.1

A vertical line shows where your slide will appear when you release the mouse button.

Vertical line ⎯

Moving mouse pointer ⎯

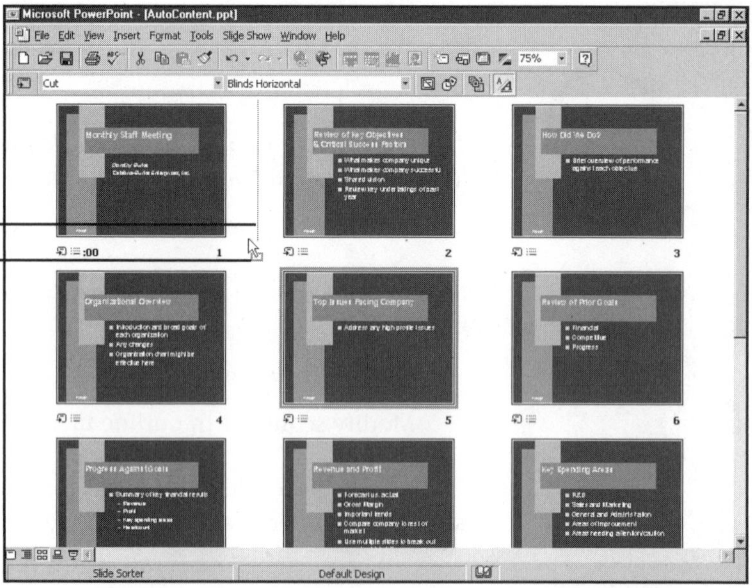

4. When the vertical line appears where you want to place the slide, release the mouse button. PowerPoint places the slide in its location and shifts the other slides to make room for the new slide. The slides are also renumbered to reflect the new order.

Copying a Slide   You can copy a slide in Slide Sorter view as easily as you can move a slide. Simply hold down the **Ctrl** key as you drag the slide. When you release the mouse button, the duplicate slide appears at the position of the vertical line.

Dragging and Dropping Between Presentations   The drag-and-drop method can be used between different presentations to copy slides from one presentation to the other. Open both presentations and then choose **Window**, **Arrange All** from the menu. The two presentation windows will appear side by side. Change to Slide Sorter view in both presentations. Now drag the slides from one presentation and drop them in the other.

Modifying Sequence in Outline Mode

In Outline view, you see the titles and text on each slide. This view gives you a clearer picture of the content and organization of your presentation than the other views, so you may prefer to rearrange your slides in Outline view. Here's how:

1. Switch to the Outline view by choosing **View**, **Outline** from the menu or clicking the **Outline View** button above the status bar.

2. For the slide you want to move, click the Slide icon to the left of the slide title. This highlights (selects) all the text of the slide.

3. Move the mouse pointer over the slide icon until the pointer becomes a four-headed arrow, hold down the left mouse button, and drag the slide up or down in the outline (see Figure 7.2).

Figure 7.2

Drag the slide until the horizontal line appears at the spot where you want to insert the slide.

Horizontal line

Slide icon

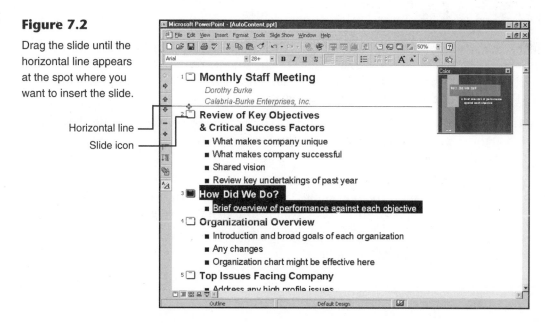

4. When the horizontal line is at the point where you want to put the slide (make sure it's not in the middle of another slide), release the mouse button. Be careful to keep the mouse pointer directly above or below the former position of the slide, because if you move it to the right or left before you release the mouse button, you might accidentally indent the entire slide.

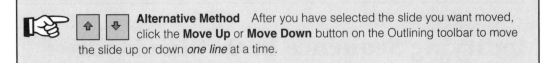

Alternative Method   After you have selected the slide you want moved, click the **Move Up** or **Move Down** button on the Outlining toolbar to move the slide up or down *one line* at a time.

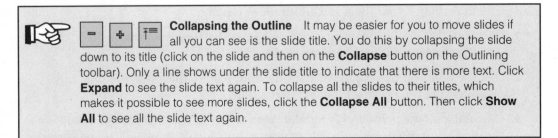

Collapsing the Outline   It may be easier for you to move slides if all you can see is the slide title. You do this by collapsing the slide down to its title (click on the slide and then on the **Collapse** button on the Outlining toolbar). Only a line shows under the slide title to indicate that there is more text. Click **Expand** to see the slide text again. To collapse all the slides to their titles, which makes it possible to see more slides, click the **Collapse All** button. Then click **Show All** to see all the slide text again.

Hiding Slides

Before you give a presentation, you should try to anticipate any questions that your audience may have and be prepared to answer those questions. You might even want to create slides to support your answers to these questions and then keep the slides hidden until you need them. To hide one or more slides, follow these steps:

1. Display or select the slide(s) you want to hide. You can do this from the Slide, Outline, or Slide Sorter views. For information on how to select multiple slides, refer to Lesson 3, "Adding and Deleting Slides."

2. Choose **Slide Show**, **Hide Slide** from the menu or right-click the slide and select **Hide** from the pop-up menu. If you're in Slide Sorter view, the hidden slide's number appears in a box with a line through it (see Figure 7.3).

3. To unhide the slide(s), display or select the hidden slide(s) and then choose **Slide Show**, **Hide Slide** again.

Presenting Hidden Slides   During the Slide Show you can display a hidden slide by right-clicking the screen and selecting **Go**, **Hidden Slide** from the pop-up menu. All hidden slides will then be visible for the remainder of the slide show.

Figure 7.3

When you hide a slide, its number appears crossed out in Slide Sorter view.

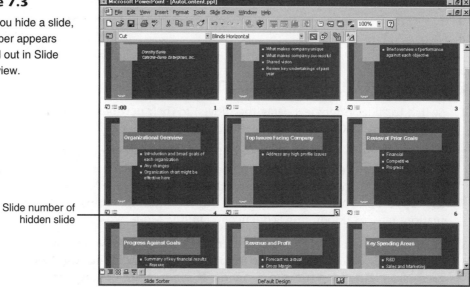

Slide number of hidden slide

 Printing Hidden Slides   When you print the presentation, select the **Print Hidden Slides** option in the Print dialog box to print the hidden slides.

Review Questions

1. How do you change the sequence of slides in a presentation using the Slide Sorter?

2. How do you change the sequence of slides while in Outline view?

3. How do you hide slides?

Review Question Answers

1. Switch to Slide Sorter view. Drag the slide(s) to their new place. For more information, refer to "Changing the Sequence of a Slide."

2. Switch to Outline view. Click to the left of the slide you want to move. Hold the mouse pointer over the slide until it becomes a four-headed arrow. Drag the slide to its new place in the outline. Alternatively, select the slide to move and click the **Move Up** or **Move Down** buttons on the Outlining toolbar. For more information, refer to "Modifying Sequence in Outline Mode."

3. In the Slide Sorter or Outline view, select the slide or slides you want to hide. Choose **Slide Show**, **Hide Slide** from the menu or right-click the slide(s) and then select **Hide** from the pop-up menu. For more information, refer to "Hiding Slides."

Practice Lab

The Microsoft Expert User Exam lists seven Required Tasks for the Skill Area "Modifying Presentations." Two of these tasks have been covered in this lesson. Following you find a practice lab for these two tasks.

Required Tasks   The Required Tasks covered in this lesson are Change the Sequence of a Slide and Modify Sequence in Outline Mode.

Change the Sequence of a Slide

Open Lesson7.ppt from the CD-ROM. In Slide Sorter view, change the order of the slides to the following:

Monthly Staff Meeting

Organizational Overview

Our Success Story

How Do We Do It?

Review of Prior Goals

Progress Against Goals

Revenue and Profit

Key Spending Areas

Headcount

Goals for Next Period

Top Issues Facing Company

Summary

Modify Sequence in Outline Mode

Switch to Outline view. Switch the order of slides so that "Top Issues Facing Company" comes before "Goals for Next Period."

To see an example of a completed exercise, open the file Lesson7a.ppt on the CD-ROM.

Finding and Replacing Text

This lesson covers one of the seven Required Tasks for the "Modifying Presentations" Skill Area.

In this lesson, you learn the following Required Task for your exam:

▶ Find and replace text

For a complete list of Required Tasks for the Skill Area "Modifying Presentations," refer to the User Skills Roadmap.

Finding and Replacing Text

If you want to find a particular word or phrase in your presentation but you can't remember or don't know where it is, have PowerPoint find the word or phrase for you. PowerPoint can also replace that word or phrase with a different word or phrase.

Finding Text

PowerPoint can search through your presentation to find occurrences of specific text. To find text, follow these steps:

1. Choose **Edit**, **Find** from the menu or press **Ctrl+F**. The Find dialog box appears (see Figure 8.1).

Figure 8.1

Enter the word or phrase you want to find in the Find What text box.

2. In the **Find What** text box, enter the text for which you're searching (the *search string*).

3. If needed, select one of the two find options:

    ▶   **Match Case**   Requires an exact match for uppercase and lowercase letters. By selecting this option, **The** will only match **The** and not **the** or **THE**.

    ▶   **Find Whole Words Only**   This will match whole words only. By selecting this check box, **the** will match only **the** and not **mother**, **these**, and so on.

4. Click **Find Next**. PowerPoint looks through the presentation for text that matches your search string. If it finds matching text, it highlights it and stops. The Find dialog box remains on the screen.

 Quick Jump to Replace   If you start out using Find and then realize that you want to replace the found word with something else, just click the **Replace** button in the Find dialog box to jump to the Replace dialog box (explained in the next section).

5. Click **Find Next** if you want to continue the search for another instance of the search string.

6. Click **Close** to close the dialog box. The found text remains highlighted.

When PowerPoint has searched the entire presentation, or if the search string cannot be found, PowerPoint displays a message informing you of the search status.

 Repeat Searches   When you open the Find dialog box, the previous search string from your current PowerPoint session (if any) will still be displayed in the **Find What** text box. This makes it easy to repeat the previous search.

 Can't find it?   If you can't find text that you're sure is in the document, check the spelling of the search string and make sure unwanted search options are not enabled.

Replacing Text

PowerPoint's Replace command enables you to search for instances of text and replace them with new text.

To replace text, do the following:

1. Choose **Edit**, **Replace** from the menu or press **Ctrl+H**. The Replace dialog box appears (see Figure 8.2).

Figure 8.2

Enter the text you want to replace in the Find What box and the replacement text in the Replace With box.

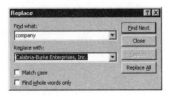

2. In the **Find What** text box, enter the text you want to replace.

3. In the **Replace With** text box, enter the replacement text.

4. If needed, select one of the two find options:

  ▶ **Match Case**   Requires an exact match for uppercase and lowercase letters. By selecting this option, **The** will only match **The** and not **the** or **THE**.

  ▶ **Find Whole Words Only**   This will match whole words only. By selecting this check box, **the** will match only **the** and not **mother**, **these**, and so on.

5. Click **Find Next** to locate and highlight the first instance of matching text. Then:

  ▶ Click **Replace** to replace the highlighted instance of matching text and then locate the next instance of it.

  ▶ Click **Find Next** to leave the highlighted instance of the matching text unchanged and to locate the next instance.

  ▶ Click **Replace All** to replace all instances of matching text in the entire document.

6. Click **Close** to close the Replace dialog box.

When PowerPoint has searched the entire presentation and replaced all the instances of the search string, or if the search string couldn't be found, PowerPoint displays a message informing you of the search status. Click **OK** to resume work on your presentation.

Review Questions

1. Explain how to find a word or phrase in your presentation.

2. How do you replace text in your presentation?

Review Question Answers

1. Choose **Edit**, **Find** from the menu or press **Ctrl+F**. Type the word or phrase in the **Find What** text box and click **Find Next**. For more information, refer to "Finding Text."

2. Choose **Edit**, **Replace** from the menu or press **Ctrl+H**. Enter the text you want to replace in the **Find What** text box and enter the text you want to appear in the **Replace With** text box. Click **Find Next**. When the first instance of the text you want to replace appears, choose **Replace** to replace the text. If you want to replace all the instances of the text without stopping at each occurrence, click **Replace All**. For more information, refer to "Replacing Text."

Practice Lab

The Microsoft Expert User Exam lists seven Required Tasks for the Skill Area "Modifying Presentations." One of these tasks has been covered in this lesson. Following you find a practice lab for that task.

 Required Tasks   The Required Task covered in this lesson is Find and Replace Text.

Find and Replace Text

Open Lesson8.ppt from the CD-ROM. Replace Calabria-Burke Enterprises with Burke-Calabria Enterprises throughout the entire presentation. Search for the word **goals**. Replace **goals** with **objectives** except where it appears on the slide "Issues Facing Company."

To see an example of a completed exercise, open the file Lesson8a.ppt on the CD-ROM.

LESSON 9

Checking Spelling

This lesson covers one of the three Required Tasks for the "Editing Presentations" Skill Area.

In this lesson, you learn the following Required Task for your exam:

▶ Using the spelling checker

For a complete list of Required Tasks for the Skill Area "Editing Presentations," refer to the User Skills Roadmap.

Using the Spelling Checker

PowerPoint uses a built-in dictionary to check the spelling in your entire presentation, including all slides, outlines, notes pages, and handout pages. The spell checker works in the Slide, Outline, Slide Sorter, and Notes Pages views.

Checking as You Type

As you enter text in your presentation, PowerPoint checks it against the dictionary. Any word that doesn't have a match in the dictionary is marked with a wavy red underline (see Figure 9.1). This doesn't mean the word is spelled incorrectly—only that the word isn't in the dictionary.

To quickly correct a word with the wavy red underline, right-click it. From the pop-up menu, select a suggested correct spelling, click **Ignore All** to skip that word throughout the presentation (such as a proper name that's spelled correctly), or click **Add** to add the word to the dictionary.

Figure 9.1

Right-click a potentially misspelled word to see a menu of spelling options.

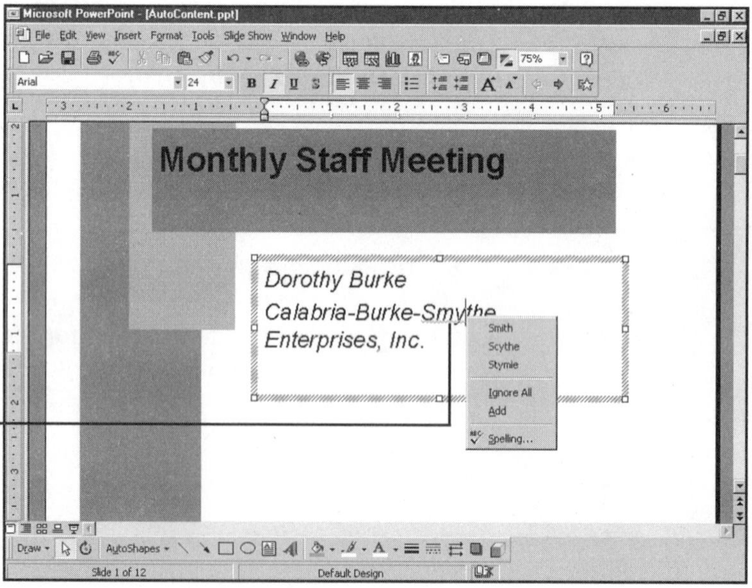

Wavy red underline ————

Checking the Entire Presentation

Follow these steps to check the spelling in your entire presentation:

1. Choose **Tools**, **Spelling** from the menu or click the **Spelling** button on the Standard toolbar or press **F7**.

2. If there are no misspellings, PowerPoint displays a dialog box saying that the spell check is complete and you must click **OK** to close the box and continue working in the presentation.

If PowerPoint detects possible misspellings, the Spelling dialog box appears (see Figure 9.2). The first suspect word PowerPoint encounters appears in the **Not in Dictionary** box.

Figure 9.2

Select the correct spelling from the Suggestions box or enter the correct text in the Change To box.

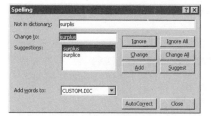

3. Select one of these options by clicking the appropriate button:

▶ **Ignore** to skip only this occurrence of the word.

▶ **Ignore All** to ignore every occurrence of the word in the presentation.

▶ **Change** to replace only this occurrence of the word with the word in the **Change To** box (type a correction in the **Change To** box or select a correct spelling from the **Suggestions** list).

▶ **Change All** to replace every occurrence of the word with the word in the **Change To** box (type a correction in the **Change To** box or select a correct spelling from the **Suggestions** list).

▶ **Add** to add the word to the dictionary, so the spell check will not question it again.

▶ **Suggest** to display a list of suggested words.

▶ **AutoCorrect** to add the misspelled word to the AutoCorrect list, with the word that appears in the **Change To** box as its correction. From then on, PowerPoint will automatically correct that misspelling if you make it again. Be careful that you spelled the word correctly before you do this!

▶ **Close** to close the Spelling dialog box without completing the spell check of the entire presentation.

4. Repeat step 3 for each possible misspelling that PowerPoint finds.

5. When the spell checker finishes checking the entire presentation, a dialog box appears telling you that the spell check is complete. Click **OK**.

Using AutoCorrect

There are certain misspellings that many people commonly make, such as transposing letters ("teh" instead of "the"), or words that are frequently misspelled (such as receive and occurrence). AutoCorrect identifies and corrects these common errors automatically as you type. You may also add your own common errors to the list.

To view and make changes to the AutoCorrect list, follow these steps:

1. Choose **Tools**, **AutoCorrect** from the menu. The AutoCorrect dialog box opens (see Figure 9.3).

Figure 9.3

Enter your own spelling error in the Replace box, type its correction in the With box, and then click Add.

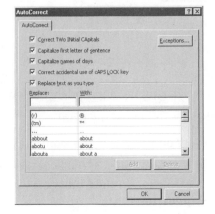

2. Do one of the following:

   ▶ Deselect any of the capitalization options—**Correct Two Initial Capitals**, **Capitalize the First Letter of Sentence**, **Capitalize Names of Days**, **Correct Accidental Use of Caps Lock Key**—at the top of the dialog box that you don't want to use. Click **Exceptions** to create a list of abbreviations and capitalization styles that you don't want to be corrected automatically.

   ▶ To add a correction to the list, type the misspelling in the **Replace** text box and the correction in the With text box. Then click the **Add** button.

   ▶ To remove a correction from the list, scroll through the list to find it, select it, and click the **Delete** button.

   ▶ To make a change to a correction, select it, make the change in the **Replace** or **With** text boxes, and then click the **Replace** button.

3. Click **OK**.

If AutoCorrect keeps correcting spelling of proper names or technical terms, remove those corrections from the replacement list. If this is not enough, you can turn AutoCorrect off by choosing **Tools**, **Options** from the menu, selecting the **Spelling** tab, and deselecting the **Spelling** option under **Check Spelling as You Type**.

 Abbreviations and Acronyms   Add abbreviations to the AutoCorrect list so PowerPoint will automatically replace the abbreviation with the full text.

Review Questions

1. How do you use the spelling checker to check for spelling errors?

2. How do you add a frequently misspelled word to the AutoCorrect list?

3. True or False: You can use AutoCorrect to replace abbreviations with the full text.

4. How do you keep AutoCorrect from treating "TNeat Company" as an error by changing it to "Tneat Company?"

Review Question Answers

1. Run the spelling checker by choosing **Tools**, **Spelling** from the menu. Alternatively, right-click the red-underlined words that are identified as potential misspellings. Choose the correct spelling or click **Ignore**. For more information, refer to "Using the Spelling Checker."

2. Choose **Tools**, **AutoCorrect** from the menu. Make sure the **Replace Text as You Type** option is selected. Enter the misspelling in the **Replace** box. Type the correct spelling in the **With** box. Click **OK**. For more information, refer to "Using AutoCorrect."

3. True. Enter the abbreviation in the **Replace** box of the AutoCorrect dialog box. Enter the full text in the **With** box. Click **OK**.

4. Either deselect the **Correct Two Initial Capitals** option in the AutoCorrect dialog box, or click the **Exceptions** button, select the **Initial Caps** tab, and enter **TNeat Company** in the **Don't Correct** box. Click **OK**.

Practice Lab

The Microsoft Expert User Exam lists three Required Tasks for the Skill Area "Editing Presentations." One of these tasks has been covered in this lesson. A practice lab for this Required Task follows.

 Required Tasks   The Required Task covered in this lesson is Using the Spelling Checker.

Using the Spelling Checker

Open the file Lesson9.ppt from the CD-ROM. Search the document for potential spelling errors by accessing the spelling checker from the menu. Correct the errors.

To see an example of a completed exercise, open the file Lesson9a.ppt on the CD-ROM.

Adding a Graph to a Slide

This lesson covers one of the twelve Required Tasks for the "Adding Visual Elements" Skill Area.

In this lesson, you learn the following Required Task for your exam:

▶ Build a graph

For a complete list of Required Tasks for the Skill Area "Adding Visual Elements," refer to the User Skills Roadmap.

Building a Graph

Microsoft packages a program called Microsoft Graph with its PowerPoint program or Office Suite. Microsoft Graph transforms raw data such as income, expenses, or demographic statistics into professional-looking graphs (or charts). When you save the graph, it appears on your slide.

To create a graph, follow these steps:

1. In the Slide view, display the slide to which you want to add the graph.

2. If you have chosen an AutoLayout for the slide, double-click in the middle of the chart placeholder. If not, choose **Insert**, **Chart** from the menu or click the **Insert Chart** button on the Standard toolbar.

3. The Microsoft Graph program starts (see Figure 10.1). Replace the sample data in the Datasheet window with your own data—just click in a cell and type to replace the data that's there. For more information on using the Datasheet, see "Editing the Datasheet" later in this lesson.

Figure 10.1

When you open Microsoft Graph, the Datasheet appears where you enter your charting information and a picture of the graph displays within a border on the screen.

Datasheet window ——

Graph ——

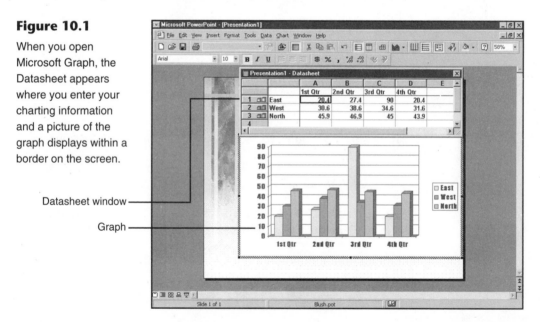

Datasheet The Datasheet is set up like a spreadsheet with rows and columns. Each rectangle in the Datasheet is a *cell* that can hold text or numbers. Microsoft Graph converts the data you enter in the Datasheet into a graph that it displays in the Graph window.

4. After you finish entering your data in the Datasheet, choose **View**, **Datasheet** from the menu to close the Datasheet window or click the **View Datasheet** button on the Standard toolbar.

   If you need to see the Datasheet again, choose **View**, **Datasheet** from the menu or click the **View Datasheet** button on the Standard toolbar.

5. Select the type of graph you want to display by clicking the down arrow next to the **Chart Type** button on the Standard toolbar and then clicking one of the chart types displayed (see Figure 10.2). See "Changing the Chart Type" later in this lesson for more information on selecting chart types.

6. To leave Microsoft Graph and return to your slide in PowerPoint, click anywhere outside the border surrounding the graph.

Figure 10.2

When you click the down arrow next to the Chart Type button, you see a selection of chart types from which to choose.

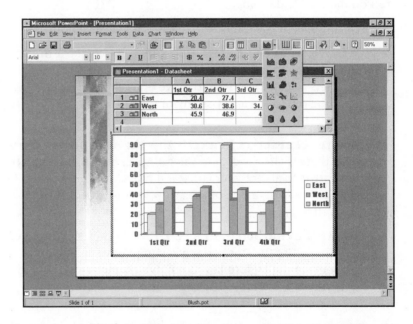

 I lost the graph tools! Did you accidentally click outside the border around the graph or outside the Datasheet? To go back to Microsoft Graph or to edit the existing graph, double-click in the middle of the graph (be sure to click on something solid, not background). When Microsoft Graph reopens, the graphing tools will also appear.

Moving and Sizing the Graph After you return to the slide, the graph will appear with handles around it. To size the graph, drag one of the handles toward or away from the center of the graph to reduce or increase its size. To move the graph, click in the middle and drag the graph to a new site on the slide.

Editing the Datasheet

If you've returned to your PowerPoint slide, double-click in the middle of the graph to open the Microsoft Graph program. Then choose **View**, **Datasheet** from the menu to open the Datasheet window if it isn't currently displayed or click the **View Datasheet** button on the Standard toolbar.

To enter or edit data in the Datasheet, follow these instructions:

▶ **To move from cell to cell**. Click any cell to make it the active cell (there is a thicker border around the active cell; the cell must be active before you can enter characters there). Press **Tab** to move one cell to the right. Press **Shift+Tab** to move one cell to the left. Use any of the arrow keys to move one cell in the direction of the arrow.

▶ **To enter characters in a cell**. After the cell is active, type your data in the cell. If there is already data in the cell, your data will automatically replace it. Press **Enter** to accept your entry and move one cell down in the column or press **Tab**, **Shift+Tab**, or one of the arrow keys to accept the entry and move to another cell.

▶ **To edit the characters in a cell**. Double-click the cell to place an insertion point there. Use the **Backspace** key to remove characters to the left of the insertion point or the **Delete** key to remove characters to the right. Use the left and right arrow keys to move back and forth. Press **Enter** to accept the changes to the cell contents.

▶ **To select cells**. To select one cell, click on it. To select several cells, drag the mouse pointer over the desired cells. To select an entire row or column, select the number to the left of the row or the letter above the column. To select all the cells, click in the upper-left square in the Datasheet.

▶ **To clear cells**. To erase the contents of cells, select the cells, and then choose **Edit**, **Clear** from the menu. Select **All** (to clear contents and formatting), **Contents** (to remove only the contents), or **Formats** (to remove the formatting but leave the contents intact). Pressing the **Delete** key clears just the contents, or right-click the cell and choose **Clear Contents** from the pop-up menu.

▶ **To cut or copy cells**. Select the cells you want to cut or copy. Then choose **Edit**, **Cut** or **Edit**, **Copy** from the menu, click the **Cut** or **Copy** button on the Standard toolbar, or right-click the selection and choose **Cut** or **Copy** from the pop-up menu.

▶ **To paste cells**. Select the cell in the upper-left corner of the area in which you want to paste the cells you previously cut or copied. Choose **Edit**, **Paste** from the menu, click the **Paste** button on the Standard toolbar, or right-click on the destination and choose **Paste** from the pop-up menu.

▶ **To insert blank cells**. To insert blank cells into your Datasheet, select the row, column, or number of cells you want to insert (rows will be inserted above the current row; columns will be inserted to the left of the current column). Choose **Insert**, **Cells** from the menu. When the Insert dialog box appears (see Figure 10.3), choose whether you want to shift the surrounding cells down or to the right and then click **OK**. Or, right-click where you want the cells to go and select **Insert** from the pop-up menu.

There's Always Undo Don't forget that if you make a mistake moving or shifting cells, you can always click the **Undo** button, press **Ctrl+Z**, or choose **Edit**, **Undo** to undo your last action.

Figure 10.3

Choose to shift cells down or to the right and then click OK.

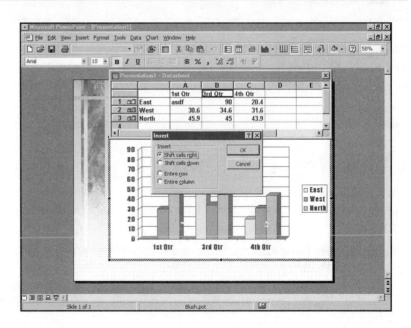

▶ **To delete rows or columns**. Select the row or column you want to delete by clicking the row number to the left of the row or the column letter at the top of the column. Choose **Edit**, **Delete** from the menu.

▶ **To change the column width**. If you type entries that are too wide for a particular column, you may want to adjust the column width (this doesn't affect the graph). Move the mouse pointer to the border on the right of the column letter cell at the top of the column. When the mouse pointer becomes a two-headed arrow, hold down the mouse button, and drag until the column is the desired width.

Changing the Data Series

When you enter data in the Datasheet, each row of data you enter is a *series*. There are times, however, when you want the series to be in columns. For example, you might have a column graph of sales figures for several salespeople over several quarters in which each column represents quarters. Then you decided that the graph would be more effective if each column represents a salesperson To fix the graph, you need to swap the data series.

 Data Series A row or column of data used to plot one line, one pie, or one set of bars or columns in a graph.

To swap data series, choose **Data**, **Series in Rows** or **Data**, **Series in Columns** from the menu, depending on which way you need the data to be graphed.

This is particularly useful if you imported data from a spreadsheet file or if you're using the same datasheet information for more than one graph, and you need to swap the series for the graph to make sense.

Changing the Chart Type

Microsoft Graph always starts with the same sample data and the same 3-D column graph in place. This helps you understand where to place data so it will appear where you want it on the graph.

Unless you were planning on creating a 3-D column graph, you will need to change the chart type. Although you can do this using the **Chart Type** button as described in "Building a Graph" earlier in this lesson, using the Chart Type dialog box gives you more choices in selecting the type appropriate for you.

There are a variety of chart types available in Microsoft Graph. Bar and column charts are useful for comparing data over a time period; line charts show trends well; pie charts show what percentage of the whole each component represents; area charts can show trends compared to expected trends; and stock charts track the opening, closing, high, and low stock prices over a period of time.

Follow these steps to choose a chart type:

1. Choose **Chart**, **Chart Type** from the menu. The Chart Type dialog box appears (see Figure 10.4).

Figure 10.4

Select the type of chart you want and then choose from the displayed sub-types.

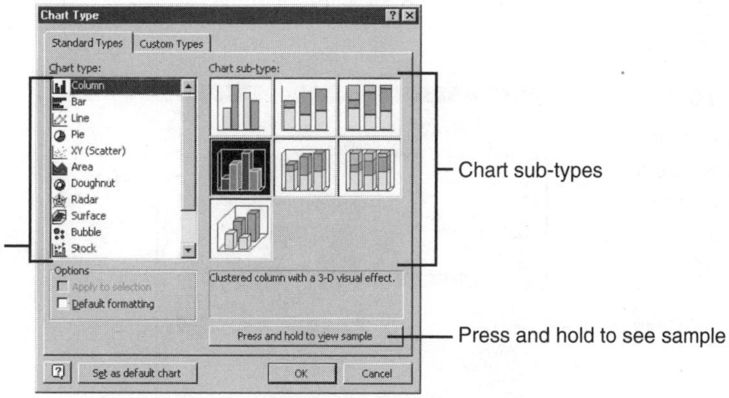

2. From the **Chart Type** list, select the type of chart you want to create.

3. Under **Chart Sub-Type**, Microsoft Graph displays several samples of the chart type you selected. Click on the example closest to what you want.

4. (Optional) To view a sample and see how it works with your data before you accept the chart, click and hold down the **Press and Hold to View Sample** button.

5. (Optional) If you want to make this type of chart the default chart that appears each time you open Microsoft Graph, click the **Set as Default Chart** button.

6. Click **OK** to apply the chart type to your data.

Setting Custom Options—Applying Custom Chart Types

Microsoft Graph comes with several predesigned chart formats that you can apply to your chart. You select the custom chart type you want, and Microsoft Graph reformats your chart, giving it a professional look. To use Custom Chart Types to select a chart design, follow these steps:

1. Choose **Chart**, **Chart Type** from the menu.

2. When the Chart Type dialog box appears, select the **Custom Types** tab (see Figure 10.5).

Figure 10.5

Select one of the predesigned chart formats from the Chart Type list.

Chart types ——

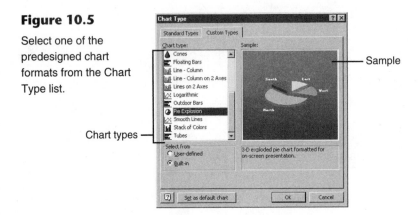

—— Sample

3. From the **Chart Type** list, select a chart type. When you select one, Microsoft Graph creates a preview of the chart type in the Sample box.

4. Click **OK**. Microsoft Graph reformats the chart using the selected custom type.

Review Questions

1. How do you add a graph to your presentation?

2. True or False: You delete a column from the datasheet by pressing the **Delete** key or by choosing **Edit**, **Cut** from the menu.

3. How do you delete a column from a datasheet?

4. If your datasheet displays the data for the quarters of the year as rows, do the labels for the quarters appear as categories on the X axis or as legends?

5. How do you make your category labels into the legend labels and your legend labels into categories?

6. How do you apply a custom chart type to your graph?

Review Question Answers

1. In Slide view, display the slide to which you want to add a graph. If you have chosen an AutoLayout for the slide, double-click in the middle of the chart placeholder. Choose **Insert**, **Chart** from the menu or click the **Insert Chart** button on the Standard toolbar. Enter your data into the Datasheet window and select the type of graph you want by clicking the **Chart Type** button on the standard toolbar. Click outside the chart area to return to your PowerPoint slide. For more information on inserting a chart in your slide, refer to "Building a Graph."

2. False. Either of those actions will not only delete the data, but will leave a blank column that translates as an empty spot in your graph.

3. Select the column by clicking the gray box at the head of the column. Choose **Edit**, **Delete** from the menu. For more information, refer to "Editing the Datasheet."

4. They appear as legends. Refer to Figure 10.1.

5. When you are in Microsoft Graph, choose **Data**, **Series in Columns** to switch them. Refer to "Changing the Data Series."

6. In the Microsoft Graph window, choose **Chart**, **Chart Type** from the menu. Select the **Custom Types** tab. Select a chart type from the **Chart Type** list. Click **OK**. Refer to "Applying Custom Chart Types."

Practice Lab

The Microsoft Expert User Exam lists twelve Required Tasks for the Skill Area "Adding Visual Elements." One of these tasks is covered in this lesson. A practice lab for this task follows.

 Required Tasks   The Required Task covered in this lesson is Build a Graph.

Build a Graph

On the "How we did it" slide, create a chart representing a large increase in sales from the years 1994 to 1997, as shown in Figure 10.6.

To see an example of a completed exercise, open the file Lesson10a.ppt from the CD-ROM.

Figure 10.6

Add a chart to the Lesson10.ppt presentation using this data.

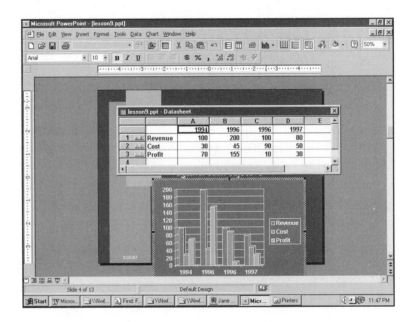

Enhancing a Graph

This lesson covers one of the twelve Required Tasks for the "Adding Visual Elements" Skill Area.

In this lesson, you learn the following Required Task for your exam:

▶ Add formatting

For a complete list of Required Tasks for the Skill Area "Adding Visual Elements," refer to the User Skills Roadmap.

What Can You Add to a Chart?

The basic graph PowerPoint builds when you enter data into the Datasheet is just the beginning. Microsoft Graph lets you format the existing elements and add others to improve the appearance and readability of the chart. Here's a list of some of the more common enhancements:

▶ **Fonts**   Specify type style, size, and attributes for the text you use in the chart.

▶ **Colors and Patterns**   Change the color of text, lines, bars, areas, and pie slices. Add patterns to bars, areas, or pie slices.

▶ **Axes**   Display or hide the lines of the Category and Value axes, change the scale of values shown, set the interval between gridlines, and format the numbers.

▶ **Titles and Labels**   Add titles to the chart or labels for the axes or data points.

▶ **Text Boxes**   Add explanatory text in a separate box.

▶ **Borders and Shading**   Add a border around the chart or background shading.

 Axis   A line that serves as a major reference for plotting data in a graph. Generally, the data values are plotted along the vertical axis, called the Y, or Value, axis, and the categories of data are plotted along the horizontal axis, called the X, or Category, axis. Where the two axes intersect is the zero (0) point of the Value axis. In a three dimensional (3-D) chart, you have a third axis that is referred to as the Z axis. The Z axis measures the depth of the 3-D object.

 Distinguishing Chart from Graph   PowerPoint uses the two terms chart and graph interchangeably. Although you use the **Insert Chart** command to add a chart, the program you create the chart in is Microsoft Graph. Don't worry about making a distinction between the two terms.

Displaying the Chart in Microsoft Graph

In order to enhance a chart, you must have the chart open in Microsoft Graph—either while you're creating the chart or when you're editing it. When you want to edit or enhance an existing chart, do the following:

1. In Slide View, display the slide that contains the graph you want to edit or enhance.

2. Select the graph by clicking it. A set of handles (small hollow boxes) appears around the chart.

3. Choose **Edit**, **Chart Object**, **Edit** from the menu.

 Quickly Return to Microsoft Graph The quickest way to open Microsoft Graph to edit or enhance an existing chart is to double-click in the middle of the graph.

Parts of a Chart

Before you start adding enhancements to a chart, you should understand that a chart is made up of several objects. By clicking an object, you make it active, and handles appear around it, as shown in Figure 11.1. You change the object's appearance by doing any of the following:

▶ Double-clicking an object to display a dialog box that enables you to change the object's appearance.

▶ Right-clicking the object and selecting the desired formatting option from the pop-up menu.

▶ Selecting the object and then selecting an option from the Format or Chart menu. The Format menu has options for changing the appearance of the object; the Chart menu enables you to add objects to a chart.

Figure 11.1

Each chart consists of several individual objects. As you point at different chart objects, a pop-up label for the object appears.

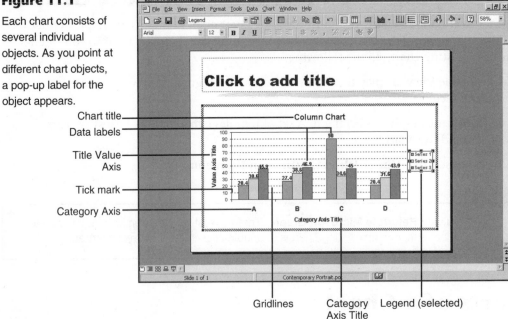

Chart title
Data labels
Title Value Axis
Tick mark
Category Axis

Gridlines   Category Axis Title   Legend (selected)

Adding Titles

There are three different titles available for each chart: the chart title, the Value Axis Title, and the Category Axis Title (refer to Figure 11.1). These are optional, and you may use all, some, or none of them.

To add titles to your chart, do the following:

1. Choose **Chart**, **Chart Options** from the menu, or right-click the chart and select **Chart Options** from the pop-up menu.

2. When the Chart Options dialog box appears, select the **Titles** tab (see Figure 11.2).

Figure 11.2

Enter the title text in the appropriate text boxes.

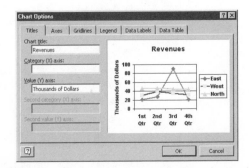

3. Enter the title you want centered at the top of the chart in the **Chart Title** box. This is the chart title, and should describe the overall purpose of the chart.

Enter the title you want to appear alongside the Value axis in the **Value (Y) Axis** box or **Value (Z) Axis** box (if the chart is 3-D). This title should provide some explanation of the data units or source.

Enter the title you want to appear beside the Category axis in the **Category (X) Axis** box. This title should explain what the categories mean.

4. Click **OK** to return to the chart window.

Adding Formatting

To add formatting to your chart, you first select the object in the chart you want to format and then select the formatting characteristics. The formatting options available depend on the object you selected. Be careful when selecting objects that have more than one "piece" in a group, such as the bars in one series of a column chart. When you click one piece in the group, all the pieces are selected and display handles. If you click the same piece again, only that piece is selected and displays handles, and all the formatting you choose will apply only to that piece.

Formatting Text on a Chart

There are two types of text on a chart:

▶ **Attached text** is any label linked to a graph object, such as an axis or data marker. Attached text moves with the item when it's repositioned, but cannot be moved independently of the graph object.

▶ **Non-attached text** is independent of the chart objects and usually appears in a text box that you added using Microsoft Graph's drawing tools. For example, you might add a comment on how good or bad a figure is, such as "Great Sales!" next to a bar or line. If you wish to make a formatting change for all the chart text at one time, the formatting won't apply to text in the text boxes. You must select the text box and format it separately.

 Text Boxes, Lines, and Arrows Microsoft Graph has a drawing toolbar that you activate by clicking the Drawing button on the Standard toolbar. It has tools that let you add text boxes, lines, arrows, and shapes to graphs in much the same way as you add them to slides. See Lesson 14, "Drawing Objects on a Slide," to learn how to use the tools on the Drawing toolbar.

To format text that's attached to the chart, do the following:

1. Select the text you want to format and then choose **Format**, **Select *Item*** (where ***Item*** is the name of the item you selected) from the menu, or right-click the text you want to format and then choose **Format *Item*** from the pop-up menu, or double-click the text (don't pause in your clicking, or Microsoft Graph will put the text in edit mode; then you'll have to drag through the text to select it). The Format *Item* dialog box appears (see Figure 11.3).

2. Select the **Font** tab to change the font, size, style, or color of the text, as shown in Figure 11.3.

Figure 11.3

Select the Font tab to change the font, size, style, or color of the text.

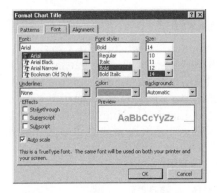

Select the **Alignment** tab (see Figure 11.4) to align the text between the left and right sides of the text box (select an option from the Horizontal drop-down list), set the position of the text between the top and bottom of the text box (select an option from the Vertical drop-down list), or choose an orientation by dragging the orientation indicator or entering a number in the Degrees box.

Figure 11.4

Select the Alignment tab to set the alignment or orientation of the text.

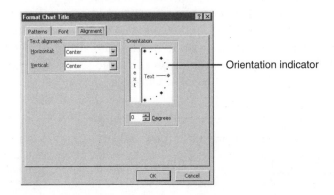

Orientation indicator

3. Click **OK** to apply the formatting to the selected text and close the dialog box.

If you have non-attached text, you can format the text in each text box separately. If you want to format more than one text box with the same formatting at the same time, click the text of the first box to select it, hold down the **Shift** key, and then click on each additional box. To format all the text in a text box, double-click the border of the box to open the Format Text Box dialog box (to format only part of the text, drag to select the text within the box you want to format and then choose **Format**, **Text Box** from the menu), in which you can set the font, color, alignment, and margins of the text within the box. You can also set the line and fill colors and patterns of the box, as well as set its size.

Formatting the Axes

Formatting the axes can involve changing the font of the labels, applying number formats to the values, setting the minimum and maximum values, setting the intervals between *tick marks*, and even changing the appearance of the axis line.

 Tick Mark   A small line that intersects an axis and marks off a category, scale, or data series. The major tick mark has a value or category label next to it. The minor tick marks fall between the major tick marks.

Follow these steps to change the axis formatting:

1. Select the axis by clicking it and then choose **Format**, **Selected Axis** from the menu, or right-click the axis and select **Format Axis** from the pop-up menu, or double-click the axis. This selects the axis line plus the text attached to it. The Format Axis dialog box appears (see Figure 11.5).

Figure 11.5

Set the formatting options for the selected axis.

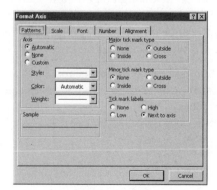

2. Select the appropriate tab to make the changes you want:

   ▶ **Patterns** Set the look of the axis line (**Style**, **Color**, and **Width**), choose what type of tick marks you want for the major and minor ticks (none, inside the axis line, outside the axis line, or crossing the axis line), and specify the position of the category or value labels in relation to the tick marks.

   ▶ **Scale** Specify the **Minimum** value (normally zero) and **Maximum** value (usually the highest number you enter in the Datasheet) to appear on the Value axis, the intervals between the **Major Units** and between the **Minor Units** (the spacing between tick marks), what numerical value the two axes cross at, whether to use a logarithmic scale instead of a linear one (a logarithmic scale doesn't have evenly spaced tick marks; the tick marks are closer together as the numbers get higher so the scale works better with larger numbers), or whether you want the scale to run in the reverse order. Figure 11.6 shows the Scale tab page for the Value axis. For the Category axis, the options are fewer: the number of categories between tick mark labels (enter 2 to show every other label), the number of categories between tick marks, where the Value and Category axis cross, and whether to run the categories in reverse order.

   ▶ **Font** Select the **Font**, **Size**, **Style**, **Color**, and Effects you want to apply to the labels along the axis. For example, if the labels are too small to read, you can choose a larger font size on this tab.

   ▶ **Number** Choose the number format you want to apply to the numbers on the Value axis. When you select a **Category**, a description appears at the bottom of the dialog box and an example shows in the Sample box (see Figure 11.7). Select the number of **Decimal Places** you want to use, the appearance of the **Negative Numbers**, currency **Symbol**, or other option specific to the format you selected.

   ▶ **Alignment** Choose the orientation (slant) of the text by dragging the orientation indicator or by entering the **Degrees** (see Figure 11.8).

3. Click **OK** to apply your choices to the selected axis.

Figure 11.6

Set the minimum and
maximum values of
the selected Value
Axis and the intervals
between tick marks.

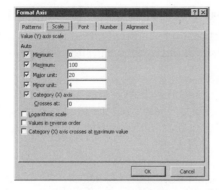

Figure 11.7

Select the number
format Category and
then set the appropri-
ate options.

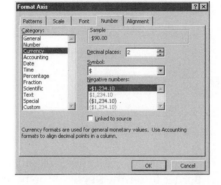

Figure 11.8

Choose the orienta-
tion of the value or
category labels in
relation to the axis.

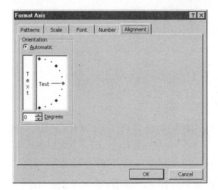

Adding Borders and Shading to Your Chart

A border around the chart or background shading behind it not only enhances the chart's appearance but makes the chart stand out against the slide background. To add a border or background, do the following:

1. Click the chart outside any specific chart object and choose **Format, Selected Chart Area** from the menu, or right-click the area and choose **Format Chart Area** from the pop-up menu, or double-click in the area. The Format Chart Area dialog box appears (see Figure 11.9).

Figure 11.9

Set the options for a border around the chart or choose a background color.

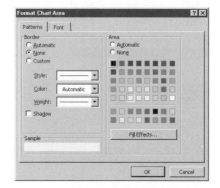

2. Select the **Patterns** tab (the **Font** tab controls the look of all the text on the chart). Make choices under Border to set the **Style** of the border line, the **Weight** of the line, and the **Color** of the line. Also, select **Shadow** to give the border a feeling of depth. Under Area select the color of the background shading. Click **Fill Effects** to select a gradient fill, a texture fill, or a pattern.

3. Click **OK**.

Placing the Legend

Although you can select the legend and drag it to a new location, using the dialog box options to position it means that it will also change to a horizontal format when placed on the top or bottom of the chart. To set the legend position, follow these steps:

1. Select the legend and choose **Format, Selected Legend** from the menu, or right-click the legend and then choose **Format Legend** from the pop-up menu, or double-click the legend.

2. When the Format Legend dialog box appears, select the **Placement** tab (use the **Font** tab to set text attributes for the legend text or the **Patterns** tab to format the box around the legend).

3. Select the placement option you want: **Top**, **Bottom**, **Left**, **Right**, or **Corner**.

4. Click **OK**.

 Formatting the Legend   In addition to setting the position of the legend in relation to the graph, the Format Legend dialog box offers options to change the font attributes of the legend text and the characteristics of the legend box fill and outline.

 Legend On/Off   To remove the legend or turn it back on, click the **Legend** button on the Standard toolbar of the Microsoft Graph window (you must be editing or creating the chart to see it).

Setting the Gridline Style

The chart gridlines are automatically solid lines. If you want dotted or dashed lines, do the following:

1. Select a gridline (not the top or bottom one, as they are considered part of the frame wall) and choose **Format**, **Selected Gridlines** from the menu, or right-click a gridline and select **Format Gridlines** from the pop-up menu, or double-click a gridline.

2. The Format Gridlines dialog box appears (see Figure 11.10). Select the **Patterns** tab (the Scale tab sets the scale options for the axis where the gridlines originate, as discussed in "Formatting the Axes").

Figure 11.10

Select the style, weight, and color of the gridlines.

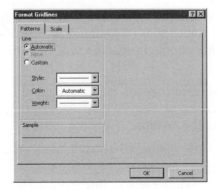

3. To set a dotted or dashed line, select one from the Style drop-down list. Pick a line Weight to make the line thicker or a line Color.

4. Click **OK**.

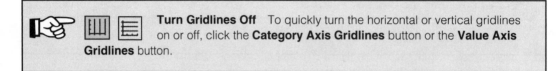 **Turn Gridlines Off** To quickly turn the horizontal or vertical gridlines on or off, click the **Category Axis Gridlines** button or the **Value Axis Gridlines** button.

Changing the Look of 3-D Charts

Three-dimensional (3-D) charts are attractive, but you may need to tilt or rotate the chart to make the various 3-D elements stand out. Here's how:

1. Choose **Chart**, **3-D View** from the menu, or right-click the chart area and choose **3-D View** from the pop-up menu. If the option is grayed, the chart is not 3-D and you can't apply 3-D formatting to it. The 3-D View dialog box appears (see Figure 11.11).

Figure 11.11

Use the Elevation and Rotation buttons to change the 3-D view.

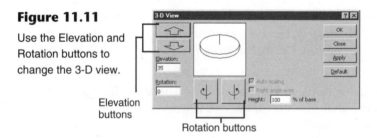

Elevation buttons

Rotation buttons

2. Click the up and down Elevation or Rotation buttons to tilt the chart towards you or away from you. As you click, the wire-frame picture of the graph reflects your changes. Type a number in the **Elevation** box to set the elevation to a specific value.

3. To change the rotation around the Z-axis, click the right or left Rotation buttons. This rotates the chart clockwise or counterclockwise. Check the wire-frame sample to see the effects of the rotation.

4. Some charts have a perspective option, in which you can change the perceived depth by clicking the up or down perspective controls.

5. To see the proposed changes on the actual chart, click the **Apply** button. Your proposed changes are shown in your graph, but not accepted until you click **OK**.

6. When you are satisfied with your selections, click **OK**.

Choosing Colors and Patterns

PowerPoint automatically assigns colors and patterns to the bars, columns, areas, or pie slices and line thickness and styles to lines in a chart. These are based on the color scheme of the presentation template. To change these colors or patterns, follow these steps:

1. Select the bars, area, columns, line, or slice you want to change and then choose **Format, Selected Data Series** or **Format, Selected Data Point** from the menu to open the Format Data Series (see Figure 11.12) or Format Data Point dialog box. Or, double-click the item to open the dialog box.

Figure 11.12

Specify the color and pattern of a bar in the Format Data Series dialog box.

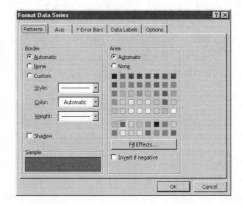

2. Select the **Patterns** tab, if it isn't already selected.

3. For objects such as slices, bars, columns, or areas, there are two sections to the Patterns page: Borders and Area. Borders are the outlines around a shape. Area is the fill of the shape. For a line chart, you will be able to choose from Line characteristics and Marker options. The choices are as individual as the different types of charts. The most common options include:

▶ **Automatic** accepts the default setting from the PowerPoint template.

▶ **None** eliminates the line, fill color or pattern, or marker.

▶ **Custom** changes the item to your settings as follows:

Border or Line **Style** includes a selection of solid or dashed lines.

Border or Line **Color** lets you set the color of the line or shape outline.

Border or Line **Weight** specifies the thickness of the line.

Marker **Style** sets how the data points on a line will look.

Marker **Size** lets you specify (in points) how large the marker should be.

Marker **Shadow** allows you to add a shadow behind the marker.

Area **Color** allows you to select one of the available colors for the fill of the item.

▶ Click **Fill Effects** to select gradient (shaded) fills, textures, patterns (checks, cross hatch, dots), or repeated pictures to fill the shape.

4. After you specify the fill, line, and marker options you want, click **OK**.

Exploding (Cutting) a Pie Slice

One way to emphasize a slice of a pie is to separate the slice from the rest of the pie. This is called "exploding" or "cutting" the slice. Because this is meant for emphasis, it's not recommended that you explode more than one or two pieces of a pie.

To explode a slice, follow these steps:

1. Select the whole pie by clicking it and then click once on the pie slice you want to explode. Only the pie slide you want to explode should now be selected.

2. Point in the middle of the pie slice, hold down the left mouse button, and drag the slice away from the center of the pie.

3. Release the mouse button.

To return the pie slice to its former position, just drag it back to the center of the pie.

Adding Data Labels

Data labels are optional. They appear at data points on your chart to show the value, percentage, or name of the data point. On bar, column, area, or line charts, they identify the exact value of the data point. On a pie chart, where legends are rarely used, the data labels identify the pie slices and note the percentages or values associated with them.

Data labels are designed to add clarity to a chart by making the value known, instead of being interpreted from their placement in relation to the axes. However, on charts with many elements, they can add clutter and make reading the chart difficult.

To add data labels to your chart, do the following:

1. Choose **Chart**, **Chart Options** from the menu, or right-click the chart and choose **Chart Options** from the pop-up menu.

2. When the Chart Options dialog box appears, select the **Data Labels** tab (see Figure 11.13).

Figure 11.13

In the Chart Options dialog box, choose to have the data point values or labels appear (or slice labels on a pie).

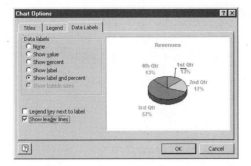

3. Select the Data Labels option you want. On most charts, you may only show the value or the label. On pie charts, you may also show the percentage or the label and the percentage.

4. On a pie chart, if you want small lines drawn between the slice and its label, select the **Show Leader Lines** option.

5. Click **OK**.

Using a Data Table

Data labels can make a chart look busy or hard to read. One solution to this is to use a *data table* instead. These tables list the values for each data point in a grid beneath the graph (this option is not available on pie charts). To add a data table, do the following:

1. Choose **Chart**, **Chart Options** from the menu, or right-click the chart and choose **Chart Options** from the pop-up menu.

2. When the Chart Options dialog box appears, select the **Data Table** tab (see Figure 11.14).

Figure 11.14

In the Chart Options dialog box, choose to have a data table appear beneath the chart.

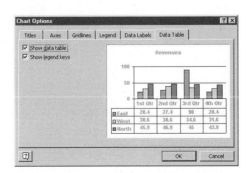

3. Select **Show Data Table**.

4. To have the legend keys also show in the data table, select the **Show Legend Keys** option to see the little boxes that display the color or line style of the data series.

5. Click **OK**.

Review Questions

1. Explain how to add a title to a chart.

2. How do you format text in a chart?

3. How do you change the scale of a Value axis?

4. Describe how to change the location of a legend.

5. How do you turn gridlines off or on, or format gridlines?

Review Question Answers

1. Choose **Chart**, **Chart Options** from the menu or right-click the chart and select **Chart** Options. Select the **Titles** tab. Enter the titles for the chart, and the X and Y axis and legend (if the chart is 3-D). Click **OK**. For more information, refer to "Adding Titles."

2. Select the text and choose **Format**, **Select _Item_** (where _Item_ is the name of the item you selected) from the menu. Alternatively, right-click the text you want to format and choose **Format _Item_**. Select the **Font** tab to change the font, size, style or color. Select the **Alignment** tab to change the alignment. Click **OK** to apply the formatting. For more information, refer to "Adding Formatting."

3. Right-click the Value axis and choose **Format Axis**. On the **Scale** tab, indicate the minimum, maximum, and major units for the scale. For more information, refer to "Formatting the Axes."

4. Right-click the legend and choose **Format Legend**. Select the **Placement** tab and set the placement option. Click **OK**. For more information, refer to "Placing the Legend."

5. Right-click the chart and select Chart Options. Select the **Gridlines** tab and indicate X and Y gridlines. To format gridlines, right-click a gridline and select Format Gridlines. Click the Patterns tab to set lines and line weights and colors. Click OK. For more information, refer to "Setting the Gridline Style."

Practice Lab

The Microsoft Expert User Exam lists twelve Required Tasks for the Skill Area "Adding Visual Elements." One of these tasks is covered in this lesson. The following section contains a practice lab for this Required Task.

 Required Tasks   The Required Task covered in this lesson is Add Formatting.

Add Formatting

Open the file Lesson11.ppt from the CD-ROM. Add a chart title and a title for the X axis. Format the Y-axis text by changing the font size, font style, and font color. Change the Y-axis scale to major units of 25. Apply a blue granite texture to the walls of the chart. Apply X-axis major gridlines.

To see an example of a completed exercise, open the file Lesson11a.ppt on the CD-ROM.

Open the file Lesson11pie.ppt. Add data labels representing the percentage of the whole that each of the three groups receives in profits. Increase the elevation 3-D level of the pie. Change the fill effect to a two-color gradient fill effect for the pie.

To see an example of a completed exercise, open the file Lesson11apie.ppt on the CD-ROM.

LESSON 12

Adding an Organizational Chart

This lesson covers one of the twelve Required Tasks for the "Adding Visual Elements" Skill Area.

In this lesson, you learn the following Required Task for your exam:

▶ Add an organizational chart

For a complete list of Required Tasks for the Skill Area "Adding Visual Elements," refer to the User Skills Roadmap.

Creating an Organizational Chart

A program called Microsoft Organization Chart comes with Microsoft PowerPoint. This program creates organizational charts that illustrate the management structure in a company, a family tree, or relationships among objects or procedures.

Before you begin creating an organizational chart, it helps to have a hand-drawn sketch of how you want it to look, so you know who goes where, how the names are spelled, what the proper titles are, and so on.

To create and place an organizational chart on a slide, follow these steps:

1. If you want to add a new slide to the presentation that has an organizational chart on it, click the **New Slide** button on the Standard toolbar and select the **Organization Chart** layout. Click **OK**. Then double-click the "Double click to add org chart" placeholder.

   If you want to change the layout of your current slide to an organizational chart layout, click the **Slide Layout** button, select the **Organization Chart** layout, and then click **Apply**. Then double-click the "Double click to add org chart" placeholder.

   If you want to add an organizational chart to your current slide (you must be in the Slide View), Choose **Insert**, **Picture**, **Organization Chart** from the menu.

2. The Microsoft Organization Chart window opens (see Figure 12.1). If the window is too small, click the **Maximize** button in the upper-right corner of the window to make the window expand to fill the screen.

3. The chart initially appears with four boxes—a single one at the top and three in the second row. Click in a box and type the person's name. Then press **Enter** to go to the next line, where you type the person's title. You may add up to two additional comment lines in each box. Press **Esc** when you've completed the entry, or click another box (you may also press **Ctrl** plus an arrow key to move to the next box in that direction).

4. To add a new box to the chart, click one of the buttons on the Icon bar (see Table 12.1 for an explanation of the buttons). Then click the box to which you want to connect the new box. When the new box appears, enter the person's information as you did in step 3.

5. When the organizational chart is complete and you want to return to your slide presentation, choose **File**, **Exit and Return to *filename*** (where *filename* is the name of your current file).

6. If asked if you want to update the image, click **Yes**.

Zoom   Icon bar

Figure 12.1

Type your entries for
name, title, and
comments for each
person in the boxes in
the organizational
chart.

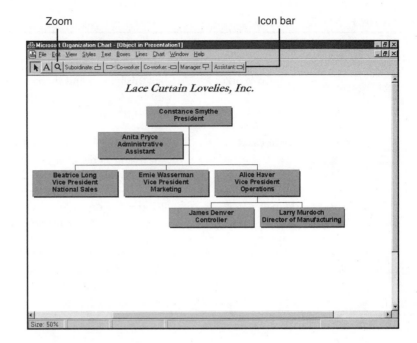

7. The organizational chart appears on the slide with handles (small boxes) around
the chart to indicate that it's selected. Point in the middle of the chart and drag
to move the chart to a different location on the slide. Drag any of the handles
away from or toward the center of the chart to size the chart.

Table 12.1 **Microsoft Organization Chart Icon Bar**

Button	Name	Description
▶	Select	Click to use your mouse pointer to select any objects on which you click.
A	Enter Text	Click on Enter Text and then click anywhere on the chart to add text outside the boxes.
Q	Zoom	Click the chart to magnify it. Click the miniature organization chart to return to the Actual Size view.
Subordinate: ⊔	Subordinate	Click this button and then click the box to which you want to add a subordinate.

continues

Table 12.1   Continued

Button	Name	Description
□+:Co-worker	Left Co-Worker	Click this button and then click the box to which you want to add a coworker on the same level, but to the left of the box.
Co-worker: –□	Right Co-Worker	Click this button and then click the box to which you want to add a coworker on the same level, but to the right of the box.
Manager: ⊡	Manager	Click this button and then click the box above where you want to add a manager box.
Assistant:□⊦	Assistant	Click this button and then click the box to which you want to add an assistant who reports directly to that person, has no subordinates, but doesn't fit with the level of the row below.

 Zoom In   In addition to using the **Zoom** button on the Icon bar, choose **View** from the menu and select a different view (**Size to Window**, **50% of Actual**, **Actual Size**, **200% of Actual**). Each view has a corresponding shortcut key, from **F9** through **F12**.

Editing an Organizational Chart

You don't have to restart the Microsoft Organization Chart program to edit your chart. If you do, you may end up with a second, empty chart on top of the first one. When you want to reopen the program to adjust, enhance, or correct an existing organizational chart, do the following:

1. Change to the Slide View of the slide containing the organizational chart.

2. Double-click the middle of the organizational chart. Microsoft Organization Chart reopens, displaying the chart for editing.

Selecting One or More Levels

As you edit, add to, or enhance an organizational chart, you need to select the boxes with which you want to work (make sure the **Select** tool is active). Do one of the following to select one or more boxes or levels:

▶ To select a single box, click it.

▶ To select more than one box, hold down the **Shift** key while clicking each box. Or, drag a rectangle around the boxes and, when you release the mouse button, all the boxes that were within that rectangle will be selected.

▶ To select a specific group of boxes (such as all the manager boxes), choose **Edit**, **Select** from the menu, and then choose the desired group.

▶ To select a specific level (row) in the organization, choose **Edit**, **Select Levels** from the menu, enter the range of levels you want to select (such as 2 through 5), and click **OK**.

Moving and Deleting Boxes

Deleting a box is a simple matter of selecting the box and pressing the **Delete** key. To rearrange your organizational chart, use Cut, Copy, and Paste:

1. Select the box or boxes you want to copy or move.

2. To move boxes, choose **Edit**, **Cut** from the menu, or right-click the boxes and choose **Cut** from the pop-up menu. To copy boxes, choose **Edit**, **Copy** from the menu, or right-click the boxes and choose **Copy** from the pop-up menu.

3. Select the box to which you want to attach the cut or copied boxes.

4. Choose **Edit**, **Paste Boxes** from the menu, which pastes the boxes to the right of or below the selected box.

 Drag and Drop   The quick way to move selected boxes is to drag and drop them on the box to which you want to connect them. If you drag close to the bottom edge of the box, they'll become subordinates; if you drag near the left or right edge of the box, they'll become coworkers.

 Undo   Undo any action immediately by selecting **Edit**, **Undo** or pressing **Ctrl+Z**. However, in Microsoft Organization Chart, you can only undo the most recent operation.

Selecting a Chart Style

The chart you create resembles a family tree. If that structure doesn't suit your needs (for all or part of the chart) or doesn't fit on the slide, select another style for your chart by following these steps:

1. Select the boxes to which you want to apply the new style. Press **Ctrl+A** to select all the boxes.

2. Choose Styles from the menu and then click the style you prefer (see Figure 12.2). These styles include horizontal boxes, vertical boxes, paired boxes, quad boxes, vertical no boxes, and vertical single box.

Figure 12.2

Select the style that best suits your needs.

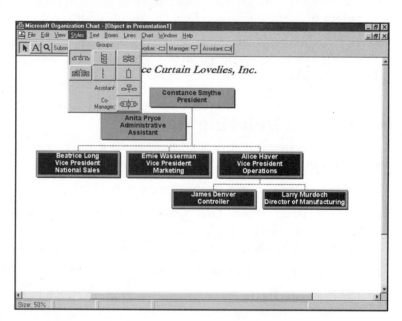

Formatting the Text

Microsoft Organization Chart enables you to format the text in the organizational chart boxes to change the font, add bold or italic, set a new font size, switch the color, or change the alignment of the text in the box. To format the text, do the following:

1. Select the text you want to format by selecting the box or boxes in which it appears or by dragging over the portion of the text that you want to format.

2. Choose **Text**, **Font** from the menu. The Font dialog box appears. Select a font, size, or style (bold or italic). Click **OK**.

3. To change the color of the text, choose **Text**, **Color** from the menu, click the desired color in the dialog box, and then click **OK**.

4. To change the alignment of the text, choose **Text** from the menu and then select **Left**, **Right**, or **Center**.

Changing the Look of Boxes and Lines

Microsoft Organization Chart formats the boxes and lines that make up the organizational chart for you, selecting colors that complement the colors in your slide template. To adjust this formatting and select your own colors, box borders and shadows, and line thickness and style, do the following:

1. Select the boxes or lines you want to format.

2. Choose **Boxes** or **Lines** from the menu.

3. From the submenu that appears, select the type of formatting you want to change. For boxes, select **Shadow**, **Border Style**, or **Border Line Style**. For lines, choose either **Thickness** or **Style**.

4. A list of available options appears in a submenu. Select the option you want to apply.

5. To change the color of the box or line, choose **Box**, **Color** or **Line**, **Color** from the menu. Select a color and click **OK**.

Review Questions

1. How do you add an organizational chart to a slide?

2. How do you edit an existing organizational chart?

3. How do you change the look of boxes in a chart?

Review Question Answers

1. Choose **Insert**, **Picture**, **Organization Chart** from the menu. Indicate the chart preferences and create the chart. For more information, refer to "Creating an Organizational Chart."

2. Switch to Slide view of the slide containing the chart. Double-click the chart and make your editing changes. For more information, refer to "Editing an Organizational Chart."

3. Select the boxes you want to format. Choose **Boxes** from the menu. Select **Shadow**, **Border Style** or **Border** Line style. To change the color, choose **Box**, **Color** from the menu. Select a color and click **OK**. For more information, refer to "Changing the Look of Boxes and Lines."

Practice Lab

The Microsoft Expert User Exam lists twelve Required Tasks for the Skill Area "Adding Visual Elements." One of these tasks has been covered in this lesson. A practice lab for that task follows.

 Required Tasks   The Required Task covered in this lesson is Add an Organizational Chart.

Add an Organizational Chart

Exercise 1: Create a new, blank presentation. Add an organizational chart using the **Insert** menu. Create a chart that represents your third-generation family tree. Using the drag-and-drop method, move some third-level members up the chart to the first level.

To see an example of a completed exercise, open the file Lesson12a.ppt on the CD-ROM.

Exercise 2: Create a new presentation that includes an organizational chart. Create a chart that represents your third-generation family tree. Using formatting options, change the colors of boxes to color-code family members and their children.

To see an example of a completed exercise, open the file Lesson12b.ppt on the CD-ROM.

Creating a Table

This lesson covers one of the twelve Required Tasks for the "Adding Visual Elements" Skill Area.

In this lesson, you learn the following Required Task for your exam:

▶ Add a table

For a complete list of Required Tasks for the Skill Area "Adding Visual Elements," refer to the User Skills Roadmap.

Adding a Table

A *table* enables you to organize information in a row and column format. Use tables for columns of numbers, lists, and anything else that requires a row and column arrangement.

Each entry in a table, called a *cell*, is independent of all other entries. You can have almost any number of rows and columns in a table. You also have a great deal of control over the size and formatting of each cell. A table cell can contain text or graphics.

 Cell The rectangle created at the intersection of a row and column. It acts as a container for text or numbers.

Change to the Slide view and then use one of these methods to create a slide with a table:

▶ To add a new slide that has a table on it, choose **Insert**, **New Slide** from the menu or click the **New Slide** button on the Standard toolbar. Select the **Table** layout and click **OK**. Double-click the "Double-click to add table" placeholder. In the Insert Word Table dialog box (see Figure 13.1), enter the number of columns and rows you want in your table and then click **OK**. A blank table appears in your document with your insertion point in the first cell.

 ▶ To change the AutoLayout of the current slide, click the **Slide Layout** button on the Standard toolbar. Select the **Table** layout and click **Apply**. Double-click the "Double-click to add table" placeholder. In the Insert Word Table dialog box (see Figure 13.1), enter the number of columns and rows you want in your table and then click **OK**. A blank table appears in your document with your insertion point in the first cell.

 ▶ To insert a table into the current slide, click the **Insert Microsoft Word Table** button. A set of boxes appears beneath the button. Drag over the boxes to select the desired number of rows and columns. When you release your mouse button, a blank table appears in your document with your insertion point in the first cell.

Figure 13.1

Enter or select the number of columns and rows you want in your table.

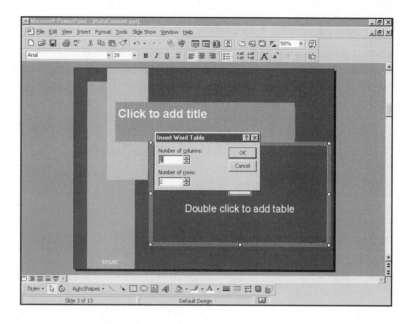

Working in a Table

When the insertion point is in a table cell, enter and edit text as you do in a word processing document. Text entered in a cell automatically wraps to the next line within the column width. Move the insertion point to any cell by clicking on that cell or by using the arrow keys. Table 13.1 shows you some keyboard shortcuts for navigating in a table.

Table 13.1   Table Keyboard Shortcuts

Press This...	To Move Here...
Tab	The next cell in the row (if you press Tab when you're in the last cell of the table, Word adds another row to the table).
Shift+Tab	The previous cell in a row.
Alt+Home	The first cell in the current row.
Alt+Page Up	The top cell in the current column.
Alt+End	The last cell in the current row.
Alt+Page Down	The last cell in the current column.

Because **Tab** moves you to the next cell, you must press **Ctrl+Tab** to insert a tab in a table cell.

Revising a Table

After you create a table and enter some information, you can edit the contents and change its appearance to suit your needs. If the table is no longer active because you clicked outside the table or went on to another slide, double-click in the middle of the table to go back to an editing mode.

In order to perform some operations on your table, you must be able to select cells, rows, and columns. Table 13.2 provides you with tips on how to select areas of your table.

Table 13.2 Selecting Table Contents

To Select...	Do This...
Cell	Click the left edge of the cell between the text and the cell border (when you see a pointer).
Row	With your insertion point in the row, choose **Table**, **Select Row** from the menu; or select the first cell and then drag across the remainder of the row.
Column	Click the column's top gridline or border when you see a down-pointing arrow; or choose **Table**, **Select Column** from the menu (with your insertion point in the column); or click in the column's top or bottom cell, hold down the **Shift** key, and press the up or down arrow key repeatedly.
Multiple cells, rows, or columns	Drag across the cell, row, or column; or select a single cell, row, or column, hold down the **Shift** key, and then click another cell, row, or column where you want the selection to end.
Text in the next cell	Press **Tab**.
Text in the previous cell	Press **Shift+Tab**.
Entire table	Click the table and then press **Alt+5** on the numeric keypad (Num Lock must be off); or choose **Table**, **Select Table** from the menu (with your insertion point somewhere in the table).

If you need to reduce a selection to fewer cells or extend a selection to adjacent cells, hold down the **Shift** key and press an arrow key repeatedly.

After you select cells, apply text formatting to the contents of those cells using the standard techniques for changing fonts and paragraph attributes.

Deleting and Inserting Cells, Rows, and Columns

Removing the contents of a cell or cells and leaving a blank cell is an easy matter of selecting the cell(s) and pressing the **Delete** key. (Click **Undo** or press **Ctrl+Z** if you didn't mean to do that.)

To remove an entire row or column (and not just the data in the cells) from the table, follow these steps:

1. Move the insertion point to any cell in the row or column to be deleted, or select the cells to be deleted.

2. Choose **Table**, **Delete Cells** from the menu. The Delete Cells dialog box appears (see Figure 13.2).

Figure 13.2

Choose Delete Entire
Row or Delete Entire
Column.

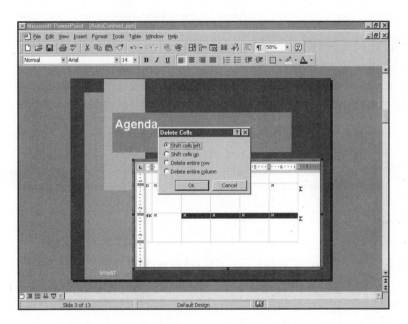

3. Select **Delete Entire Row** or **Delete Entire Column** (PowerPoint does offer the option of removing just selected cells. This shifts the other cells over into the empty spots and makes uneven rows or columns).

4. Click **OK**. The row or column is deleted.

 Recovery   Remember that you can undo table-editing actions with the **Edit**, **Undo** command on the menu or by clicking the **Undo** button on the Standard toolbar or by pressing **Ctrl+Z**.

To insert rows or columns into a table, follow these steps:

1. Select the column to the right of where you want to insert new columns or select the row below where you want to insert new rows (to insert just one row, have your insertion point in the row below where you want the new row). To insert more than one column or row, select the same number of rows or columns that you want to insert.

2. Choose **Table**, **Insert Columns** to insert a new, blank column (or the same number of columns as you selected) to the left of the selected column. Choose **Table**, **Insert Rows** to insert a new, blank row (or the same number of rows as you selected) above the selected row.

 Appending Rows or Columns To add a row at the bottom of the table, move the insertion point to the last cell in the table and press **Tab**. To add a column after the last column on the right, click just outside the table's right border, choose **Table**, **Select Column** from the menu, and then choose **Table**, **Insert Columns**.

 Changing Commands The commands on the Table menu change according to circumstances because they are context-sensitive. For example, if you select a column in a table, the Insert Columns command is displayed but the Insert Rows command is not.

Moving or Copying Columns and Rows

Here's how to copy or move an entire column or row from one location in a table to another:

1. Select the column or row you want to move or copy.

 2. To *copy* the selected row or column, click the **Copy** button on the Standard toolbar or press **Ctrl+C**.

 To *move* the selected row or column, click the **Cut** button on the Standard toolbar or press **Ctrl+X**.

3. Move your insertion point to the new location for the row or column. It will be inserted above or to the left of the location of the insertion point.

 4. Click the **Paste** button on the Standard toolbar, choose **Edit**, **Paste** from the menu, or press **Ctrl+V**.

Adding Borders and Shading to a Table

PowerPoint normally doesn't place any borders or shading on the table. If you want to add borders around the table or the cells to add color, clarity, or emphasis, here are the steps involved:

1. Select the table cells whose borders you want to modify.

2. Choose **Format**, **Borders and Shading** from the menu to display the Borders and Shading dialog box.

3. Select the **Borders** tab to work with border options (see Figure 13.3):

    ▶ Under Setting, select one of the preset border options: **None** to remove all borders from the selected cells, **Box** to insert a box border around the selected cells, **All** to insert a box border around the selected cells and apply preset shadow formatting to the border, **Grid** to insert a box border around the selection and apply preset 3-D border formatting, or **Custom** to create a border using the options you click in the Preview window. When you choose any of these settings, the current selections in Style, Color, and Width apply to the borders.

    ▶ From the **Style** list, select the type of line you want to use for the border, including dotted, dashed, and wavy lines.

    ▶ Click the **Color** drop-down list to select a color to apply to the border.

    ▶ From the **Width** drop-down list, choose the thickness of the border line from 1/4-point to 6 points.

    ▶ In the Preview box, click the individual border lines or use the border line buttons to apply or remove borders or change the attributes for a particular border (select the attributes first and then add the border).

    ▶ From the **Apply To** drop-down list, select whether to apply the border to the entire **Table** or a selected **Cell** or cells.

4. Select the **Shading** tab to choose shading options (see Figure 13.4):

    ▶ Under Fill, select the color or shade of gray with which you want to fill the selection.

    ▶ From the **Patterns Style** drop-down list, choose a shading percentage for the color you selected under **Fill** or a pattern of lines such as **Lt Horizontal** or **Dk Trellis**.

    ▶ If you selected a pattern of lines, select the **Color** of the lines from the drop-down list. The fill color then becomes the background color for the pattern.

> From the **Apply To** drop-down list select whether to apply the shading options to the entire **Table** or a selected **Cell** or cells.

Figure 13.3

Select the Borders tab to set the options for the lines around the cells.

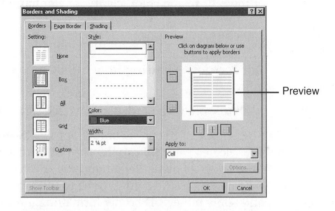

Preview

Figure 13.4

Select the background color for the selection from the Fill colors.

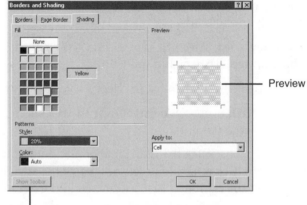

Preview

Click here to see the Tables and Borders toolbar

5. Click **OK**.

In a table with no borders, you can display non-printing gridlines on-screen to make it easier to work with the table. Choose **Table**, **Show Gridlines** to display the gridlines and **Table**, **Hide Gridlines** to turn the gridlines off.

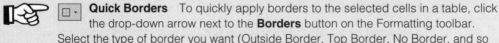 **Quick Borders** To quickly apply borders to the selected cells in a table, click the drop-down arrow next to the **Borders** button on the Formatting toolbar. Select the type of border you want (Outside Border, Top Border, No Border, and so on) and Word applies a single thin border to the selection as designated.

When you're choosing border and shading options and you want the ease of working with a toolbar, click the **Tables and Borders** button on the Standard toolbar (or click **Show Toolbar** when you're in the Borders and Shading dialog box). The Tables and Borders toolbar appears (see Figure 13.5). Click the appropriate buttons to apply border and shading attributes to selected cells.

Figure 13.5

Use the Tables and Borders toolbar when you're drawing tables, as well as choosing borders and shading for selected cells.

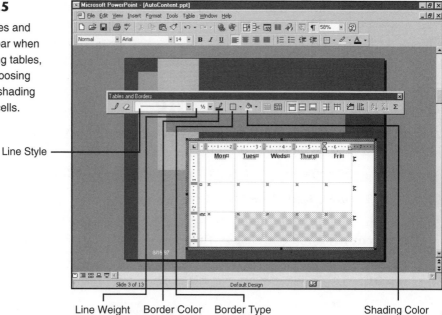

Line Style

Line Weight   Border Color   Border Type   Shading Color

Automatic Table Formatting

PowerPoint provides a variety of predefined table formats. Using these formats makes it easy to apply attractive formatting to any table. To apply automatic formatting to an existing table:

1. Place the insertion point anywhere in the table.

2. Choose **Table**, **Table AutoFormat** from the menu. The Table AutoFormat dialog box appears (see Figure 13.6). This is the same dialog box you see if you select **AutoFormat** in the Insert Table dialog box when first creating a table.

3. The **Formats** list shows the available table formats. As you scroll through the list, the Preview box shows the appearance of the highlighted format.

4. Select or deselect the formatting check boxes as needed until the Preview shows the table appearance you want.

5. Click **OK**. The selected formatting is applied to the table.

Figure 13.6

The AutoFormat dialog box offers several preset formats that you may apply to your table.

Formats list —

Select or deselect formats to apply

— Preview

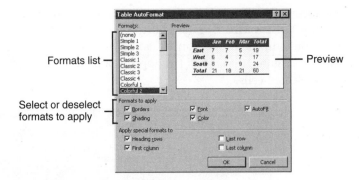

Rotating Text in a Table

Because horizontal space may be at a premium, you may want to have some of your table text appear in a vertical orientation. To do this:

1. Select the text you want to rotate (this will affect only the cell selected).

2. Choose **Format**, **Text Direction** from the menu.

3. When the Text Direction—Table Cell dialog box appears (see Figure 13.7), click the **Orientation** you want to use. The Preview window shows you how it will look.

4. Click **OK**.

Figure 13.7

Select the orientation you want to make your text display vertically.

Vertical orientations

— Preview

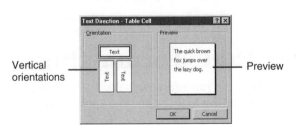

Modifying Table Structure

The width of columns and the height of rows in Word tables are adjustable. Cells can be split into more cells or merged together in one cell.

Changing Column Width

You can quickly change the width of a column using the mouse in one of two ways (see Figure 13.8):

▶ Point at the right border of the column whose width you want to change. The mouse pointer changes to a pair of thin vertical lines with arrowheads pointing left and right. Drag the column border to the desired width.

▶ The ruler shows the column separators. Point to the column separator over the right border of the column until the mouse pointer becomes a two-headed arrow. Then drag the separator until the column is the desired width.

Figure 13.8

To change the column width, drag the border between the columns or drag the column separator on the ruler.

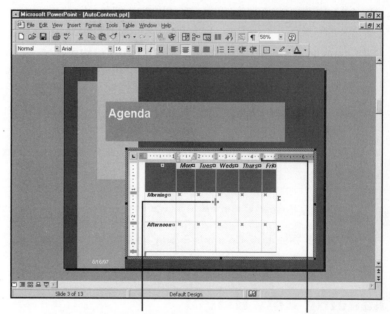

Mouse pointer for dragging column border   Column separator on ruler

When you want to be more exact in setting the column size, use the Cell Height and Width dialog box to change the width:

1. Move the insertion point to any cell in the column you want to change.

2. Choose **Table**, **Cell Height and Width** from the menu. The Cell Height and Width dialog box appears. Select the **Column** tab (see Figure 13.9).

Figure 13.9

Enter the column width
in inches or click
Autofit to have
PowerPoint adjust the
column to the length of
the widest entry.

3. In the **Width of Column** text box, enter the desired column width or click the arrows to change the setting. Note that the label identifies which column you are working on by number. To automatically adjust the column width to fit the widest cell entry in that column, click the **Autofit** button.

4. Change the value in the **Space Between Columns** text box to modify spacing between columns. Changing this setting increases or decreases the amount of space between the text in each cell and the cell's left and right borders.

5. Click **Next Column** or **Previous Column** to change the settings for other columns in the table.

6. Click **OK**. The table changes to reflect the new column settings.

 Evenly Spaced Columns   To evenly space two or more adjacent columns over their entire width and make them the same width, select the columns and then choose **Table, Distribute Columns Evenly** from the menu.

Changing Row Height

Row height in a table is usually based on the font size or the greatest number of lines in any cell in that row. To adjust the row height using the mouse:

▶ Point at the top or bottom border of the row whose height you want to change. The mouse pointer changes to a pair of thin horizontal lines with arrowheads pointing up and down (see Figure 13.10). Drag the row border to the desired height.

▶ The vertical ruler shows the row separators. Point to the row separator over the border of the row until the mouse pointer becomes a two-headed arrow. Then drag the separator until the row is the desired height.

Figure 13.10

Drag the border of the row or the row separator on the ruler.

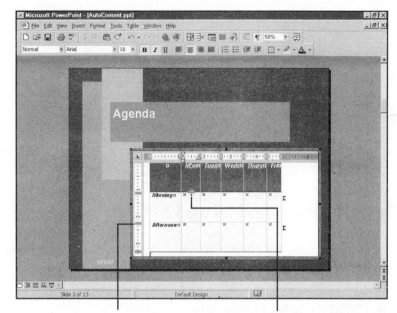

Agenda

Row sparator on ruler   Mouse pointer for dragging the row border

To change the row height using the Cell Height and Width dialog box:

1. Select the rows that you want to change.

2. Choose **Table**, **Cell Height and Width** from the menu to open the Cell Height and Width dialog box. Select the **Row** tab (see Figure 13.11).

Figure 13.11

In addition to row height, you can set the alignment of the table on the slide, indent the table from the left margin, or allow a row to break across pages.

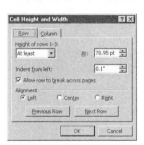

3. From the **Height of Rows** drop-down list, select **Auto** to adjust automatically to the height of the tallest cell in the row, choose **At Least** to specify a minimum row height (entered in the **At** box, in points) that automatically adjusts to a larger size to fit the row contents, or select **Exactly** to specify a fixed row height (entered in the **At** box, in points). When you use **Exactly**, PowerPoint prints only the contents that fit in that specified height.

4. Click **Previous Row** or **Next Row** to set the row height for other rows in the table.

5. Click **OK**. The table adjusts to match your settings.

 Evenly Spaced Rows To evenly space two or more adjacent rows over their entire height and make them the same height, select the rows and then choose **Table**, **Distribute Rows Evenly** from the menu.

Merging and Splitting Cells

Tables have the flexibility to enable you to merge several cells into one. The cells must be adjoining cells—sharing a border horizontally or vertically such as cells in the same row, cells in the same column, or cells that make a rectangle. Adjacent or adjoining cells are often referred to as contiguous cells. To merge cells, follow these steps:

1. Select the cells you want to merge.

2. Choose **Table**, **Merge Cells** from the menu.

Conversely, you can split cells into more than one cell:

1. Select the cell or cells you want to split (it doesn't have to be a cell that was merged earlier).

2. Choose **Table**, **Split Cells** from the menu. The Split Cells dialog box appears (see Figure 13.12).

Figure 13.12

Enter the number of rows or columns into which you want to split the selected cell(s).

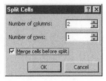

3. Enter the number of rows or columns into which you want to split the cell.

4. Click **OK**.

Review Questions

1. How do you add a table to a new slide?

2. Explain how to delete rows or columns.

3. How do you append a row or column?

4. How do you add shading to a table?

5. How do you apply Automatic Table Formatting to a table?

6. How do you merge cells?

Review Question Answers

1. Choose **Insert**, **New Slide** from the menu or click the **New Slide** button on the Standard toolbar. Select the **Table** layout and click **OK**. Indicate the number of rows and columns and click **OK**. For more information, refer to "Adding a Table."

2. Move the insertion point to any cell in the row or column to be deleted, or select the row or column. Choose **Table**, **Delete Cells** from the menu. Select **Delete Entire Row** or **Delete Entire Column**. Click **OK**. For more information, refer to "Deleting and Inserting Cells, Rows, and Columns."

3. To add a row, move the insertion point to the last cell in the table and press the **Tab** key. To add a column, click just outside of the table right border and choose **Table**, **Select Column** from the menu, then choose **Table**, **Insert Columns**. For more information, refer to "Deleting and Inserting Cells, Rows, and Columns."

4. Select the table cells to be shaded. Choose **Format**, **Borders and Shading** from the menu. Select the **Shading** tab and choose shading options. For more information, refer to "Adding Borders and Shading to a Table."

5. Place the insertion point anywhere in the table. Choose **Table**, **Table AutoFormat** from the menu. Select or deselect the formatting check boxes until the table has the appearance you want. Click **OK**. For more information, refer to "Automatic Table Formatting."

6. Select the cells to be merged. Choose **Table**, **Merge Cells** from the menu. For more information, refer to "Merging and Splitting Cells."

Practice Lab

The Microsoft Expert User Exam lists twelve Required Tasks for the Skill Area "Adding Visual Elements." One of these tasks has been covered in this lesson. A practice lab for that task follows.

 Required Tasks   The Required Task covered in this lesson is Add a Table.

Add a Table

Create a new presentation using the table layout. Edit the table to represent the TV programming grid for the evening. Use the newspaper TV section to help if you can't remember how the programs are listed. Use half-hour time slots in your table. Merge cells when programs exceed the half-hour time slot. Use shading and borders to accent and separate programs.

To see an example of a completed exercise, open the file Lesson13a.ppt on the CD-ROM.

Drawing Objects on a Slide

This chapter covers three of the twelve Required Tasks for the "Adding Visual Elements" Skill Area.

In this lesson, you learn the following Required Tasks for your exam:

▶ Draw an object

▶ Add shapes

▶ Check styles

For a complete list of Required Tasks for the Skill Area "Adding Visual Elements," refer to the User Skills Roadmap.

PowerPoint's Drawing Tools

Although PowerPoint is not a drawing program per se, it still has a fairly complete set of drawing tools. With them, you can draw diagrams such as the one in Figure 14.1, create simple logos, or accent your slide with lines or arrows.

PowerPoint's drawing tools are available from the Drawing toolbar at the bottom of the screen, as shown in Figure 14.1. If you don't see the toolbar, choose **View**, **Toolbars**, **Drawing** from the menu. Table 14.1 lists the various tools and describes their use.

Figure 14.1

The Drawing toolbar is at the bottom of the PowerPoint window.

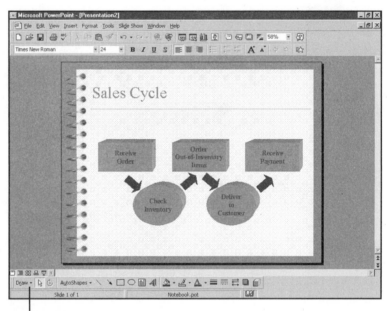

Drawing toolbar

Table 14.1 PowerPoint's Drawing Tools

Button	Name	Description
Draw ▾	Draw	Displays a menu of drawing commands.
⏳	Select Objects	Selects drawing objects.
⟳	Free Rotate	Rotates objects to any angle.
AutoShapes ▾	AutoShapes	Displays a pop-up menu of different shapes.

Button	Name	Description
	Line	Draws straight lines.
	Arrow	Draws arrows.
	Rectangle	Draws rectangles and squares.
	Oval	Draws ovals and circles.
	Text Box	Creates text anywhere without attaching it to an object.
	Insert WordArt	Creates a WordArt object in your document.
	Fill Color	Applies fill colors or attributes to selected objects.
	Line Color	Applies color or patterns to selected lines or outlines.
	Font Color	Applies color to selected text.
	Line Style	Applies a line thickness or style to a selected line or outline.
	Dash Style	Applies a dashed line style to a selected line or outline.
	Arrow Style	Applies an arrow style or direction to a selected line or arrow.
	Shadow	Applies a shadow to a selected object.
	3-D	Applies a three-dimensional (3-D) setting to a selected object.

Drawing an Object

To create lines, arrows, rectangles, or ovals, follow these simple instructions:

▶ To draw a line or arrow, click the **Line** or **Arrow** button on the Drawing toolbar, position the mouse pointer (a cross hair) where you want the line or arrow to start, hold down the mouse button and drag to the end of the line or arrow, and release the mouse button. Hold down the **Shift** key as you drag to make a straight horizontal or vertical line or arrow.

▶ To draw a rectangle, click the **Rectangle** tool on the Drawing toolbar, position the mouse pointer (a crosshair) where you want one corner of the rectangle to be, hold down the mouse button and drag diagonally to the opposite corner, and then release the mouse button. Hold down the **Shift** key as you drag if you want to draw a square. Hold down the **Ctrl** key to draw the rectangle out from the center point (hold **Ctrl+Shift** to draw a square out from the center point).

▶ To draw an oval, click the **Oval** tool on the Drawing toolbar, position the mouse pointer (a crosshair) where you would imagine one corner of a rectangle surrounding the oval to be, hold down the mouse button and drag diagonally to the opposite corner, and then release the mouse button. Hold down the **Shift** key as you drag if you want to draw a circle. Hold down the **Ctrl** key to draw the oval out from the center point (hold **Ctrl+Shift** to draw a circle out from the center point).

Adding Shapes

PowerPoint comes with several pre-drawn objects, called AutoShapes, which save you from having to create complex shapes with the tools at hand. To draw one of these objects, do the following:

AutoShapes ▾

1. Click the **AutoShapes** tool on the Drawing toolbar. A menu of shape types appears.

2. Select the type of shape you want to draw. A palette of that type of object appears, as shown in Figure 14.2.

3. Click the shape you want to draw.

4. Move the mouse pointer to where you want the corner of the shape to be.

5. Hold down the mouse button and drag the mouse diagonally to draw the object. Hold down the **Shift** key as you drag to keep the object's height and width in the same proportion as shown on the AutoShapes palette. Hold down the **Ctrl** key to draw the shape out from the center point.

6. When you release the mouse button, the shape appears.

Figure 14.2

Select the shape you want to draw from the AutoShapes palette.

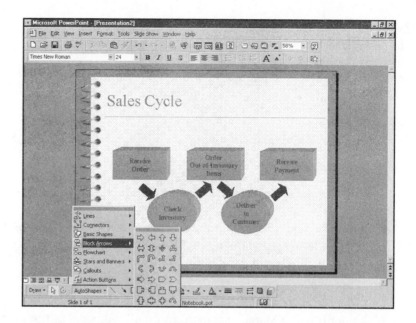

 Changing an Existing Shape   To change an existing shape into a different shape, select the existing shape, click the **Draw** button on the Drawing toolbar, select **Change AutoShape**, and then click on new shape you want.

Adding Text to an Object

Except for lines and arrows, you can add text to any object you draw, such as a box in a diagram. The text stays with the shape when you move it. To insert text into an object, do the following:

1. Select the object into which you want to insert text.

2. Type the text. As you type, the text appears in a single line across the object.

3. Click outside the object to deselect it.

To define how the text fits within the shape, follow these steps:

1. Select the object with the text in it.

2. Choose **Format**, **AutoShape** from the menu.

3. When the Format AutoShape dialog box appears, select the **Text Box** tab (see Figure 14.3).

Figure 14.3

The Anchor Point option specifies how to position the text within the shape.

4. From the Text Anchor Point drop-down list, choose a position for the text in relation to the shape (**Top**, **Middle**, **Bottom**, **Top Centered**, **Middle Centered**, or **Bottom Centered**). This position (text anchor) setting does not affect the horizontal text alignment (if the text is left-aligned, the left edges of the text still line up).

5. Under Internal Margin, set margins for all four sides of the shape, establishing how much white space will be left between the edges of the shape and the text.

6. Select any of the following options:

    ▶ **Word Wrap Text in AutoShape**   Wraps text to another line if the text is wider than the shape.

    ▶ **Resize AutoShape to Fit Text**   Makes the shape larger or smaller so the text fits exactly within the margins you specified in step 5.

    ▶ **Rotate Text Within AutoShape by 90°** Rotates the text to run the other way (usually vertically) to help it fit better in the shape.

 Viewing the Effects of Your Changes   Drag the title bar of the dialog box to move the box away from the object. Click **Preview** to view the effects of your changes.

7. Click **OK** to save your changes.

Tips for Working with Objects

Here are some quick tips that can save you some time and reduce frustration as you begin working with objects. You'll learn more about manipulating objects in Lesson 15, "Positioning and Sizing Objects."

▶ If you're going to use the same tool to draw several objects in a row, double-click on the tool. The tool stays selected and you don't have to re-click it after you draw each shape. Click another tool to turn it off.

▶ To draw an object out from the center rather than from a corner, hold down the **Ctrl** key while dragging.

▶ To select an object, click it.

▶ To delete an object, select it and press the **Delete** key.

▶ To move an object, select it and then drag it to its new location (if the object doesn't have a fill, drag it by the outline).

▶ To resize or reshape an object, select it and drag one of its handles. To keep an object from being distorted when you size it, hold down the Shift key and drag one of the corner handles toward or away from the center of the object. Using the shift key in this way, you can keep your perfect circle or square without turning it into an oval or rectangle.

▶ To copy an object, hold down the **Ctrl** key while dragging it.

Checking Styles

When you add drawings or pre-drawn objects to your slide presentation, or you change fonts and colors on your slides, you change the format established by the slide master. Some of these changes may be very good for your presentation, but some may be haphazard and ill-planned. PowerPoint's Style Checker performs a consistency check for you, to help avoid a presentation that looks like you just learned all the new PowerPoint features and wanted to try them out in one place.

To check your presentation for consistency and style, do the following:

1. Open the presentation you want to check.

2. Choose **Tools, Style Checker** from the menu to open the Style Checker dialog box (see Figure 14.4).

Figure 14.4

Select which of the three listed items you want to check.

3. Select the items you want to check:

   ▶ **Spelling**   Checks for spelling errors.

   ▶ **Visual Clarity**   Checks your presentation for appropriate font usage and for legibility of slide titles and body text.

   ▶ **Case and End Punctuation**   Checks your presentation for consistency of capitalization and end punctuation in slide titles and body text (for example, did you put a period after every bullet paragraph?).

4. Click **Options** to set more specific options. The Style Checker Options dialog box appears (see Figure 14.5).

Figure 14.5

Select the specific items that you want the Style Checker to look for.

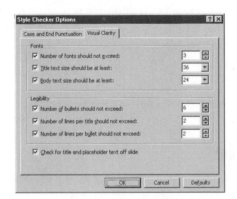

5. Select the **Visual Clarity** tab or the **Case and End Punctuation** tab to specify exactly what you want to check. Then click **OK**.

6. Click **Start**.

7. Each time the Style Checker meets a problem that you should correct, a dialog box appears with a description of the problem (see Figure 14.6). Click **Change** to follow the Style Checker's suggestion to fix the problem, **Change All** to fix all such instances, **Ignore** to ignore this problem and go on, or **Ignore All** to ignore all similar problems. The Style Checker may also alert you to style problems that you should fix after the check is completed, such as the text is too small on a slide.

8. PowerPoint alerts you when the Style Check is complete. Click **OK**.

Figure 14.6

The Style Checker alerts you to problems and gives you the opportunity to fix them.

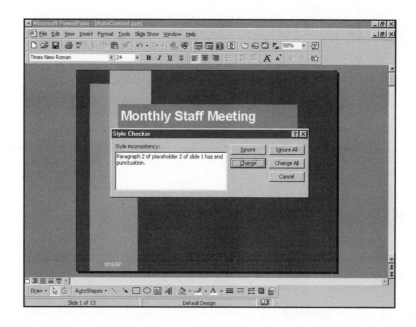

Of course, there is no substitute for good proofreading, as these automatic checkers won't catch everything. Always look your work over carefully and, when possible, have another person read it .

Review Questions

1. Explain how to draw an arrow on a slide.

2. Explain how to draw a circle on a slide.

3. How do you add a box and text to a slide?

4. How do you check the styles you have applied to your worksheet?

Review Question Answers

1. Display the drawing toolbar and click the Arrow button on the toolbar. Position the cursor where you want the arrow to begin and hold down the mouse key, releasing where you want the arrow to end. For more information, refer to "Drawing an Object."

2. Click the Oval tool on the Drawing toolbar and position your cursor where you want the circle to be. Hold down the **Shift** key and the mouse button, and then drag the circle to the size you desire. Release the mouse. For more information, refer to "Drawing an Object."

3. Use the AutoShapes tool to draw the box. Select the box and type the text. Choose **Format**, **AutoShape** from the menu to format the text. For more information, refer to "Adding Shapes."

4. Choose **Tools**, **Style Checker** from the menu. Select the items you want to check and click **Start**. PowerPoint alerts you when the Style Check is complete. Click **OK**. For more information, refer to "Checking Styles."

Practice Lab

The Microsoft Expert User Exam lists twelve Required Tasks for the Skill Area "Adding Visual Elements." Three of these tasks have been covered in this lesson. A practice lab for each of these three tasks follows.

Required Tasks   The Required Tasks covered in this lesson are Add Shapes, Draw an Object, and Check Styles.

Add Shapes

Start a new PowerPoint presentation and draw the boxes and ovals as displayed in Figure 14.1. Add text to the boxes and change the box colors and format the text to appear in different colors in the boxes and in the ovals.

Draw an Object

Draw the arrows as shown in Figure 14.1. Format the arrows so that they appear as thick as the arrows in the figure and format the arrow colors.

Check Styles

Run the Style Checker to check the visual clarity of your presentation.

To see an example of the completed exercise, open the file Lesson14a.ppt on the CD-ROM.

Positioning and Sizing Objects

This lesson covers two of the twelve Required Tasks for the "Adding Visual Elements" Skill Area.

In this lesson you learn the following Required Tasks for your exam:

▶ Rotate and fill an object

▶ Scale and size an object

For a complete list of Required Tasks for the Skill Area "Adding Visual Elements," refer to the User Skills Roadmap.

Selecting Objects

Before copying, moving, rotating, or resizing an object, you must select the object (rectangle, oval, arrow, line, or text box). Change to Slide view and do one of the following:

▶ To select a single object, click it (if you click text, a frame appears around the text; click the frame to select the text object). Handles (small boxes) appear around a selected object, as shown in Figure 15.1.

Figure 15.1

Small boxes, or handles, appear around a selected object. In this case, an oval has been selected.

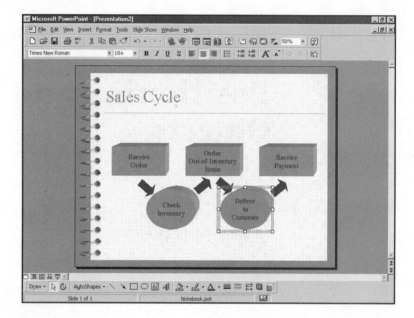

▶ To select more than one object, hold down the **Shift** key while clicking on each object.

▶ To select several objects that are close together or on top of each other, click the **Select Objects** button on the Drawing toolbar and drag a selection box around the objects. When you release the mouse button, all the objects within the selection box display handles, indicating that they are all selected, and the selection box disappears.

▶ To deselect selected objects, click anywhere outside the selected objects. To deselect just one of several selected objects, hold down the **Shift** key and click the object you want to deselect.

Working with Layers of Objects

As you place objects on your slide, they may start to overlap with the most recently drawn object being on top of the ones drawn before it. This makes it difficult or impossible to select the objects in lower layers, or to see those objects. To change the position of objects stacked in this fashion, do the following:

1. Click the object you want to move up or down in the stack.

2. Click the **Draw** button on the Drawing toolbar. From the menu that appears, select **Order** (see Figure 15.2).

Figure 15.2

When you want to move an item up or down in a stack, click Draw, choose Order, and then select one of the available options.

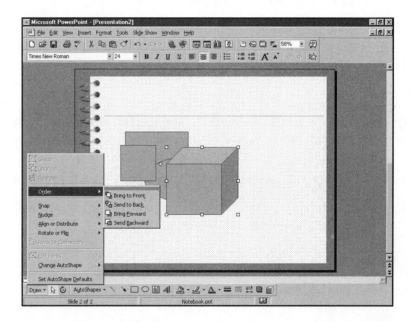

3. Then select one of the following options:

   ▶ **Bring to Front** brings the object to the top of the stack.

   ▶ **Send to Back** sends the object to the bottom of the stack.

   ▶ **Bring Forward** brings the object up one layer.

   ▶ **Send Backward** sends the object back one layer.

You can also select the object and right-click it to access the **Order** submenu without going to the Drawing toolbar.

Grouping and Ungrouping Objects

Each object you draw is independent of the other objects on your slide. However, sometimes you want two or more objects to act together—you may want to make sure they don't separate if you move them. Grouping also lets you size, cut, copy, or delete them as one piece (be careful formatting, or all the objects in the group could become one color). For example, if you've drawn a bullseye, which is a set of concentric circles of alternating colors, you need to keep them together in order to size them and move them as if they were one object.

To treat two or more objects as a group, follow these steps:

1. Select the objects you want to group together.

2. Click the **Draw** button on the Drawing toolbar.

3. Select **Group** from the menu that pops up.

To return a group to a set of independent objects, select any object in the group, click the **Draw** button on the Drawing toolbar, and then select **Ungroup**. Or, click the group with the right mouse button and select **Ungroup** from the pop-up menu.

Cutting, Copying, and Pasting Objects

To rearrange objects on a slide, duplicate objects, or copy or move objects from one slide to another, use the **Cut**, **Copy**, and **Paste** commands.

> **Cut**   When you cut an object, PowerPoint removes it from the slide and stores it in the Clipboard.
>
> **Copy**   When you copy an object, PowerPoint places a duplicate of it in the Clipboard but leaves the original on the slide.
>
> **Paste**   When you paste an object, a copy of the Clipboard contents appears on your slide.
>
> **Clipboard**   A temporary memory holding area for items you have cut or copied. The items remain in the Clipboard until you cut or copy another item or until you shutdown your computer. They can be pasted again and again, provided you do not cut or copy anything else in the meantime.

To move or copy an object, perform the following steps:

1. Select the object or objects you want to move or copy.

2. To copy, choose **Edit**, **Copy** from the menu, or right-click the object(s) and select **Copy** from the pop-up menu, or click the **Copy** button on the Standard toolbar (or press **Ctrl+C**).

To cut, choose **Edit**, **Cut** or right-click the object(s) and select **Cut** from the pop-up menu, or click the **Cut** button on the Standard toolbar (or press **Ctrl+X**).

3. In the Slide view, display the slide in which you want to put the object(s).

4. Choose **Edit**, **Paste** from the menu, or click the **Paste** button on the Standard toolbar, or press **Ctrl+V**.

Dragging and Dropping Objects The quickest way to copy or move objects is to drag and drop them. Select the objects you want to move, position the mouse pointer over any of the selected objects, and drag the objects where you want them. To copy the objects, hold down the **Ctrl** key while dragging.

Duplicating and Aligning Objects

The Cut and Copy commands both involve the Clipboard, but PowerPoint has another method for copying objects that doesn't use the Clipboard and gives you the added benefit of automatically spacing the objects as you go. The only limitation of this method is that you must stay on the same slide, but it really helps when you're making diagrams and need a series of the same objects. This method also assures you that you won't lose whatever you have cut or copied to your Clipboard.

To copy and space objects, follow these steps:

1. Select the object or objects you want to copy.

2. Choose **Edit**, **Duplicate** from the menu or press **Ctrl+D**.

3. A copy of the object(s) appears slightly to the right and down from the original. Move that duplicate object to its correct position.

4. To make another copy, leave the duplicated object(s) selected and choose **Edit**, **Duplicate** from the menu or press **Ctrl+D**. The new object(s) appears the same spatial distance from the last duplicate as it did from the original. For example, if you duplicated a rectangle and placed the duplicate an inch to the right of the first rectangle, the new duplicate appears one inch to the right of the first duplicate.

To align objects in a row or column and make them evenly spaced, do the following:

1. If you want a row or column of objects to be evenly spaced, move the first object and the last object in the row or column to locations where you want the row or column to begin and end. This isn't necessary if you're simply aligning objects.

2. Select the objects.

3. Click the **Draw** button on the Drawing toolbar. Select **Align or Distribute** from the menu that pops up.

4. Make the appropriate selection, using the pictures next to the options to guide you (see Figure 15.3).

Figure 15.3

Select the appropriate alignment or distribution option for the selected objects.

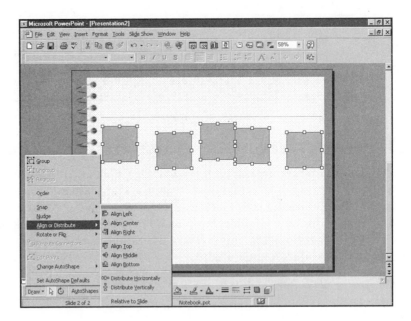

5. Repeat steps 2 through 4 if you need to align and distribute the objects.

Scaling and Sizing Objects

There are times when an object you create or import is not the right size for your slide. You change the size of the object by following these steps:

1. Select the object you want to resize. The handles appear around the object.

2. Drag one of the handles toward or away from the center of the object. The top and bottom handles make the object shorter or taller, the left and right handles make the object wider or narrower, and the corner handles change both.

3. An outline appears as you drag, representing the final size of the object. Release the mouse button when the outline is the shape and size you desire.

The problem with the previous method is that you can distort clip art and images, and make people too wide or buildings too short and so on. To maintain the proportions of the object (the *aspect ratio*) while resizing it, which is referring to as "scaling," do one of the following:

▶ To scale the object proportionally, hold down the **Shift** key and drag a corner handle (with PowerPoint clip art, you don't need to hold down the **Shift** key).

▶ To scale an object vertically, horizontally, or diagonally from the center out, hold down the **Ctrl** key and drag a sizing handle.

▶ To scale an object proportionally from the center outward, hold down **Ctrl+Shift** and drag a corner sizing handle.

 Aspect Ratio The aspect ratio is the ratio or proportion between the height and width of an object. For example, if an object is one inch high and two inches wide, the aspect ratio is 1:2. Therefore, if you want to maintain the aspect ratio so the object doesn't become distorted, and you want to make it twice as high, the newly sized object would be 2 inches high and four inches wide.

Rotating and Filling Objects

PowerPoint enables you to set objects at an angle, including text (the text inside a shape rotates with the shape), or add colors, patterns, textures, or gradient fills to the objects.

Rotating an Object

A PowerPoint object rotates around its center point, as if you had a pin stuck in the center of a card and spun the card with your finger. In Figure 15.1, for example, the arrows were rotated to put them at an angle. To rotate an object, do the following:

1. Select the object you want to rotate (you can't rotate clip art unless you ungroup the clip art first and then group it again).

 2. Click the **Free Rotate** tool on the Drawing toolbar. The selection handles disappear, and four small circles show up at the corners of the object (or two circles at either end of a line or arrow).

3. Move the mouse pointer over one of the round handles and drag in a circular fashion. An outline of the object rotates (see Figure 15.4).

Figure 15.4

Drag one of the circular handles until the outline is in the correct position.

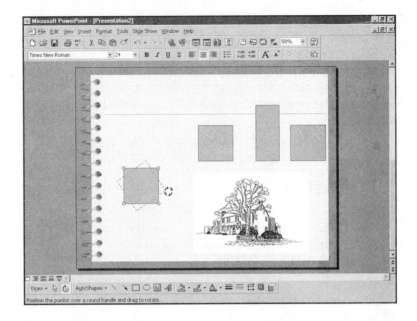

4. When the outline is at the angle you want, release the mouse button.

Other Rotation Options Click the **Draw** button on the Drawing toolbar, select **Rotate or Flip**, and choose an option to rotate the selected object: **Rotate Left** (rotates 90° counterclockwise), **Rotate Right** (rotates 90° clockwise), **Flip Horizontal** (flips left to right to make a mirror image), or **Flip Vertical** (flips top to bottom to make a mirror image).

Filling an Object

In addition to solid color, PowerPoint offers several types of fills for objects: textures, gradients, and patterns. Fills can help make your presentations easier to interpret. You might need to fill areas of a pie chart, for example, when you want to differentiate more clearly the different parts of the pie.

To add a fill to an object, select it and then do one of the following:

▶ To apply the current fill color, click the **Fill Color** button.

▶ To apply a different color, click the down arrow next to the **Fill Color** button, and then click one of the colors shown (see Figure 15.5). Click **More Fill Colors** to see a larger selection. Click **No Fill** to remove the fill from the object.

Figure 15.5

Click the arrow next to the Fill Color button to see a selection of colors.

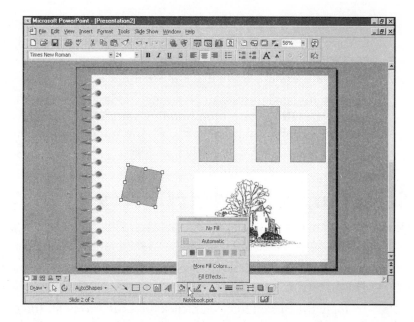

▶ To apply a gradient fill, click the down arrow next to the **Fill Color** button, and then click **Fill Effects**. Select the **Gradient** tab on the Fill Effects dialog box (see Figure 15.6). Choose **One Color**, **Two Colors**, or **Preset** gradient. Select the colors from the drop-down boxes on the right or set the lightness/darkness by dragging the box in the scroll bar, and then click a shading style. Click **OK**.

Figure 15.6

Select the type of gradient you want, the colors involved, and the shading style.

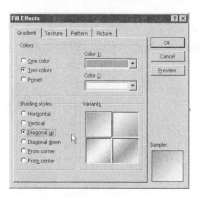

▶ To add a texture to the object, click the down arrow next to the **Fill Color** button, and then click **Fill Effects**. Select the **Texture** tab on the Fill Effects dialog box. Click one of the textures, such as Green Marble or Granite, and then click **OK**.

▶ To add a pattern to the object, click the down arrow next to the **Fill Color** button, and then click **Fill Effects**. Select the **Pattern** tab on the Fill Effects dialog box. Select a Foreground and Background color and then click the pattern you want (lines, dots, crosshatch). Click **OK**.

▶ To add a repeated picture (such as a logo) to the object, click the down arrow next to the **Fill Color** button, and then click **Fill Effects**. Select the **Picture** tab on the Fill Effects dialog box. Click the **Select Picture** button, specify the picture file you want to use, and click **OK**.

Selecting Line Attributes

Lines, arrows, and outlines around objects all have line attributes such as thickness, style, dashing, and color. Arrows also have different arrowheads to choose.

To change the attributes of a line, arrow, or outline, do one of the following to the selected item or items:

▶ To apply the current line color, click the **Line Color** button on the Drawing toolbar.

▶ To change the color of the line, click down arrow next to the **Line Color** button on the Drawing toolbar and select one of the colors (see Figure 15.7). Click **More Line Colors** to see a bigger selection. Click **No Line** to have the line disappear.

Figure 15.7

Click Line Color and choose from the selection of colors.

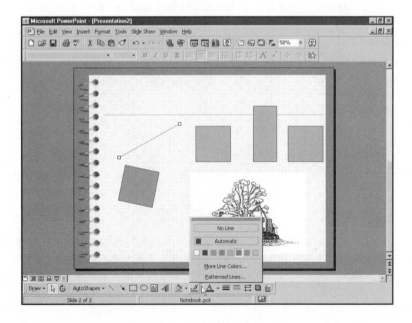

▶ To select a pattern for the line, click the down arrow next to the Line Color button and click Patterned Lines. When the Patterned Lines dialog box appears (see Figure 15.8), select Foreground and Background colors, click the pattern you want, and click OK.

Figure 15.8

Select the pattern you want to apply to the line.

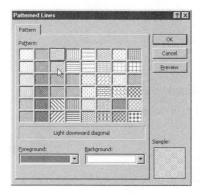

▶ To change the line thickness or change to double lines, click the **Line Style** button and select one of the options.

▶ If you want a dotted or dashed line, click the **Dash Style** button and select the type of dashing you want.

▶ For an arrow, click the **Arrow Style** button to see a selection of arrows. Click the one you want or click **More Arrows** to mix and match starting and ending arrow styles.

Cropping a Picture

If the object you're working with is an image, such as a scanned picture of your company president or logo, you may want to trim some unnecessary background from the picture.

Trimming a picture is called cropping, and here's how you do it:

1. Select the picture you want to crop. The Picture toolbar appears (see Figure 15.9).

2. Click the **Crop** button on the Picture toolbar.

3. Move the mouse pointer (now shaped like the cropping tool) over one of the handles.

4. Hold down the mouse button, and drag toward the center of the picture.

5. When the crop lines are where you want the picture trimmed, release the mouse button.

Figure 15.9

Position the mouse pointer over a handle and drag toward the center of the picture until the crop line is where you to crop.

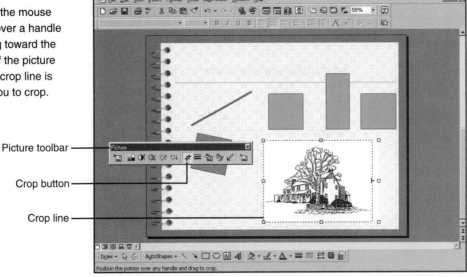

Picture toolbar ——

Crop button ——

Crop line ——

Uncropping Choose **Edit**, **Undo** from the menu or click the **Undo** button to return the picture to its full size immediately after you've cropped it. At any time, you remove the cropping by doing the same steps you performed to crop the picture, but dragging away from the center of the picture until it's full size again.

Review Questions

1. How do you rotate an object?

2. How do you fill an object?

3. How do you scale an object?

4. True or False: When you group objects, you can move and size them together.

5. What happens when you crop a picture?

Review Question Answers

1. Select the object you want to rotate. Click the **Free Rotate** tool on the Drawing toolbar. Move the mouse pointer over one of the round handles and drag in a circular motion. When the outline of the object appears at the angle you want, release the mouse button. For more information, refer to "Rotating an Object."

2. Select the object and click the **Fill Color** button. Select a color or a gradient fill or a Fill Effect. Click **OK**. For more information, see "Filling an Object."

3. Select the object and position your cursor over one of the sizing handles. Click and drag the mouse until the object is the size you want. Release the mouse button. For more information, refer to "Scaling and Sizing Objects."

4. True. Grouping causes the objects to act like one. For more information, refer to "Grouping and Ungrouping Objects."

5. You trim away the parts of the background you don't need. For more information, refer to "Cropping a Picture."

Practice Lab

The Microsoft Expert User Exam lists twelve Required Tasks for the Skill Area "Adding Visual Elements." Two of these tasks have been covered in this lesson. A practice lab for these two tasks follows.

 Required Tasks   The Required Tasks covered in this lesson are Rotate and Fill an Object, and Scale and Size an Object.

Rotate and Fill an Object

Open the file Lesson15.ppt from the CD-ROM. Rotate the arrow so that it is pointing to the left of the slide. Change the fill effects of the box to two colors and select the colors.

Scale and Size an Object

Change the size of the 3-D star so that it is much smaller (half of its current size).

To see an example of a completed exercise, open the file Lesson15a.ppt.

Adding Pictures, Sounds, and Movies

This lesson covers three of the six Required Tasks for the "Importing and Exporting Data" Skill Area.

In this lesson, you learn the following Required Tasks for your exam:

- ▶ Add clip art
- ▶ Add scanned images
- ▶ Add sound and movies

For a complete list of the Required Tasks for the Skill Area "Importing and Exporting Data," refer to the User Skills Roadmap.

Introducing the Clip Gallery

Using clip art, pictures, videos, or sounds adds excitement and interest to your presentation. Microsoft PowerPoint manages pictures, clip art, videos (movies), and sounds in the Clip Gallery (see Figure 16.1). Most of the items in the Clip Gallery are packaged with PowerPoint and installed when you install PowerPoint, although there are additional files available on the Office CD-ROM. You may add other clip art, pictures, videos, or sounds to the Clip Gallery.

Figure 16.1

Select the tab for the type of item you want, select a category if necessary, click the item, and then click Insert.

Categories

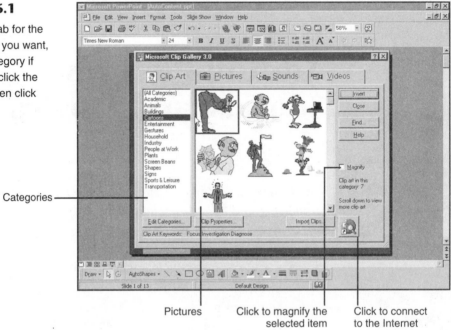

Pictures   Click to magnify the selected item   Click to connect to the Internet

 Clip Art A collection of previously created pictures or images available for use without infringement of the artist's copyright.

 PowerPoint on the Web Click the Internet icon in the lower-right corner of the Clip Gallery 3.0 dialog box (refer to Figure 16.1) to connect to Microsoft's Web site and download additional clip art.

Adding Clip Art

Adding clip art to your slide helps illustrate your points, adds a touch of humor, or just gives a little visual interest. PowerPoint has clip art incorporated into some of the AutoLayouts, in which you double-click the clip art placeholder to open the Clip Gallery. To add clip art on any slide, do the following:

1. Change to Slide view.

2. Display the slide in which you want to place the clip art.

 3. Choose **Insert**, **Picture**, **Clip Art** from the menu or click the **Insert Clip Art** button on the Standard toolbar. The Microsoft Clip Gallery 3.0 dialog box opens (refer to Figure 16.1).

4. Select the **Clip Art** tab to select a drawing or the **Pictures** tab to select an image.

5. On the left side, select a category for the type of pictures you want to use.

6. On the right side, click the picture you want to select.

7. Click **Insert**.

8. The picture appears in the middle of the slide. Move it and size it to fit your needs (refer to Lesson 15, "Positioning and Sizing Objects," for more information on moving and sizing objects).

 File Size on the Web Artwork, movies, and sounds can really add a lot to a PowerPoint presentation on the Web, but they also add to the size of the file and, consequently, to the time it will take a reader to download it. For this reason, try to be judicious in your use of media on presentations designed for the Web.

Adding Scanned Images

There is a great deal of clip art available on the market, beyond what PowerPoint has. If you can't find it at the local computer store, your favorite computer magazine probably has ads for clip art catalogs. Most of this is now on CDs. There are also a lot of photograph collections for sale on CDs. The price of color scanners has moved into the "reasonable" range, so many people are scanning their own artwork. Your company logo, for instance, may be in a scanned file. Or, you might have a picture of your company headquarters that was taken with a digital camera and saved as a file.

How do you place this non-PowerPoint art or the pictures you scanned into your slide? Follow these directions:

1. Change to Slide view.

2. Display the slide in which you want to place the picture.

3. Choose **Insert**, **Picture**, **From File** from the menu. The Insert Picture dialog box appears (see Figure 16.2).

Figure 16.2

Select the picture file and click Insert.

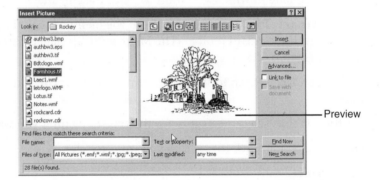

Preview

4. Select the picture you want to use. A preview of the picture appears on the right side of the dialog box (click the **Preview** button if the picture doesn't appear).

5. Click **Insert**.

6. The picture appears in the middle of the slide. Move it and size it to fit your needs (refer to Lesson 15 for more information on moving and sizing objects).

 Adding Pictures to the Clip Gallery   If you find yourself inserting the same picture in presentation after presentation, you should add it to the Clip Gallery. When you have the Clip Gallery open, click the **Import Clips** button, select the file you want to add, and click **Open**. Select a category and click **OK**.

Adding Sounds and Movies

Adding sounds and video clips (movies) to your slides makes your presentation more interesting, although the slide show has to be projected using a multimedia computer (able to play sound and videos). It's a wonderful way to have an expert deliver comments even though she can't be at the presentation in person.

To add a sound or movie to your slide, follow these steps:

1. Change to Slide view.

2. Display the slide in which you want to place the sound or movie.

3. Choose **Insert**, **Movies and Sounds** from the menu.

4. Select **Sound from Gallery** or **Movie from Gallery** from the submenu. The Clip Gallery appears (see Figure 16.3).

Figure 16.3

To hear the sound or see the movie before inserting it into your slide, click Play.

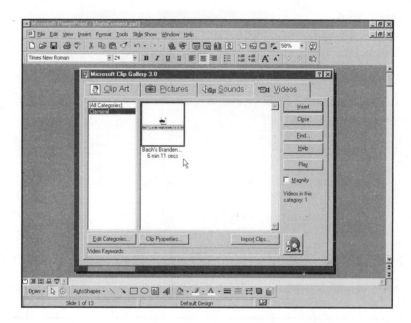

5. Choose a category on the left of the dialog box.

6. Select a sound or movie on the right. Click **Play** to play the sound or the movie.

7. Click **Insert**. A small symbol appears in the middle of the slide. Move it to a better location.

Making Movies and Sounds Play Automatically

Slides are static, for the most part. They appear and then they sit there. Movies and sounds, on the other hand, are dynamic.

Normally, when you place a sound or movie on a slide, the object doesn't activate until you click on it. For example, as the presenter you want to control when the narration about a procedural diagram starts by clicking on the sound icon when you're ready for it.

However, you may want some sounds or movies to play automatically at certain times in the presentation, such as when you open a particular slide. To control this, follow these steps:

1. Click the object (the sound icon or the movie image) on the slide.

2. Choose **Slide Show**, **Custom Animation** from the menu.

3. When the Custom Animation dialog box opens (see Figure 16.4), select the **Timing** tab.

Figure 16.4

Select Animate and then Automatically to make the sound or movie run without the presenter clicking on the icon.

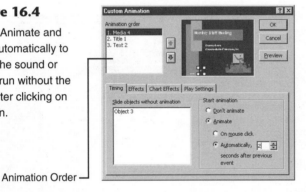

Animation Order

4. Select **Animate** to indicate that you want the sound or movie to play on the slide.

5. Select **Automatically** to indicate you want it to play without user intervention, and then in the text box enter the number of seconds that PowerPoint should pause after the previous event before playing the sound or movie.

 Previous Event   If this is the only media clip on this slide, the previous event is the slide itself being displayed. If there is more than one media clip on the slide, you control in which order they activate by switching around the order in the Animation Order list.

6. Click **OK**.

7. Switch to the Slide Show view to test the slide, making sure you have set up the sound or movie to play when you want.

 Continuous Play   Set a sound or movie to loop continuously by clicking the **Play Settings** tab in the Custom Animation dialog box and then the **More Options** button. Select both the **Loop Until Stopped** and **Rewind Movie When Done Playing** options.

Review Questions

1. How do you add clip art to your presentation?

2. How do you add a scanned image to your presentation?

3. Explain how you add sound and movies to your presentation.

4. How do you set a movie to play continuously during your presentation?

Review Question Answers

1. In Slide view, display the slide where you want to place the clip art. Choose **Insert**, **Picture**, **Clip Art** from the menu or click the **Insert Clip Art** button on the standard toolbar. Select the clip art to insert, and click **Insert**. For more information, refer to "Adding Clip Art."

2. In Slide view, display the slide where you want to place the clip art. Choose **Insert**, **Picture**, **From File**. Select the file to insert, and click **Insert.** For more information, refer to "Adding Scanned Images."

3. In Slide view, display the slide where you want to place the clip art. Choose **Insert**, **Movies and Sounds** from the menu. Select the movie or sound to insert, and click **Insert**. For more information, refer to "Adding Sound and Movies."

4. Click the object (the movie icon) and choose **Slide Show**, **Custom Animation**. Click **More Options** and select the **Loop Until Stopped** and the **Rewind Move When Done Playing** options. For more information, refer to "Making Movies and Sounds Play Automatically."

Practice Lab

The Microsoft Expert User Exam lists six Required Tasks for the Skill Area "Importing and Exporting Data." Three of these tasks have been covered in this lesson. A practice lab for each of these three tasks follows.

 Required Tasks   The Required Tasks covered in this lesson are Add Clip Art, Add Scanned Images, and Add Sound and Movies.

Add Clip Art

Create a new presentation. Select an AutoFormat that includes a clip art placeholder. Add clip art to that placeholder. Also add any suitable text. Add a new slide that has no placeholder, and add another piece of clip art from the Gallery.

Add Scanned Images

On a new slide, add a scanned picture—either one you scanned yourself or one you have from a library of images. There are some images (usually JPG or GIF files) on the Microsoft Office CD-ROM. The authors used one from the Photo folder in the Clip art folder, called Garden.Jpg. You may also find some in the Microsoft Office Clip art folder on your own computer. Try the CDonline folder.

Add Sound and Movies

On the slide with the picture, add a sound or video clip (if you have one). There are sound files on the Microsoft Office CD-ROM, in the Microsoft Office folder, or in the Windows folder. To play the sound, you must run the Slide Show (click to advance the slides) and click the Sound or Video icon when it appears. This will only work if you have a computer that can play sound.

To see an example of a completed exercise, open the file Lesson16a.ppt on the CD-ROM.

Editing Objects

This lesson covers two of the seven Required Tasks for the "Customizing Presentations" Skill Area.

In this lesson, you learn the following Required Tasks for your exam:

▶ Customize clip art and other objects

▶ Recolor and edit objects

For a complete list of the Required Tasks for the Skill Area "Customizing Presentations," refer to the User Skills Roadmap.

Recoloring and Editing Objects

Although the attributes of objects can be modified using the Fill Color, Line Color, Line Style, Dash Style, Arrow Style, Shadow, and 3-D tools, changing the colors used in clip art or modifying the shape of a drawn object is a little different.

Creating and Editing Freeform Objects

The objects you draw on a slide can be enhanced with new fill or line attributes, sized, rotated, or flipped. The basic shapes, however, remain the same. Only objects created with the Curve, Scribble, and Freeform tools can have their basic shapes altered.

To use the Curve, Scribble, or Freeform tools, click the **AutoShapes** button on the Drawing toolbar, select **Lines** from the menu that pops up, and then click the tool you want (see Figure 17.1).

Figure 17.1

The Curve, Scribble, and Freeform tools are AutoShapes.

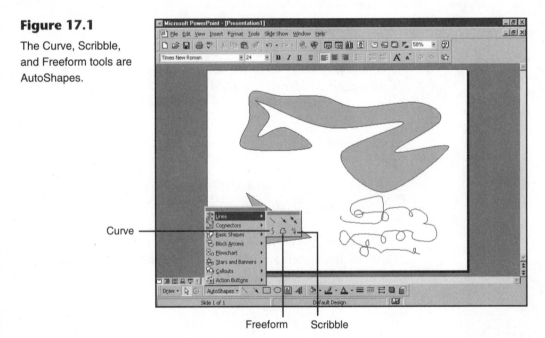

With the Curve tool, you draw a smooth, curved shape, clicking at each point where you want the line to change direction and double-clicking to end the drawing. Drawing with the Scribble tool creates an object that looks as if it were drawn on the screen with a pencil (you drag the mouse pointer across the screen to draw). The Freeform tool has two uses: When you drag the tool, it creates objects with smoother curves than the Scribble tool; when you click the icon, it creates straight lines between your clicks.

As these three tools draw, PowerPoint marks any change in the direction of a curve or line with a *point*. Moving, deleting, or adding points changes the shape of the object.

To change the shape of one of these objects, do the following:

1. Select the object.

2. Click the **Draw** button on the Drawing toolbar.

3. From the menu that appears, select **Edit Points**.

4. Do one of the following:

   ▶ To add a point to a line or curve segment, hold down the **Ctrl** key and click where you want the new point.

   ▶ To move a point, click and drag the point until the dotted line outline is in the position you want and then release the mouse button (see Figure 17.2).

   ▶ To delete a point, hold down the **Ctrl** key and click the point when the **X** appears.

   ▶ To adjust the curve between two points, drag the curve line.

Figure 17.2

When you drag a point, a dotted outline shows how the curve or line will look when you release the mouse button.

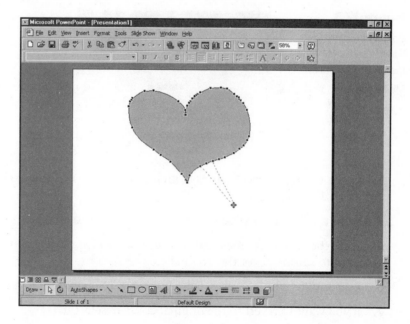

5. When your editing is complete, click an empty portion of the slide to deselect the points.

Recoloring Objects

Drawings from the Microsoft Clip Gallery clip art already have colors assigned to them when you insert them in your slide. These colors may not be compatible with your slide background or other objects on the slide. However, when you choose a different fill color, either that color is applied to the background behind the drawing or the entire drawing becomes the same color.

To change the color of a clip art picture, follow these steps:

1. Select the picture.

2. Do one of the following to open the Recolor Picture dialog box (see Figure 17.3):

   ▶ Click the **Recolor Picture** button on the Picture toolbar. If the Picture toolbar isn't showing, right-click the picture and select **Show Picture Toolbar**.

   ▶ Choose **Format**, **Colors and Lines** from the menu. When the Format Picture dialog box appears, select the **Picture** tab and then click the **Recolor** button.

Figure 17.3

Select the colors you want to substitute for the original colors in the picture.

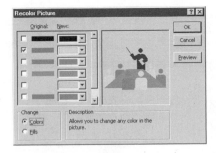

3. Under Change, select **Colors** to change any color or **Fills** to change only background or fill colors.

4. From the Original list, select the color you want to change.

5. From the New drop-down list next to the selected color, choose the color you want to substitute for the original.

6. Repeat steps 3 to 5 for each color you want to change.

7. If you want to revert to the original color, deselect it.

8. Click **OK** to apply your new colors to the picture.

Customizing Clip Art and Other Objects

The Recolor feature allows you to change the color of clip art, but it doesn't allow you to add a pattern to a woman's dress or to eliminate parts of the clip art that you don't want.

Clip art is a combination of many objects grouped together. Therefore, to modify clip art, you must ungroup it as follows:

1. In Slide view, display the slide that has the clip art you want to modify.

2. Select the clip art by clicking on it. Handles appear around the clip art to indicate that it's selected.

 3. Click the **Draw** button on the Drawing toolbar.

4. Select **Ungroup** from the menu that pops up.

 Bitmap Images   You can't ungroup a bitmap image. A bitmap image is artwork created in paint programs such as Windows Paint (*.bmp), saved in an image editing program such as Adobe PhotoShop, or captured by a scanner (*.tif). These programs color each pixel of the image and map those pixels to save them. There are no separate objects that make up the image, and therefore nothing to ungroup.

5. PowerPoint displays a warning that the selected artwork is an imported object, not a group, and that linking information will be lost. Click **Yes** to continue.

 What links will I destroy?   Normally, PowerPoint clip art maintains a link back to the Clip Gallery. If you double-click a piece of clip art, the Clip Gallery opens. Then, if you so choose, you can select another piece of clip art to replace the one on your slide. If you ungroup clip art, you sever the link to the Clip Gallery, so you have to delete the current picture and insert a new one when you want to replace the clip art.

6. The individual pieces within the clip art become individual groups or objects, with handles around each one. If necessary, select a group and ungroup it to work with one of the objects within it.

7. After you have the object you want selected, delete it, move it, fill it, change the line style, rotate it, or flip it.

8. To bring the individual objects back into one group again, click **Draw** on the Drawing toolbar and select **Group**.

Even though you can't ungroup and modify bitmap images the way you can PowerPoint clip art, there are still some modifications available to you.

The tools you need are on the Picture toolbar. (If the Picture toolbar doesn't appear when you select the image, right-click the picture and then select **Show Picture Toolbar**.) Table 17.1 lists a description of the tools. To use a tool, select the image and then click the tool.

Table 17.1   Tools on the Picture Toolbar

Button	Name	Description
	Insert Picture	Inserts an existing picture from a file into the current slide.
	Image Control	Converts the image to grayscale (changes colors to levels of gray), black-and-white (line drawing), or watermark (low-density coloring so image can be placed behind other objects on a slide). Automatic is the default setting.
	More Contrast	Increases the saturation, or intensity, of the colors in the selected picture.
	Less Contrast	Decreases the saturation, or intensity, of the colors in the selected picture.
	More Brightness	Adds white to lighten the colors in the selected picture.
	Less Brightness	Adds black to darken the colors in the selected picture.
	Crop	Trims a picture (see Lesson 15, "Positioning and Sizing Objects").
	Line Style	Selects a width or style of line to use as a border for the image.
	Recolor Picture	Lets you substitute colors for the original colors in the picture (not available for bitmaps).

Button	Name	Description
	Format Picture	Opens the Format Picture dialog box in which you select options for the line, color, fill and pattern, size, position, brightness, contrast, trim, and so on.
	Set Transparent Color	Sets the transparent color for the selected bitmap. Click the color you want to make transparent, so the slide background shows through. This tool works only on bitmap images.
	Reset Picture	Removes cropping from the selected picture and returns the color, brightness, and contrast to the original settings.

Review Questions

1. Explain how to draw a curve.

2. How do you change the shape of a freeform drawing?

3. How do you add points when editing a shape?

4. How do you change a color in PowerPoint's clip art?

5. Describe how to change the fill type in part of a clip art picture.

6. How do you change a scanned photograph to grayscale?

7. How do you adjust the contrast of a scanned photograph?

Review Question Answers

1. Click the **AutoShapes** tool on the Drawing toolbar, select **Lines**, and then choose **Curve**. Drag to draw the curve, clicking at each point where you want the curve to change direction. For more information, refer to "Creating and Editing Freeform Objects."

2. First, select the freeform drawing. Click the **Draw** button on the Drawing toolbar and then select **Edit Points**. Drag one of the points to a new location. For more information, refer to "Creating and Editing Freeform Objects."

3. Hold down the **Ctrl** key and click the curve or line where you want to add the new point. For more information, refer to "Creating and Editing Freeform Objects."

4. Click the Recolor button on the Picture toolbar or choose **Format**, **Colors and Lines** from the menu. When the Format Picture dialog box appears, select the **Picture** tab and then click the **Recolor** button. Under Change, select **Colors** to change any color or **Fills** to change only background or fill colors. From the Original list, select the color you want to change. From the New drop-down list next to the selected color, choose the color you want to substitute for the original. Click **OK**. For more information, refer to "Recoloring Objects."

5. Select the clip art picture. Click the **Draw** button on the Drawing toolbar and choose **Ungroup** from the menu that pops up. Ungroup again if you need to, until the part of the drawing you want to change is independent of the rest of the clip art. Then select that piece and change the fill color. For more information, refer to "Customizing Clip Art and Other Objects."

6. Select the photograph. Click the **Image Control** button on the Picture toolbar and then select **Grayscale**. For more information, refer to "Customizing Clip Art and Other Objects."

7. Select the photograph. Click the **More Contrast** or **Less Contrast** button on the Picture toolbar. For more information, refer to "Customizing Clip Art and Other Objects."

Practice Lab

The Microsoft Expert User Exam lists seven Required Tasks for the Skill Area "Customizing Presentations." Two of these tasks have been covered in this lesson. Following you will find a practice lab for each of these tasks.

Required Tasks   The Required Tasks covered in this lesson are Recolor and Edit Objects, and Customize Clip Art and Other Objects.

Recolor and Edit Objects

Open the file Lesson17.ppt from the CD-ROM. Change the red rose on Slide 2 to a yellow rose. On Slide 3, change Shape A to look like Shape B.

Customize Clip Art and Other Objects

On Slide 4, eliminate the man in the middle of the picture so that all you see is the one man shaking hands with the woman. On Slide 5, crop the black border from the picture, add more contrast, and decrease the brightness. Open the file Lesson17a.ppt on the CD-ROM to see an example of how your changes would affect the presentation.

LESSON 18

Importing and Exporting Data

This lesson covers three of the six Required Tasks for the "Importing and Exporting Data" Skill Area.

In this lesson, you learn the following Required Tasks for your exam:

- ▶ Insert a Microsoft Excel chart
- ▶ Import text from Microsoft Word
- ▶ Export an outline to Word

For a complete list of Required Tasks for the Skill Area "Importing and Exporting Data," refer to the User Skills Roadmap.

Inserting a Microsoft Excel Chart

You don't need to re-create a chart in PowerPoint that you already made in Microsoft Excel. Instead, you can import the chart to PowerPoint. There are three ways to do this:

▶ Select the chart in the Excel worksheet and choose **Edit**, **Copy** from the menu. Then display the slide in PowerPoint where you want the chart placed and choose **Edit**, **Paste**. Size and move the chart as you would any other object on the slide. Because PowerPoint automatically embeds a Microsoft Chart when you import it, just double-click the chart to format it (see Figure 18.1).

If the data is on the same worksheet or another worksheet in the Excel workbook, it's also possible to edit the data by going to that portion of the embedded worksheet and changing the figures. The change will not affect the original (source) Excel workbook.

Figure 18.1

This chart was copied from an Excel worksheet and pasted into PowerPoint. Double-clicking the chart makes it possible to edit the data in the worksheet and format the chart.

Embedded chart —

Excel Chart toolbar —

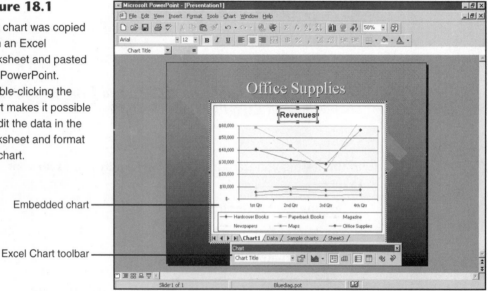

▶ Select the chart in the Excel worksheet and choose **Edit**, **Copy** from the menu. Then display the slide in PowerPoint where you want the chart placed and choose **Edit**, **Paste Special**. When the Paste Special dialog box appears (see Figure 18.2), select the **Paste Link** option to have the chart updated each time the data in the source workbook is changed. Click **OK**.

Size and move the chart as you would any other object on the slide. When you double-click the chart, you jump to Microsoft Excel for editing or formatting. Modify the chart or the chart data and save the workbook. Switch back to PowerPoint to view the effects of your changes on the chart.

Figure 18.2

Choose Paste Link to have the chart automatically updated when changes are made to the chart or chart data in the source workbook.

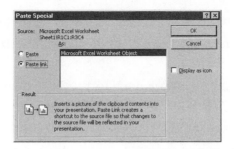

> ▶ From PowerPoint, choose **Insert**, **Object**. When the Insert Object dialog box appears (see Figure 18.3), select the **Create From File** option (**Create New** inserts a new, blank workbook into the slide; you have to enter the data and then create the slide from there). In the **File** text box, enter the name and path of the workbook file where the chart is stored or click **Browse** to specify the name and location of the file.
>
> Select the **Link** option if you just want to link the file to the source workbook as you did with the Paste Link option in the Paste Special dialog box; deselect that option to embed the chart in the slide. Click **OK**. When the chart appears on the slide, move or size it as you do any object. If the chart isn't located on its own worksheet, you may see parts of the worksheet on your slide. Double-click the slide to return to Microsoft Excel to edit or format the chart.

Figure 18.3

Using the Insert, Object command embeds the chart in the slide unless you select the Link option.

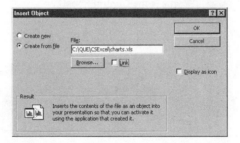

Importing Text from Microsoft Word

When you import text from a Microsoft Word document, there are two possible destinations in PowerPoint: directly onto a slide or into the outline.

Importing Text into a Slide

If you want to bring the Word text directly into the current slide (the one you're displaying in Slide view), follow these steps:

1. Choose **Insert**, **Object** from the menu to display the Insert Object dialog box (refer to Figure 18.3).

2. Select **Create From File**.

3. In the **File** box, enter the name and path of the file or click **Browse** to select the file.

4. Select the **Link** option if you just want to link the file to the source document; deselect that option to embed the document in the slide.

5. Click **OK**. The text appears on the slide. Move it or size it as you do any object.

6. To edit the text, double-click in the middle of the object. If you chose the Link option, you jump back to Microsoft Word. If you deselected the **Link** option, the Word toolbars and menus appear in PowerPoint (see Figure 18.4). Make your changes, save the file, and click outside the border to return to the slide or switch back from Microsoft Word to PowerPoint.

Figure 18.4

Double-click the inserted text object to edit and enhance it.

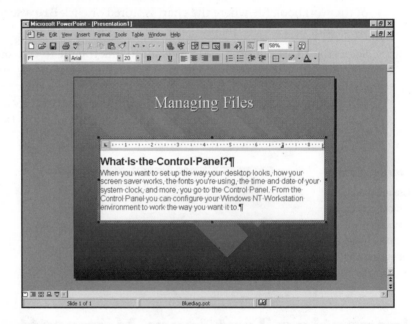

 Copy and Paste   If you don't want all the text in the document to be inserted, open the document in Word and select the portion you want. Choose **Edit**, **Copy** or click the **Copy** button on the Standard toolbar. Switch to PowerPoint and display the slide where you want the text to go. Choose **Edit**, **Paste**. Double-click the text object to edit or enhance it. To maintain a link back to the original document so the text updates when the document changes, choose **Edit**, **Paste Link** when you place the text on the slide.

Importing Text into a PowerPoint Outline

The other method for importing text into PowerPoint is to bring it into the outline where you can quickly edit it and reformat it for the presentation. There are three options for bringing a Word document into Outline view:

▶ **Start a new presentation by importing a Word outline**. Choose **File**, **Open** from the menu to display the Open dialog box (see Figure 18.5). From the **Files of Type** drop-down list, select **All Outlines**. Select the file you want and then click **Open**. The text appears in Outline view.

Figure 18.5

Select All Outlines as the file type and then choose the file you want to use.

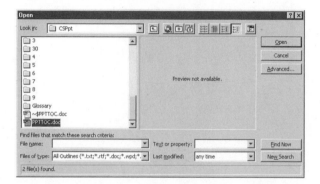

▶ **Insert text into an existing presentation outline**. Place your insertion point in the outline where you want to add the Word text. Choose **Insert**, **Slides from Outline** from the menu to display the Insert Outline dialog box (see Figure 18.6). From the **Files of Type** drop-down list, select **All Outlines**. Choose the file you want to use and click **Insert**.

Figure 18.6

Select the file you want to add to the Outline and click Insert.

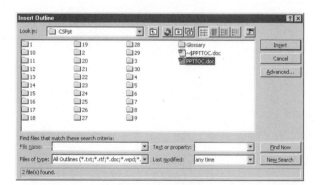

▶ **Create a presentation from a Word document**. Open the document in Word that you want to use to create a presentation. Choose **File**, **Send To**, **Microsoft PowerPoint** from the menu. A new PowerPoint presentation starts up and the Word document becomes the presentation outline.

Exporting an Outline to Word

Although you can copy and paste the outline into a Word document, try using PowerPoint's Write-Up feature to send your outline to Word. In addition to the outline text, Write-Up can send the slides and notes.

To use Write-Up to send your outline to Word, do the following:

1. Choose **File**, **Send To**, **Microsoft Word** from the menu. The Write-Up dialog box appears (see Figure 18.7).

Figure 18.7

To send the outline to Word, select Outline Only.

2. Select **Outline Only**.

3. Click **OK**.

4. A new Word document opens with the outline text in it.

Review Questions

1. How do you add a Microsoft Excel chart to a slide so the chart automatically updates when changes are made to the chart or chart data in the source workbook?

2. How do you edit an embedded Microsoft Excel chart? Will these changes be incorporated into the original Excel document?

3. Describe how to place text from Microsoft Word on a PowerPoint slide.

4. How do you start a new presentation by importing a Word outline into PowerPoint?

5. How do you create a Microsoft Word document from your presentation outline?

Review Question Answers

1. Select the chart in the Excel workbook. Copy it to the Clipboard. In PowerPoint, choose **Edit**, **Paste Special** to paste it onto the current slide. Select the Paste Link option and click OK. For more information, refer to "Inserting a Microsoft Excel Chart."

2. Double-click in the middle of the chart to make the Excel toolbar available to you. Then make any changes to the graph just as you would in Excel. Click outside the chart area to return to PowerPoint. These changes are not made in the original Excel document. For more information, refer to "Inserting a Microsoft Excel Chart."

3. In PowerPoint, choose **Insert**, **Object**, **Create from File**. Specify the name of the file and its location. Click **OK**. For more information, refer to "Importing Text from Microsoft Word."

4. In PowerPoint, choose **File**, **Open** from the menu. From the Files of Type dropdown list, select **All Outlines**. Select the file you want and then click **Open**. The text appears in the Outline view. For more information, refer to "Importing Text from Microsoft Word."

5. In PowerPoint, choose **File**, **Send To**, **Microsoft Word** from the menu. Select **Outline Only** and click **OK**. For more information, refer to "Exporting an Outline to Word."

Practice Lab

The Microsoft Expert User Exam lists six Required Tasks for the Skill Area "Importing and Exporting Data." Three of these tasks have been covered in this lesson. Following you will find a practice lab for these three tasks.

 Required Tasks The Required Tasks covered in this lesson are Insert a Microsoft Excel Chart Import, Text from Microsoft Word, and Export an Outline to Word.

Insert a Microsoft Excel Chart

Open the file Lesson18.ppt from the CD-ROM. On Slide 2, insert a Microsoft Excel chart from the file Lesson18.xls. The chart is called "Total Revenues by Category" and is found on the Chart 1 worksheet.

Import Text from Microsoft Word

On Slide 3, import text from the Microsoft Word file Lesson18.doc.

Export an Outline to Word

Export the outline from the presentation as an outline to Microsoft Word. Save the file as Present1.rtf.

Open the file Lesson18a.ppt on the CD-ROM to see an example of the changed presentation. Lesson18a.rtf is an example of how the presentation outline would look when converted to a Microsoft Word document.

Changing a Presentation's Look

This lesson covers one of the seven Required Tasks for the "Modifying Presentations" Skill Area.

In this lesson, you learn the following Required Task for your exam:

▶ Modify the slide master

For a complete list of Required Tasks for the Skill Area "Modifying Presentations," refer to the User Skills Roadmap.

Giving Your Slides a Professional Look

PowerPoint comes with dozens of professional slide designs that become the templates for your own presentations. That is, you may apply one of these designs to an already existing presentation to give the slides in your presentation a consistent look.

 Template A presentation design that affects the color scheme, fonts, and layouts of each slide in your presentation.

The basic color scheme, font choices, and layout of a template are embodied in the master slide of your presentation. Although you attach a template to a presentation, you are able to modify the master slide to get the look you want. The alterations you make to the master slide affect the entire presentation but don't change the original template, so you may use that template again to set the look of other presentations.

Applying a Presentation Design Template

When you start your presentation, you begin by selecting the AutoContent Wizard, by choosing a template, or by working with a blank presentation (refer to Lesson 1, "Creating a Presentation"). If you start from the AutoContent Wizard, a template is automatically selected for your presentation. The blank presentation is a template without a background and minimal formatting. However you started out, your presentation has a template controlling the overall design.

PowerPoint lets you change your presentation template at any time, no matter which method you used to start your presentation. To change your template, follow these steps:

1. Click the **Apply Design** button on the Standard toolbar, or choose **Format**, **Apply Design** from the menu, or right-click the slide and select **Apply Design** from the pop-up menu. The Apply Design dialog box appears (see Figure 19.1).

2. From the list of templates on the left side of the dialog box, select a template to use. When you select a template, a preview of a bulleted list slide appears on the right side of the dialog box.

3. Click **Apply** to apply the selected template to your presentation.

Figure 19.1

Select the template
you want to use from
the list and a preview
of it appears on the
right.

 Things Aren't Where They Should Be When you switch templates, items in place-holders that use the placeholder default formatting will convert easily from one design to another. But if you've added any objects or modified any of the formats, your modifications might not look as well with the new design. Make sure you review your entire presentation and correct any pieces that no longer match.

Using AutoLayouts

Although templates control the color and overall design of your presentation, the layout of each slide depends on the AutoLayout you apply to the slide. AutoLayouts structure the placement of graphs, organization charts, clip art, objects, tables, and so on. AutoLayouts provide placeholders for you to help you design your slides quickly, in almost fill-in-the-blanks style. There is also a blank AutoLayout to use if you want to lay out the slide elements yourself.

PowerPoint provides 24 AutoLayouts for each presentation, and the AutoLayouts work within the style guidelines of the template, so the placement and coloring of a graph in the AutoLayout in the Bedrock template will look different than one in the Blush template.

To apply an AutoLayout to a slide, do the following:

1. In the Slide view, display the slide you want to change.

2. Choose **Format**, **Slide Layout** from the menu, or click the **Slide Layout** button on the Standard toolbar, or right-click the slide and select **Slide Layout** from the pop-up menu. The Slide Layout dialog box appears (see Figure 19.2).

3. Click the desired layout shown under **Change the Layout of the Slide To**. The name of the layout appears at the bottom right of the dialog box.

4. Click **Apply**. PowerPoint applies the selected layout to the current slide.

Figure 19.2

Select the AutoLayout you want to use with the current slide.

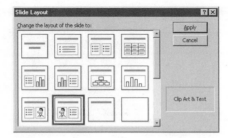

Modifying the Slide Master

Every presentation has a slide master that controls the overall appearance and layout of each slide. The slide master contains all the formatting information that the template brings to the presentation, such as colors and background patterns, and it also marks where the elements you use from the AutoLayout feature will appear on the slide. Changes you make to the slide master will alter all the slides in the presentation, except the title slide which has its own title master.

To make changes to the slide master for your presentation, follow these steps:

1. Choose **View**, **Master**, **Slide Master** from the menu. The slide master appears (see Figure 19.3).

Figure 19.3

Modify the slide master formatting and objects to change all the slides in the presentation.

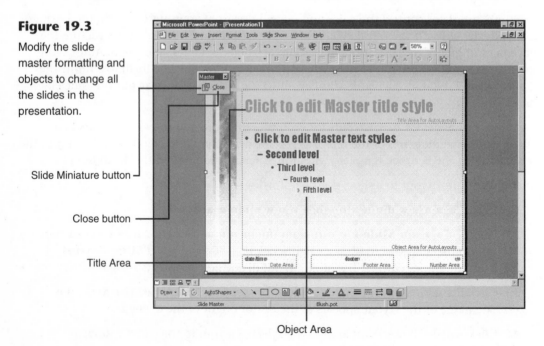

Object Area

2. Make any changes to the slide master that you want to appear on every slide in your presentation (add a logo, add drawn objects, change the background color, change fonts, select different bullets, and so on).

3. When you're done working with the slide master, click the **Close** button on the Master toolbar to return to the view you had open before you switched to the slide master (to see the Master toolbar, choose **View**, **Toolbars**, **Master**), or choose **View**, **Slide** to return to the Slide view.

The two most important elements on the slide master are the *title area* and the *object area* for the AutoLayout objects. The title area contains the formatting specifications for each slide's title—font, size, style, alignment, and color. The object area contains the formatting specifications for all remaining text on the slide, especially for the different levels for bulleted lists—the type of bullet, type styles, sizes, and indents for each bullet level.

The slide master also holds borders, page numbers, company logos, clip art objects, and any other elements you want to appear on each page.

You modify the slide master as you do any slide in the presentation. Just keep in mind that the changes have far-reaching effects, as changes to the slide master will modify all the slides in the presentation except the title slide.

 Headers, Footers, Dates, and Slide Numbers Areas for these items appear on the slide master, but they are meant for formatting and not for entering the text. To enter the text for these items, choose **View**, **Header and Footer**. Select the items you want to show and enter the text you need.

Review Questions

1. How do you change the design template of your presentation?

2. How do you apply an AutoLayout to a slide?

3. How do you add a picture to every slide in your presentation?

4. How do you change the title font and color for every slide?

Review Question Answers

1. Click the **Apply Design** button or choose **Format**, **Apply Design** from the menu. Select a template from the list on the left side of the Apply Design dialog box. Click **Apply**. For more information, refer to "Applying a Presentation Design Template."

2. Choose **Format**, **Slide Layout** from the menu or click the **Slide Layout** button. Click the layout you want to use and then click **Apply**. For more information, refer to "Using AutoLayouts."

3. Choose **View**, **Master**, **Slide Master** to view the slide master for the presentation. Then choose **Insert**, **Picture** from the menu. Select **From File** or **Clip Art**, depending on where your picture is stored. Select the picture or the picture file name and click **OK**. Position and size the picture so it will look well on every slide. For more information, refer to "Modifying the Slide Master."

4. Choose **View**, **Master**, **Slide Master** to view the slide master for the presentation. Select the title text, change the font, and apply a new color. For more information, refer to "Modifying the Slide Master."

Practice Lab

The Microsoft Expert User Exam lists seven Required Tasks for the Skill Area "Modifying Presentations." One of these tasks has been covered in this lesson. Following you will find a practice lab for this task.

 Required Tasks   The Required Task covered in this lesson is Modify the Slide Master.

Modify the Slide Master

Open the file Lesson19.ppt from the CD-ROM. Add a clip art picture that you want to show on every page. Change the font and color of the title. Change the style of the bullets. Save the file as Master1.ppt.

An example of how the your changes might affect the presentation is shown in the Lesson19a.ppt file on the CD-ROM.

Working with Presentation Colors and Backgrounds

This lesson covers two of the seven Required Tasks for the "Customizing Presentations" Skill Area.

In this lesson, you learn the following Required Tasks for your exam:

▶ Customize a color scheme

▶ Create a custom background

For a complete list of Required Tasks for the Skill Area "Customizing Presentations," refer to the User Skills Roadmap.

Understanding Color Schemes and Backgrounds

Color schemes are sets of professionally selected complementary colors assigned to different elements in the presentation. Each color scheme controls the color of the background, lines, text, shadows, fills, and other items on a slide. Using one of these color schemes ensures that your presentation looks appealing and professional.

Backgrounds are the colors, patterns, textures, or gradients that fill the slide. All other items on the slide appear in front of this fill.

 Gradient Fill A *gradient* is where the background starts out one color on one side of the slide and gradually changes to another color. When one of the colors is white or black, the shading is called a *one-color gradient*. When neither color is white or black, the gradient is *two-color*.

When you change the color scheme and background for the slide master, which controls the look of all the slides in the presentation, you change the overall look of the presentation. If you apply a background or color scheme to all the slides in the presentation, you override the slide master settings for all the slides. Changing the slide background and color scheme for an individual slide makes that one slide different from the rest of the presentation.

Selecting a Color Scheme

The basic color scheme of your presentation depends on the active design template. Design templates include both color schemes and backgrounds.

Within each design template, there are several variations of one color scheme. All the color schemes in a template use the same basic colors, but each color scheme arranges its colors differently. For example, for on-screen viewing, the color scheme is a dark background and light text; for printing on a color printer, a light background and dark text; and, for printing on a one-color printer, a black-and-white color scheme.

When you select a color scheme, it may be for one slide or all the slides in the presentation. To select a color scheme, do the following:

1. If you don't want to change all the slides in the presentation, display or select the slide(s) with the color scheme you want to change (it's easiest to do this from Slide Sorter view).

2. Choose **Format**, **Slide Color Scheme** from the menu. The Color Scheme dialog box appears (see Figure 20.1).

Figure 20.1

Click Preview to see how the color scheme you selected affects the slide.

3. Select the **Standard** tab. The dialog box displays the color schemes available for the current design template.

4. Click the color scheme you want to use.

5. Click **Apply** to apply the color scheme to the current or selected slide(s). Click **Apply to All** to apply the color scheme to all the slides in the presentation.

Customizing a Color Scheme

Even though each template comes with its own color schemes, you can customize the scheme for a presentation by adjusting the individual colors or radically changing them all.

To customize a color scheme, follow these steps:

1. If you don't want to change all the slides in the presentation, display or select the slide(s) with the color scheme you want to change (selecting multiple slides is probably easiest from Slide Sorter view).

2. Choose **Format**, **Slide Color Scheme** from the menu.

3. When the Color Scheme dialog box appears (see Figure 20.2), select the **Custom** tab.

4. Click one of the colors for the individual elements involved in the color scheme and then click **Change Color**.

5. When the dialog box appears showing the range of available colors (see the colors for the background in Figure 20.3), click the color you want to use and then click **OK**. Change to the **Custom** tab only if the color you want isn't offered on the Standard page, and you need to create the color.

Figure 20.2

Change the colors
applied to the
elements of the
presentation in order
to change the scheme.

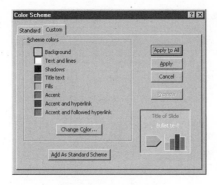

Figure 20.3

Select the color you
want to apply to the
slide element—in this
case, the background.

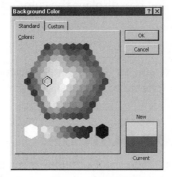

6. Repeat steps 4 and 5 for each color you want to change. The sample in the lower-right corner gives you a quick look at how you're changing the scheme. Click **Preview** to see how your changes affect the slide.

7. Click **Apply** to apply them only to the current or selected slide(s).Click **Apply to All** to apply the new colors to every slide in the presentation. If you want to use this scheme again, click the **Add as Standard Scheme** button on the Standard tab.

 Stay Consistent Be careful when you change the colors on a single slide. You don't want one slide to clash with the rest of your slides.

Copying a Slide's Color Scheme to Another Slide

If you want to change the color scheme for an entire presentation, it's best to make the changes to the slide master. However, if you want to change several slides, but not all of them, make the changes to a single slide and then copy that slide's color scheme to the others. Follow these steps to copy a slide's color scheme:

1. Display your presentation in Slide Sorter view.

2. Select the slide containing the color scheme you want to copy.

3. Click the **Format Painter** button on the Standard toolbar.

4. Click the slide that you want to receive the color scheme.

5. Repeat steps 2 through 4 for each slide you want to change.

Creating a Custom Background

An effective background adds a professional look to any presentation. PowerPoint enables you to set the background to any color, and to add patterns, textures, and shadings to it.

To change the background for a slide or for the entire presentation, follow these steps:

1. Display or select the slide with the background you want to change. To change the slide background in the entire presentation, display the slide master.

2. Choose **Format**, **Background** from the menu or right-click the background and select **Background** from the pop-up menu. The Background dialog box appears (see Figure 20.4).

Figure 20.4

Select Fill Effects to choose patterns, textures, or gradient fills.

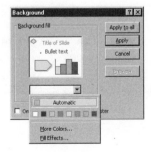

3. From the drop-down list under **Background Fill**, select one of the following options:

   ▶ **Automatic** sets the background to whatever the slide master currently shows as the background.

   ▶ A solid color sets the background to that color.

   ▶ **More Colors** opens a Colors dialog box similar to the one shown in Figure 20.3, in which you choose from a color assortment.

   ▶ **Fill Effects** opens a dialog box (see Figure 20.5) in which you choose from many special effects such as a gradient fill, textured backgrounds, or pictures used as backgrounds.

Figure 20.5

Select the tab for the type of fill you want for your background and then specify the options you want.

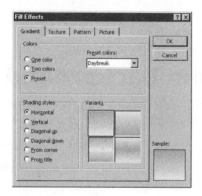

4. Click **Apply** to apply the background to the current or selected slide. Click **Apply to All** to apply the background to all the slides in the presentation.

 PowerPoint on the Web   If you are creating a presentation for use on the Web, try to keep the background light-colored. It will be easier for your readers to view on their monitors this way. Save dark backgrounds for slides designed to be shown on larger screens.

Review Questions

1. How would you change the color scheme for five slides from a 20-slide presentation?

2. Explain how to customize a color scheme for the entire presentation.

3. How do you apply the custom color scheme of one slide to another slide in the presentation?

4. How do you add a custom background to a slide?

Review Question Answers

1. From the Slide Sorter view, select the slides that you want to change. Choose **Format**, **Slide Color Scheme** from the menu. Select the **Standard** tab in the dialog box. Click the color scheme you want to use. Click **Apply**. For more information, refer to "Selecting a Color Scheme."

2. Select the slide(s) that you want to change. Choose **Format**, **Slide Color Scheme** from the menu. Select the **Custom** tab in the dialog box. Click one of the colors and then click **Change Color**. Select the color you want to use and click **OK**. Do the same for each color you want to change. Click **Apply to All** to apply the new colors to every slide in the presentation. For more information, refer to "Customizing a Color Scheme."

3. In the Slide Sorter view, select the slide that has the color scheme you want to copy. Click the **Format Painter** button. Click the slide to which you want to copy the color scheme. For more information, refer to "Copying a Slide's Color Scheme to Another Slide."

4. Select the slide to which you want to apply the new background. Choose **Format**, **Background** from the menu or right-click the background and select **Background** from the pop-up menu. From the Background Fill drop-down list, select the type of fill you want to use. Specify the options for the fill you want and click **Apply**. For more information, refer to "Creating a Custom Background."

Practice Lab

The Microsoft Expert User Exam lists seven Required Tasks for the Skill Area "Customizing Presentations." Two of these tasks have been covered in this lesson. Following you will find a practice lab for those two tasks.

 Required Tasks The Required Tasks covered in this lesson are Customize a Color Scheme and Create a Custom Background.

Customize a Color Scheme

Open the file Lesson20.ppt on the CD-ROM. Create a custom color scheme for Slide 7 using shades of blue.

Create a Custom Background

Change the slide background of Slide 7 by applying a texture. Save the file as Texture.ppt. To see an example of a finished file, open Lesson20a.ppt on the CD-ROM.

Creating a Template

This lesson covers one of the seven Required Tasks for the "Customizing Presentations" Skill Area.

In this lesson, you will learn the following Required Task for your exam:

▶ Apply a template from another presentation

For a complete list of Required Tasks for the Skill Area "Customizing Presentations," refer to the User Skills Roadmap.

Saving Your Presentation as a Template

Many companies prefer to design their own templates, with perhaps their logos appearing as part of the background, which are used by all their employees. This keeps all the presentations in the organization consistent.

If you want to design your own template, either start with a presentation in which you can edit the current master slide, make alterations to an existing design template, or start with a blank presentation and create the template from scratch.

To create your own design template, do the following:

1. Open the existing presentation you want to use as the basis for your template, or start a new presentation using a design template close to what you need, or start a blank presentation.

2. Change to the slide master by choosing **View**, **Master**, **Slide Master** from the menu.

3. Make changes to the color scheme and background, add text you want to appear on each slide, change the format of the title and body text, or add art (such as a logo). For more information on modifying the slide master, refer to Lesson 20 "Working with Presentation Colors and Backgrounds."

4. When you've completed your modifications, delete any slides you made from the presentation. This is a design template, not a contents template, so all you want are the background colors, color scheme, and background elements (such as boxes, lines, and pictures).

5. Choose **File**, **Save As** from the menu. The Save As dialog box appears (see Figure 21.1).

Figure 21.1

Change Save As Type to Presentation Template.

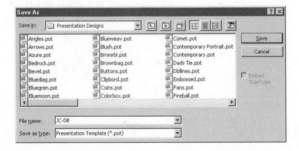

6. From the **Save as Type** drop-down box, select **Presentation Templates**.

7. Double-click the folder where you want to store your new template (design templates are usually stored in the Presentation Designs folder).

8. Enter a name for the template in the **File Name** box.

9. Click **Save**.

 Contents Template If you want to save a contents template instead of a design template, follow the same steps but don't delete the slides from the file. Leave any generic text and charts you'll be using each time you start a presentation using this template, so you only have to add new text or text specific to the current presentation. Instead of saving the presentation in the Presentation Designs folder, save it in the Presentations folder with the other contents templates (normally used with the AutoContent Wizard).

Applying a Template from Another Presentation

After you've saved your design or contents template, you may apply it to a new presentation (refer to Lesson 1, "Creating a Presentation," for further information):

1. Choose **File**, **New** from the menu.

2. When the New Presentation dialog box appears (see Figure 21.2), select the **Presentation Designs** tab for a design template or the **Presentations** tab for a contents template.

Figure 21.2

Select your template from the New Presentation dialog box.

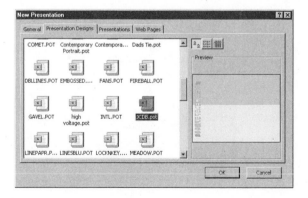

3. Click the icon for your template.

4. Click **OK**.

If you need to edit a template, you can open it (the files are in the Templates folder inside the Microsoft Office folder; the file type is Presentation Template *.pot), make your modifications, and save it again.

Review Questions

1. How do you save an existing presentation as a template?

2. How do you apply the template from another presentation to a new presentation?

Review Question Answers

1. Open the presentation and make any changes to the background, color scheme, or master slide you want to add to your template. Choose **File**, **Save As** from the menu. In the Save As dialog box, select **Presentation Templates** from the **Save as Type** drop-down box. Double-click the folder where you want to store your new template. Enter a name for the template in the **File Name** box. Click **Save**. For more information, refer to "Saving Your Presentation as a Template."

2. Choose **File**, **New** from the menu. Click the **Presentation Designs** tab. Click the icon for your template. Click **OK**. For more information, refer to "Applying a Template from Another Presentation."

Practice Lab

The Microsoft Expert User Exam lists seven Required Tasks for the Skill Area "Customizing Presentations." One of them is covered in this lesson. Following you will find a practice lab for this area.

Required Tasks The Required Task covered in this lesson is Apply a Template from Another Presentation.

Apply a Template from Another Presentation

Open the file Lesson21.ppt from the CD-ROM. Change the slide background or color scheme (or both) and add a piece of clip art to the master slide so it appears on every slide. Save the file as a template and call it MyTemplate.pot. Then start a new file and apply that template to your new file.

On the CD-ROM is a file titled Lesson21a.ppt, which shows you what can be done in designing your own template. Copy that file to the Presentation Designs folder in the Templates folder under Microsoft Office. Then start a new file using that template to see how it works.

Creating Speaker's Notes

This lesson covers one of the three Required Tasks for the "Editing Presentations" Skill Area.

In this lesson, you learn the following Required Task for your exam:

▶ Add speaker's notes

For a complete list of Required Tasks for the Skill Area "Editing Presentations," refer to the User Skills Roadmap.

Understanding Speaker's Notes

The problem with many presentations is that the presenter merely flips from one slide to the next, without telling the audience the point or providing an overview that adds meaning. The speaker ends up reading the slide to the audience. To make your slide show a success, you should put together a set of speaker's notes pages to help you deliver an effective, coherent presentation. You use the notes to rehearse your presentation or refer to the notes during the presentation as a guide.

PowerPoint provides a Notes Pages view for creating your speaker's notes pages. Each page is divided into two parts. A small version of the slide appears at the top of the page, and your notes appear below it (see Figure 22.1).

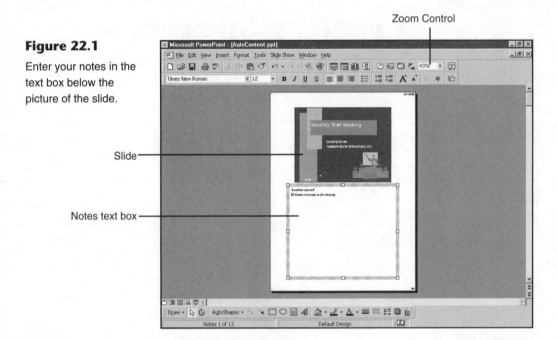

Zoom Control

Figure 22.1

Enter your notes in the text box below the picture of the slide.

Slide

Notes text box

Adding Speaker's Notes

You already have the slide part of the speaker's notes pages. All you need to do is type the notes. You type the notes in the Notes Pages view. Follow these steps to add speaker's notes:

1. Open the presentation for which you want to create notes pages.

2. Click the **Notes Pages View** button at the bottom of the presentation window or choose **View**, **Notes Pages** from the menu.

3. The currently selected slide appears in Notes Pages view (refer to Figure 22.1). Click the Notes text box in the lower half of the notes page to select it.

4. To see what you typed, click the drop-down arrow next to the **Zoom Control** button on the Standard toolbar and select a higher percentage (such as 100%).

5. Type the text that you want to use as notes material for this slide. Include reminders, jokes, supporting data, relevant quotes, summaries, or explanations about how the slide fits in with the presentation's big picture.

6. Format the text so it is large enough for you to see as you give your talk.

7. Press the Page Up or Page Down key to move to another notes page (click outside the text box to deselect it if Page Up or Page Down doesn't respond). Then repeat steps 5 and 6. You don't have to add notes to every slide.

8. Save the presentation to save your notes.

 Quick Notes   As you're creating your slides, you may think of comments or information you want to include in your notes pages. You don't have to change to Notes Pages view to quickly write these thoughts down. Choose **View**, **Speaker Notes** from the menu (see Figure 22.2). Type your notes for that slide and click **Close**. Whatever you typed appears on the notes page for that slide, where you can edit and format it if necessary.

Figure 22.2

Choose View, Speaker Notes to quickly write notes while in the Slide, Slide Sorter, or Outline views.

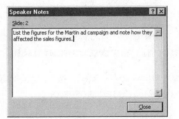

Changing the Size of the Slide and Text Box

As explained earlier, each notes page contains two objects: a slide and a text box. You change the size of either object just as you change the size of any object in PowerPoint:

1. Click the slide picture or on the text box to select it. If you clicked the text box, click the frame around it to see the handles. The handles appear on the slide picture as soon as you click it.

2. Move the mouse pointer over one of the object's handles. Use a corner handle to change both the width and height of the object. Use a side handle to change the width; use the top or bottom handles to change the height.

3. Hold down the mouse button and drag the handle until the object is the size you want.

4. Release the mouse button.

 Consistent Notes Pages   To keep the size of the slides and note text boxes consistent on all notes pages, change the size on the notes master (see the next section).

Working with the Notes Master

Just as the presentation has a slide master that contains the background and layout for all the slides in the presentation, notes pages has a notes master feature that contains the background and layout for all your notes pages. Use the notes master to do the following:

▶ Add background information (such as date, time, or page numbers) that you want to appear on all notes pages.

▶ Add a picture, such as a company logo, that you want to appear on each notes page.

▶ Move or resize objects on the notes pages.

▶ Choose a color scheme or background for the slide (this affects the look of the slide only on the notes pages, not in the presentation itself).

▶ Set up the body area of the notes master to control the general layout and formatting of the text in the notes area of each notes page.

To change the notes master, do the following:

1. Choose **View**, **Master**, **Notes Master** from the menu, or hold down **Shift** as you click the **Notes Pages View** button. The notes master appears (see Figure 22.3).

2. Change any of the elements of the notes master as you do in the slide master.

3. When you are finished, click **Close** on the Master toolbar.

Figure 22.3

Change the size or position of any of the objects on the notes master to create a consistent look for all the notes pages.

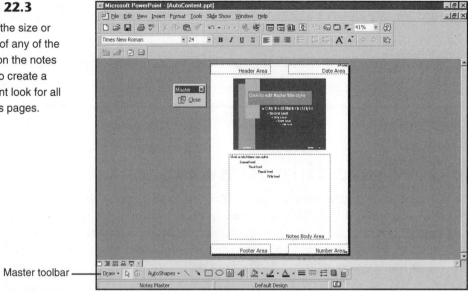

Master toolbar

To add the text for headers, footers, dates, and slide numbers, choose **View**, **Header and Footer** from the menu. Click the **Notes and Handouts** tab (see Figure 22.4). Select the items you want to show and enter the appropriate text. Click OK. Then format the text and position it on the notes master.

Figure 22.4

Enter the text for the header and footer in the dialog box. Format it on the notes master.

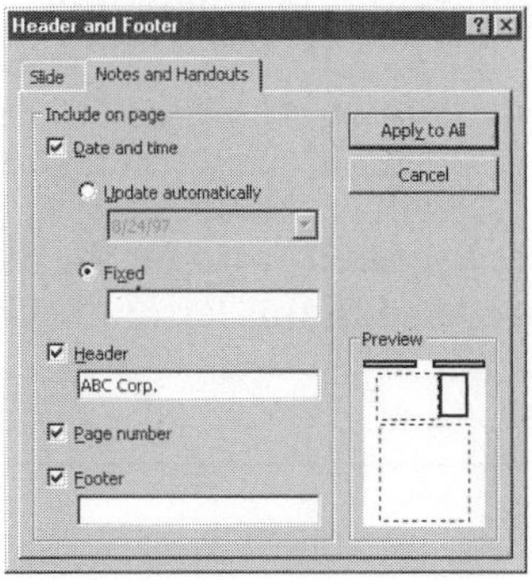

Review Questions

1. How do you add speaker's notes to a slide in your presentation?

2. How do you make the size of the text larger for all the notes pages?

3. Explain how to add page numbers and header text to the notes pages.

Review Question Answers

1. Display or select the slide to which you want to add notes. Switch to the Notes Pages view by clicking the **Notes Pages View** button. Click the Notes text box in the lower half of the notes page to select it. Type the text that you want to use as notes material for this slide. Save the presentation to save your notes. For more information, refer to "Adding Speaker's Notes."

2. Go to the notes master by choosing **View**, **Master**, **Notes Master** from the menu. Select the text box. Increase the font size. For more information, refer to "Working with the Notes Master."

3. Choose **View**, **Header and Footer** from the menu. Click the **Notes and Handouts** tab. Select the items you want to show and enter the appropriate text. Click **OK**. Then format the text and position it on the notes master. For more information, refer to "Working with the Notes Master."

Practice Lab

The Microsoft Expert User Exam lists three Required Tasks for the Skill Area "Editing Presentations." One of these tasks has been covered in this lesson. Following you will find a practice lab for that task.

 Required Tasks   The Required Task covered in this lesson is Add Speaker's Notes.

Add Speaker's Notes

Open the file Lesson22.ppt on the CD-ROM. Add the following speaker's notes to the presentation:

Slide 1—Welcome. Today we're going to discuss the business plan for Francine's Fancies. We'll look at where we've been and where we're planning to go.

Slide 2—We're selling quality. That's our real product. If we don't have quality, our customers will find a cheaper version of what we're trying to sell them.

Slide 3—These are the people at the top, but every employee has made contributions to improve the quality of our products, to create new products, and improve the efficiency of our operations.

Slide 6—All we think about is quality!

Change the Notes Master to make the text larger and easier to read. Add page numbers to each notes page and a header that reads **Francine's Fancies Business Plan**.

To see how the final presentation might appear, check the notes pages in Lesson22a.ppt on the CD-ROM.

Viewing a Slide Show

This lesson covers three of the eleven Required Tasks for the "Delivering Presentations" Skill Area.

In this lesson, you learn the following Required Tasks for your exam:

▶ Start a slide show from any slide

▶ Use on-screen navigation tools

▶ Save a presentation to use on another computer

For a complete list of Required Tasks for the Skill Area "Delivering Presentations," refer to the User Skills Roadmap.

Starting a Slide Show from Any Slide

Any presentation is immediately a slide show, because it can be displayed on-screen as well as printed or made into 35mm slides. Even if you intend to print the final version of the presentation, use the slide show to see your slides in full screen. It's a good way to check continuity and proof your slides.

 You start the slide show at any time by clicking the **Slide Show** view button at the bottom of the Presentation window. The currently displayed or selected slide is shown full screen; therefore you should go to Slide 1 before you click the **Slide Show** button if you want to start the slide show at the beginning of the presentation.

Once the slide show begins, do the following:

▶ To go to the next slide, click the left mouse button, press **Enter**, press the **Page Down** key, or press the Spacebar or the right arrow or down arrow keys.

▶ To go back to the previous slide, click the right mouse button and then choose **Previous** from the pop-up menu, press the **Page Up** key, or press the left arrow or up arrow keys.

▶ To quit the slide show, press **Esc**.

Start the Show!   Clicking the **Slide Show** button is the fastest way to start a slide show. Other ways to start a slide show include choosing **View**, **Slide Show** or **Slide Show**, **View Show** from the menu.

Using On-Screen Navigation Tools

While you view the slide show, you aren't restricted to moving forward or backward from slide to slide. Once you move your mouse, a triangle in a box appears in the bottom left corner of the slide show screen (see Figure 23.1). Click the triangle to see a pop-up menu that contains commands to use while you're giving the presentation:

▶ **Next** takes you to the next slide.

▶ **Previous** takes you to the previous slide.

▶ **Go** presents a submenu. Select **Slide Navigator** to see a dialog box listing every slide in the presentation (see Figure 23.2). Select the name of the slide you want to see and click **Go To** to jump to the slide you selected. If you know the title of the slide you want to jump to, choose **By Title** from the submenu, and then click on the title of the slide from the next submenu.

Figure 23.1

Click the triangle to
see commands to use
while showing the
presentation.

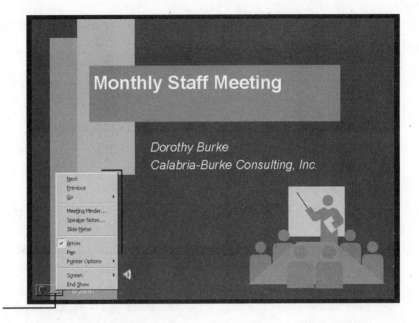

Click here to see menu ——

Figure 23.2

Select the slide to
which you want to
jump.

▶ **Meeting Minder** brings up a window where you can take notes about the
meeting at which the presentation is being given. This is particularly useful at
decision-making meetings in which you want to record the input of all the attendees. You export the minutes to a Word document for printing (see Lesson
27, "Taking Notes During a Slide Show," for more information on using the
Meeting Minder).

▶ **Speaker Notes** lets you review your notes for the presentation in a window in
the middle of the screen. This is helpful when you're rehearsing the slide show,
because you can also modify the notes in the window.

▶ **Slide Meter** opens a dialog box that lets you see how much time the slide show
is taking (the time on the bottom) and how much time you're spending on the
current slide (the top time). That way you know if you need to hurry up to finish
the presentation on time. This only appears on your PC; the audience doesn't see it.

▶ **Arrow** is the default mouse option. When this option is selected, the mouse serves as a pointer on your screen and activates sound, video, and animation objects.

▶ **Pen** is the other mouse option. When selected, the mouse writes on-screen. This is useful for circling important items and drawing arrows or lines during the slide show as emphasis, but it's very difficult to write text with the Pen. The Pen writing disappears from the slide as soon as you move to another slide. To turn off the Pen, move to the next slide or right-click the screen and select **Arrow** from the pop-up menu.

▶ **Pointer Options** lets you choose a color for the Pen and whether to display or hide the pointer. **Hide Now** makes the pointer disappear until you move the mouse again; **Hide Always** makes it disappear for the rest of the slide show.

▶ **Screen** opens a submenu that enables you to pause the show, blank the screen, and erase any pen marks you made on the screen. Click the screen to return to the slide show.

▶ **End Show** closes the slide show and takes you back to PowerPoint's slide editing window.

Setting Slide Show Options

Depending on the type of show you're presenting, you may find it useful to make some adjustments to the way the show runs, such as making it run in a window (the default is full-screen) or showing only certain slides. You'll find these controls and more in the Set Up Show dialog box (see Figure 23.3). To open it, choose **Slide Show**, **Set Up Show** from the menu.

Figure 23.3

Use the Set Up Show dialog box to give PowerPoint some basic instructions on how to present your slide show.

In this dialog box, the choices available to you are:

▶ How the presentation is presented:

  ▹ **Presented by a Speaker (Full Screen)** shows the slide show in the traditional full-screen manner. You advance the slides and animation manually or set automatic timings.

  ▹ **Browsed by an Individual (Window)** runs the slide show in a standard window. Menus and commands help the viewer to browse your presentation.

  ▹ **Browsed at a Kiosk (Full Screen)** displays the slide show full screen. It runs as a self-running show that restarts after five minutes of inactivity. Viewers can advance the slides or click hyperlinks and action buttons but can't modify the presentation.

▶ **Loop Continuously Until 'Esc'**   The show runs through to its end and then begins again until someone presses the Esc key. This option is automatically selected when you choose the **Browsed at a Kiosk** option.

▶ **Show Without Narrations**   If you created narrations for the slide show, click this option to run it without playing the voice narrations (to record narrations for the slide show, choose **Slide Show**, **Record Narration** from the menu).

▶ **Show Without Animation**   The slides appear as they would after all the animation effects had run and all items were in their final positions. You may want to choose this option when the viewers will be browsing your presentation.

▶ **Show Scrollbar**   This option is available when you select the **Browsed by an Individual** option. It adds a scrollbar to the slide show window.

▶ **Slides**   Choose to show **All** the slides, a range of slides specified by the slide numbers you enter in the **From** and **To** boxes, or **Custom Shows** to run the custom slide show (a presentation within a presentation) that you select from the drop-down list. The Custom Shows option is available only if you have created custom shows for your presentation.

▶ **Advance Slides**   Choose to run the slide show **Manually** (using mouse or keyboard directions) or by **Using Timings, If Present** (slides change automatically based on times you assigned each slide).

▶ **Pen Color**   Select a color for the Pen from the drop-down list. This option is only available when you choose **Presented by a Speaker**.

Click **OK** to close the dialog box and apply your choices to the slide show.

Adding Action Buttons on Slides

Adding slide timings to a slide advances the slides automatically, which you may want to do if you are running a show in a continuous loop (see Lesson 25, "Working with Slide Timings," to learn more about adding timing to slides). It isn't recommended when you have a speaker, however, because you can't anticipate the length of questions or possible interruptions. Likewise, in a kiosk situation, you want the readers to advance the slides at their own pace.

To advance the slides manually, use the methods listed at the beginning of this lesson. They work well in most cases, except when you want to easily jump to special slides in the presentation or in kiosk situations when you don't want the readers to have access to the keyboard.

The alternative is to add action buttons to the slides. The users click the buttons to advance the slides, go to the previous slide, jump to a particular slide, start a custom show, and so on. To add action buttons to slides, follow these steps:

1. In Slide view, display the slide to which you want to add action buttons (if you want to add the same controls to all the slides in the show, display the slide master by choosing **View**, **Master**, **Slide Master** from the menu).

2. Choose **Slide Show**, **Action Buttons** from the menu. Pick a button from the submenu (see Figure 23.4).

 Which button should I choose? Choose any button you like. At this point you are only choosing a picture to show on the button, not any particular function for it. However, you might consider the action that you want the button to perform, and then pick a button that matches it well.

Figure 23.4

Select a button that closely matches the action it will perform.

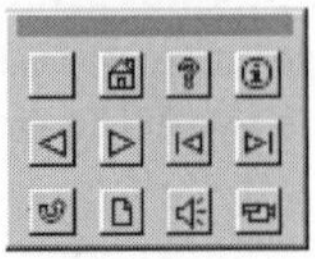

3. Your mouse pointer becomes a crosshair. Drag to draw a box on the slide where you want the button to appear (you resize the box as you would any graphic object). PowerPoint draws the button on the slide and opens the Action Settings dialog box (see Figure 23.5).

4. If you want the action to be initiated by a mouse click, select the **Mouse Click** tab. If you want the action to be initiated when the mouse points at the action button, select the **Mouse Over** tab.

Figure 23.5

Use the Action
Settings dialog box to
define what will
happen when an
action button is
activated.

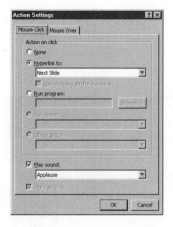

5. Choose the type of action you want to happen when the user clicks the button
    or points the mouse at the button:

    ▶ **None**   Use this to deactivate a button so nothing happens when you click
    or point at it.

    ▶ **Hyperlink To**   This can be a slide, an Web address (URL), a document on
    your computer—anything on the drop-down list.

    ▶ **Run Program**   Choose to have a program start when the button is
    activated.

    ▶ **Run Macro**   If you have recorded a macro, have the user run it from the
    button.

    ▶ **Object Action**   If you have embedded an object in the presentation, the
    user can activate it with the action button.

6. Open the drop-down list for the type of action you chose, and select the exact
    action (for instance, **Next Slide**). Or, if you chose **Run Program**, click the
    Browse button and locate the program to be run.

7. (Optional) If you want a sound to play when the user activates the button, select
    the **Play Sound** option and choose a sound from the drop-down list.

8. (Optional) If you want the button to look highlighted when the user clicks it or
    points to it, select the **Highlight Click** or **Highlight When Mouse Over**
    option.

9. Click **OK**.

Figure 23.6 shows four buttons added to a slide. These were added on the slide master, so the same buttons appear on each slide in the presentation. However, when you add buttons to the slide master, they don't appear on the title slide. You must add those buttons separately on that slide.

Figure 23.6

These action buttons help you navigate the presentation.

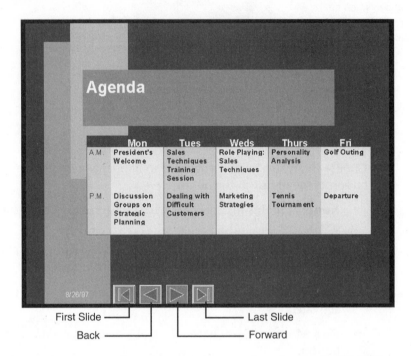

Saving a Presentation to Use on Another Computer

Although you can copy a presentation file to another computer in order to show the slides there, you run the risk of forgetting any linked files needed for that particular presentation. And what if you send the file to someone who doesn't have PowerPoint?

The best way to pass along a presentation file, and all the linked files that go with it, is to use the Pack and Go Wizard. The wizard not only copies all the files and fonts used in the presentation to a disk, but includes the PowerPoint Viewer if the destination computer doesn't have PowerPoint. The PowerPoint Viewer is a small program that has enough of the PowerPoint program to show the presentation slide show.

If you change the presentation after you run the Pack and Go Wizard, just run the wizard again to update the files.

To package your presentation for use on another computer, follow these steps:

1. Choose **File**, **Pack and Go** from the menu.

2. When the Pack and Go Wizard opens, click **Next** to continue.

3. The wizard asks which presentation you want to pack: the active presentation or another presentation. If you have the presentation open that you want to pack, select **Active Presentation**. If you want to specify a different presentation, select **Other Presentation(s)** and specify the filename and path of the presentation (or click **Browse** and select the file). Click **Next** to continue (or **Back** to go back to the previous step).

4. Choose the drive where you want to store the files by selecting **A:\ Drive**, **B:\Drive** (if you have one), or **Choose Destination**. In the last case you must specify the drive and directory (folder) where you want to store the files, such as a network drive. Click **Browse** to help select a destination. Click **Next** to continue.

5. If there are files linked to your presentation (such as spreadsheets or charts), select the **Include Linked Files** option to have the Pack and Go Wizard also copy those files to the destination disk. Select **Embed TrueType Fonts** if you used TrueType fonts in your presentation and you're not sure if the user on the other end has the same font files. Click **Next** to continue.

6. If you know that the user receiving the disk has PowerPoint on the computer, select **Don't Include the Viewer**. If you're not sure or you know the person doesn't have PowerPoint, select **Viewer for Windows 95 or NT** (if the machine isn't Windows 95 or NT, it cannot run the slide show anyway). Click **Next**.

7. The Pack and Go Wizard confirms that it will compress the files for your presentation on the disk you designated. Click **Finish** to have it perform the operation.

When a user receives the presentation you packaged, someone must perform the following steps in order to run the slide show:

1. Insert the disk that contains the presentation files.

2. From the Windows Explorer, select the drive where the disk is loaded and then double-click the **Pngsetup** icon.

3. Enter the destination on the computer where you want the files copied.

4. To run the show, open the folder (directory) where you copied the files and double-click the PowerPoint viewer file **Ppview32**.

5. Click the presentation you want to run.

Review Questions

1. How do you start a Slide Show from any slide?

2. How do you use the on-screen navigation tools to go to a specific slide?

3. How do you write on the screen during a slide show?

4. Explain how to set the slide show options to have the show loop continuously until you press **Esc**.

5. How do you add an action button to a slide?

6. How do you save a slide show for use on another computer?

Review Question Answers

1. Click the **Slide Show View** button. Click the left mouse button to go forward and the right mouse button and choose **Previous** to go backward. For more information, refer to "Starting the Slide Show from Any Slide."

2. Begin the slide show. Move the mouse to make the navigation tools visible and then click the triangle. On the menu, click **Go**, and choose **By Title**. Select the title of the slide you want to see. For more information, refer to "Using On-Screen Navigation Tools."

3. When the slide show is running, move the mouse. Click the triangle that appears. Choose Pen from the menu. Drag to write on the screen. For more information, refer to "Using On-Screen Navigation Tools."

4. Choose **Slide Show**, **Set Up Show** from the menu. Check the **Loop Continuously Until 'Esc'** option. Click **OK**. For more information, refer to "Setting Slide Show Options."

5. Display the slide in Slide view. Choose **Slide Show**, **Action Buttons**, and then select a button. Drag a rectangle on the slide where the button will appear. Select the **Mouse Click** or **Mouse Over** tab. Select an action and click **OK**. For more information, refer to "Adding Action Buttons on Slides."

6. Choose **File**, **Pack and Go**. Follow the steps in the Pack and Go Wizard, clicking **Finish** when you're done. For more information, refer to "Saving a Presentation to Use on Another Computer."

Practice Lab

The Microsoft Expert User Exam lists eleven Required Tasks for the Skill Area "Delivering Presentations." Three of these tasks have been covered in this lesson. Following you will find a practice lab for these three tasks.

 Required Tasks   The Required Tasks covered in this lesson are Start a Slide Show from any Slide, Use On-Screen Navigation Tools, and Save a Presentation to Use on Another Computer.

Start a Slide Show from Any Slide

Open the file Lesson23.ppt from the CD-ROM. Start the slide show. View all the slides in the slide show. Exit the Slide show, but leave the file open.

Use On-Screen Navigation Tools

Start the slide show again. From the first slide, jump to Slide 10. Using the Pen, circle "R&D" on that slide. Go to Slide 7. Exit the slide show, but keep the file open.

Add action buttons on every slide to go to the next slide or the previous slide.

Save a Presentation to Use on Another Computer

Save the presentation so it may be used on another computer. Include linked files and embed any TrueType fonts. Don't include the Viewer.

Open the file Lesson23a.ppt to see a finished example of the presentation and run the slide show. Double-click the file Pngsetup.exe to open the version of the presentation saved by Pack and Go.

Transitions and Animation

This lesson covers two of the twelve Required Tasks for the "Adding Visual Elements" Skill Area.

In this lesson, you learn the following Required Tasks for your exam:

▶ Add transitions

▶ Animate objects

For a complete list of Required Tasks for the Skill Area "Adding Visual Elements," refer to the User Skills Roadmap.

Adding Transitions

With an on-screen slide show, PowerPoint has impressive and professional visual methods (transitions and effects) that provide smooth and attention-getting movements from one slide or object to the next.

> **Transitions and Effects** A *transition* is a way of moving from one slide to the next. For example, with a vertical blinds transition, the slide takes on the look of window blinds that turn to reveal the next slide. An *effect* is also an animated movement from one item to another, but it pertains to individual objects on the slide, such as a bulleted list or a movie, rather than to the appearance or disappearance of the entire slide.

A transition is the animation of movement from one slide to the next, and the default transition in PowerPoint is for one slide to simply vanish and the next slide to appear in its place.

To apply a slide transition to a slide, do the following:

1. Open the presentation to which you want to add transitions.

2. Switch to the Slide Sorter view (see Figure 24.1) by clicking the **Slide Sorter View** button or choosing **View, Slide Sorter** from the menu.

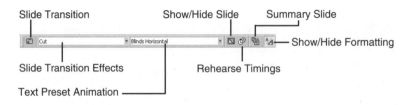

Figure 24.1

Use the Slide Sorter toolbar to control the transitions and effects in your slide show.

3. Select the slide to which you want to add a transition by clicking on it. To select more than one slide, hold down the **Shift** key as you click each slide you want. Press **Ctrl+A** or choose **Edit, Select All** to select all the slides.

4. Choose **Slide Show, Slide Transitions** or click the **Slide Transition** button on the Slide Sorter toolbar. The Slide Transition dialog box appears (see Figure 24.2).

5. From the **Effect** drop-down list, select a transition effect. Watch the preview area to see a demonstration of the transition effect (click the preview picture to see it again if you missed it).

Figure 24.2

Select the transition
you want to apply to
the slide.

6. Set the speed at which the transition takes effect by selecting **Slow**, **Medium**, or **Fast**.

7. Set the method you want to use to advance to the next slide: **On Mouse Click** advances the slide only when you click the mouse or press a key; **Automatically After** lets you specify the number of **Seconds** delay before the slide show moves on to the next slide.

8. To associate a sound with the transition, select one from the **Sound** drop-down list (to loop the sound so it plays over and over, select the **Loop Until Next Sound** option).

9. Click **Apply** to apply the settings to the slide(s) you selected, or click **Apply to All** to apply the settings to all slides in the presentation.

Slides to which you have applied transition effects display a small Transition Effect icon beneath the slide in the slide sorter (see Figure 24.3).

Figure 24.3

Each slide to which
you added a transition
effect displays an icon
beneath the slide.

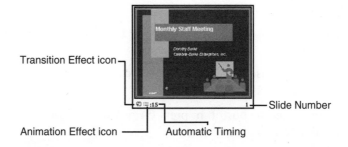

Transition Effect icon

Slide Number

Animation Effect icon

Automatic Timing

 Quick Transition Setup To quickly apply a transition (without being able to set the speed, timing, or sound association), select one from the **Slide Transition Effects** drop-down list on the Slide Sorter toolbar. Watch the slide as you do, and you'll see a demonstration of the effect.

Animating Objects

Transitions affect an entire slide, but animation effects apply to individual elements on the slide. For instance, you might want the slide's background and title to appear first and then have the items on the bulleted list appear one at a time.

 Animation When most people think of animation, they think of cartoons. PowerPoint refers to animation as the movement on-screen that acts as a transition from one object on the slide to the next.

Animating the Text on a Slide

The simplest form of animation is to animate the text on a slide separately from its title and background. When you choose one of these effects, the title and background appear as specified by the transition effect, and then the rest of the slide's text appears, paragraph by paragraph, using the chosen effect.

To apply simple animation effects to an object on a slide, follow these steps:

1. Switch to the Slide Sorter view.

2. Select the slide that contains the text you want to animate.

3. From the **Text Preset Animation** drop-down list on the Slide Sorter toolbar, select an animation effect for the text on that slide such as the Drive-In Effect, the Flying Effect, the Camera Effect, the Flash Once Effect, the Laser Text Effect, the Typewriter Text Effect, or the Drop In Effect (you need to test each one to understand how they work).

4. Switch to the Slide Show view to preview the effect. The title and background of the slide appear.

5. Click the left mouse button or press **Page Down** to have the first paragraph appear using the effect you selected.

6. Click the left mouse button or press **Page Down** again for each paragraph until all of the slide's text is on-screen.

7. Press **Esc** to return to the Slide Sorter view.

Using Custom Animation

If you want to get more detailed animation, and especially if you want to animate objects other than the text, such as drawn objects or multimedia objects, you must use custom animation. Here's how:

1. Switch to the Slide view and go to the slide to which you want to add animation.

2. Choose **Slide Show, Custom Animation** from the menu or click the **Custom Animation** button on the Animation Effects toolbar (to see the Animation Effects toolbar, click the **Animation Effects** button on the Formatting toolbar). The Custom Animation dialog box appears (see Figure 24.4).

Figure 24.4

Select the object you want to animate from the Slide Objects Without Animation list.

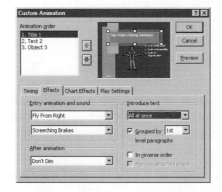

3. Select the **Timing** tab.

4. From the **Slide Objects Without Animation** list, select the object you want to animate.

5. Under Animation, select the **Animate** option. The selected object moves from the Slide Objects Without Animation list to the Animation Order list.

6. Specify when animation should take place:

   ▶ Select **On Mouse Click** to have the animation happen when you click the mouse.

   ▶ Select **Automatically** to have the animation happen when the number of seconds specified elapses following the previous animation.

7. Repeat steps 4 through 6 for each object you want to animate.

8. Use the up and down arrows to the right of the list to rearrange the objects in the **Animation Order** list. The slide "builds" in the order you specify in the list.

9. From the **Animation Order** list, select the object to which you want to apply an animation effect. The slide preview shows the object as being selected.

10. Select the **Effects** tab (see Figure 24.5).

Figure 24.5

Use the Effects options to specify what animation will occur and what sound will be associated with it.

11. In the **Entry Animation and Sound** section, choose the animation effect from the top drop-down list and the sound you want to associate with it from the second drop-down list (the After Animation option is covered in the next section).

12. (Optional) If the object you selected is a chart, select the **Chart Effects** tab and select options there to control the animation of the chart. If the object is a movie, select the **Play Settings** tab and select options to specify when the movie will start and stop.

13. Click **Preview** to test your settings.

14. Click **OK**.

Using Other Animation Options

There are many more options in the Custom Animation dialog box for setting up your animation. Experiment with them and find your favorite special effects. Here are some ideas to get you started:

▶ From the **Introduce Text** drop-down list, choose whether you want the text to appear all at once, word by word, or letter by letter.

▶ If you have multiple levels of bullet points in your text, animate by a different level than first by choosing it from the **Grouped By** drop-down list.

▶ Build text from the bottom to the top by selecting the **In Reverse Order** option.

▶ From the **After Animation** drop-down list, choose to dim an object after it has completed its animation. This is useful for bulleted lists, because the point you're discussing is bright compared to the previous points.

A quick way to apply animation effects is to use the Animation Effects toolbar (see Figure 24.6). To see the Animation Effects toolbar, click the **Animation Effects** button on the Formatting toolbar.

Figure 24.6

Use the buttons on the Animation Effects toolbar to quickly apply animation effects.

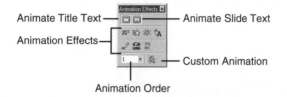

To use the Animation Effects toolbar, do the following:

1. Display the slide in Slide View that you want to animate.

2. Select an object on the slide to which you want to apply animation effects.

3. Click one of the animation effects:

   ▶ **Drive-In Effect**   Drives in like a car and screeches to a halt.

   ▶ **Flying Effect**   Flies in from the side of the screen.

   ▶ **Camera Effect**   Irises like a camera lens.

   ▶ **Flash Once**   Flashes on the screen once.

   ▶ **Laser Text Effect**   Appears as if being written by a laser gun.

   ▶ **Typewriter Text Effect**   Types in one character at a time with typewriter sounds.

   ▶ **Drop In**   Drops in one character at a time.

   When you apply an effect to the title text, the **Animate Title Text** button is depressed automatically. When you apply an effect to the slide text, the **Animate Slide Text** button is selected automatically.

4. The animation order is automatically set in the order that you assign automation effects to objects on the slide. To change the animation order, select a different order number from the **Animation Order** drop-down list.

5. To add more complicated effects and timing, click the **Custom Animation** button.

Review Questions

1. How do you add a transition to a slide?

2. How do you set the speed at which the transition occurs?

3. How do you add a sound to the transition?

4. Explain how to quickly animate the text on the slide.

5. Describe how to add animation effects to objects.

Review Question Answers

1. Change to the Slide Sorter view. Select the slide. Select the effect you want from the **Slide Transition Effects** drop-down list on the Slide Sorter toolbar. For more information, refer to "Adding Transitions."

2. Change to the Slide Sorter view. Select the slide. Click the **Slide Transition** button. Choose **Slow**, **Medium**, or **Fast**. Click **Apply**. For more information, refer to "Adding Transitions."

3. Change to the Slide Sorter view. Select the slide. Click the **Slide Transition** button. Choose a sound from the Sound drop-down list. Click **Apply**. For more information, refer to "Adding Transitions."

4. Change to the Slide Sorter view. Select the slide. Select an animation type from the **Text Preset Animation** drop-down list on the Slide Sorter toolbar. For more information, refer to "Animating Objects."

5. Choose **Slide Show**, **Custom Animation** from the menu or click the **Custom Animation** button on the Animation Effects toolbar. Select the **Timing** tab. From the Slide Objects Without Animation list, select the object you want to animate. Under **Animation**, select the **Animate** option. The selected object moves from the Slide Objects Without Animation list to the Animation Order list. Specify whether the animation should take place on a mouse click or automatically after a specified number of seconds. From the Animation Order list, select the object to which you want to apply an animation effect. Select the **Effects** tab. In the **Entry Animation and Sound** section, choose the animation effect from the top drop-down list and the sound you want to associate with it from the bottom drop-down list. Click **OK**. For more information, refer to "Animating Objects."

Practice Lab

The Microsoft Expert User Exam lists twelve Required Tasks for the Skill Area "Adding Visual Elements." Two of these tasks have been covered in this lesson. Following you will find a practice lab for these tasks.

 Required Tasks   The Required Tasks covered in this lesson are Add Transitions and Animate Objects.

Add Transitions

Open the file Lesson24.ppt from the CD-ROM. Add transitions to each slide in the presentation. Set the speed of some of the transitions to slow and add sounds to some of the transitions. Don't expect to hear the sounds if you don't have a multimedia computer that has speakers.

Animate Objects

Animate the text on the slides and add animation effects to the charts, including sounds.

The file Lesson24a.ppt on the CD-ROM shows an example of an animated slide show.

Working with Slide Timings

This lesson covers one of the three Required Tasks for the "Editing Presentations" Skill Area.

In this lesson, you learn the following Required Task for your exam:

▶ Set automatic slide timing

For a complete list of Required Tasks for the Skill Area "Editing Presentations," refer to the User Skills Roadmap.

Setting Automatic Slide Timing

Automatic slide timing allows you to set your slides to automatically advance at a specified time. You don't always want to use slide timing because it is difficult to pace a speaker and allow time for questions and other interruptions. However, some shows are run without user intervention (such as a slide show that runs on a continuous loop while your audience is settling in or a slide show that runs at a kiosk). In these cases, you can set the timings manually or automatically as you rehearse the slide show.

 Specific Slides You can also set slide timings on specific slides within a presentation and keep the others at manual advance.

Setting the Slide Timings Manually

If you want to use slide timing to advance your slides automatically (instead of having to click or press a key to make the slide show move forward) in the slide show (for a self-running or kiosk presentation), you specify the time for each slide by doing the following:

1. Open the presentation to which you want to add slide timings.

 2. Switch to the Slide Sorter view by choosing **View**, **Slide Sorter** from the menu or by clicking the **Slide Sorter View** button.

3. Select the slide(s) for which you want to specify the timing. To select more than one slide, hold down the **Shift** key as you click on each slide you want. To select all the slides, press **Ctrl+A** or choose **Edit**, **Select All**.

 4. Choose **Slide Show**, **Slide Transition** from the menu or click the **Slide Transition** button on the Slide Sorter toolbar. The Slide Transition dialog box appears (see Figure 25.1).

Figure 25.1

Enter the number of seconds before the next slide appears.

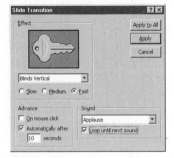

5. Under **Advance**, select the **Automatically After** option and enter the number of **Seconds** before the next transition.

6. Click **Apply** to apply the slide timing to the selected slide(s) or **Apply to All** to apply the timing to all the slides in the slide show.

7. To have the slide show use the slide timings you set, choose **Slide Show**, **Set Up Show** from the menu to open the Set Up Show dialog box (see Figure 25.2).

Figure 25.2

Specify that you want to use the slide timings when you run the slide show.

8. Under Advance Slides, select the **Use Timings, If Present** option.

9. Click **OK**. When you run the slide show, the slides will automatically advance at the time intervals you set.

Setting the Slide Timings as You Rehearse

If you want the slides to automatically advance at the proper time in your narration, you may want to rehearse the timing. Rehearsing the timing also gives you the total time for the presentation, as well as for each slide.

To set the timing as you rehearse, do the following:

1. Open the presentation for which you want to set the timings.

2. Change to the Slide Sorter view.

3. Choose **Slide Show**, **Rehearse Timings** from the menu or click the **Rehearse Timings** button on the Slide Sorter toolbar.

4. The Slide Show begins, with the Rehearsal dialog box showing on-screen (see Figure 25.3). This dialog box keeps track of the elapsed time of the slide show and the elapsed time of the current slide. As you rehearse, click the **Advance** button to move on to the next animation or the next slide.

5. When you finish the last slide in the slide show, a dialog box appears asking if you want to record the timings for the slide show. Click **Yes**.

6. Another dialog box appears asking if you want to review the timings in the Slide Sorter. Click **Yes** to return to the Slide Sorter view.

Figure 25.3

The Rehearsal dialog box lets you record the time you spend on each slide as well as keep track of the total time it takes you to give the entire presentation.

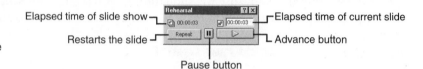

Elapsed time of slide show — ⌐ Elapsed time of current slide

Restarts the slide — ⌐ Advance button

Pause button

Viewing Rehearsed Timings During a Slide Show

Even if you rehearse timings, you may not want to advance the slides automatically based on those timings. If you set up the show to use manual timings, you may want to view the Slide Meter as you give your presentation to see how you're doing against your rehearsed times. Before giving your presentation, follow these steps:

1. Click the **Slide Show** button to begin viewing the slide show.

2. Right-click the slide and select **Slide Meter** from the pop-up menu (see the Slide Meter in Figure 25.4).

Figure 25.4

The numbers at the top of the Slide Meter show the elapsed time for the current slide.

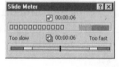

The elapsed time for the current slide shows at the top of the meter. The elapsed time for the slide show appears near the bottom. A progress bar in the middle shows how you're doing compared to your rehearsed timing. When you're within the rehearsed time, green boxes appear. The boxes are yellow if you go beyond the rehearsed time. Red boxes mean you've gone far beyond the rehearsed time. Along the bottom of the meter is a bar that indicates whether you're going too fast or too slow in comparison with your rehearsed time.

Review Questions

1. Explain how to assign automatic slide timing to the slides in your presentation.

2. How do you set up the slide show to use the automatic timings?

3. How do you assign automatic timings as you rehearse the slides?

4. How do you view the rehearsed slide timings during the slide show?

Review Question Answers

1. Open the presentation to which you want to add slide timings. Switch to the Slide Sorter view. Select the slide(s) for which you want to specify the timing. Choose **Slide Show**, **Slide Transition** from the menu or click the **Slide Transition** button on the Slide Sorter toolbar. In the dialog box, select the **Automatically After** option and enter the number of **Seconds** before the next transition. Click **Apply** to apply the slide timing to the selected slide(s) or **Apply to All** to apply the timing to all the slides in the slide show. For more information, refer to "Setting Automatic Slide Timing."

2. Choose **Slide Show**, **Set Up Show** from the menu to open the Set Up Show dialog box. Under Advance Slides, select the **Use Timings, If Present** option. Click **OK**. For more information, refer to "Setting Automatic Slide Timing."

3. Open the presentation for which you want to set the timings. Change to the Slide Sorter view. Choose **Slide Show**, **Rehearse Timings** from the menu or click the **Rehearse Timings** button on the Slide Sorter toolbar. The Slide Show begins, with the Rehearsal dialog box showing on-screen. As you rehearse, click the **Advance** button to move on to the next animation or the next slide. When you finish the last slide in the slide show, a dialog box appears asking if you want to record the timings for the slide show. Click **Yes**. For more information, refer to "Setting Automatic Slide Timing."

4. Click the **Slide Show** button to begin viewing the slide show. Right-click the slide and select Slide Meter from the pop-up menu. For more information, refer to "Viewing Rehearsed Timings During a Slide Show."

Practice Lab

The Microsoft Expert User Exam lists three Required Tasks for the Skill Area "Editing Presentations." One of these tasks is covered in this lesson. Following you will find a practice lab for that task.

 Required Tasks The Required Task covered in this lesson is Set Automatic Slide Timing.

Set Automatic Slide Timing

Open the file Lesson25.ppt on the CD-ROM. Assign automatic timings to all the slides. Change the slide show options to use the automatic timings. Save the file as Show25.ppt.

To see an example of a slide show that runs continuously and uses slide timings, open Lesson 25a.ppt on the CD-ROM.

Customizing Slide Shows

This lesson covers two of the seven Required Tasks for the "Customizing Presentations" Skill Area.

In this lesson, you learn the following Required Tasks for your exam:

▶ Add links to other slides within the presentation

▶ Hide slides

For a complete list of Required Tasks for the Skill Area "Customizing Presentations," refer to the User Skills Roadmap.

Adding Links to Other Slides Within the Presentation

For presentations you plan to show on the Web, or in a kiosk setting, adding links to other slides in the presentation or to other presentations is particularly useful. Even in a speaker-led presentation, it helps the presenter to be able to jump to a particular slide when necessary.

Any object on a slide—text, shapes, tables, charts, pictures—can serve as the hyperlink to other slides or presentations (or, for that matter, other programs or an address on the Internet). You attach an action to the object, and the link is activated when you click the object or move the mouse over it (depending on the option you choose) during a slide show.

Hyperlink   A hyperlink is a graphical object or colored and underlined text that you click in order to jump to a different location in the file, to a different file, to an HTML page on the World Wide Web, or to an HTML page on an intranet.

HyperText Markup Language (HTML)   HTML is a collection of instructions, or *tags*, that tell a browser how to display a document—when the text is bold, italic, and so on.

A hyperlink must have a destination, a location to which you jump. The path to that destination can be an absolute link or a relative link. An absolute link contains the full path name or address of a file such as **C:\Myweb\logo.gif** or **http://www.mywebsite.com/images/logo.gif**. A relative link contains a partial path name or address such as **/images/logo.gif**. When the path is a relative link, the file that contains the hyperlink and the destination can be moved without severing the link, provided you move them together.

Follow these steps to add a link between slides to your presentation:

1. Save the presentation prior to adding a hyperlink. Otherwise, you won't be able to create a relative link.

2. In the Slide view, select the text or object (picture, clip art, shape, and so on) you want to use for the hyperlink.

3. Choose **Slide Show**, **Action Settings**. The Action Settings dialog box appears (see Figure 26.1).

4. If you want to activate the hyperlink by clicking on the object, select the **Mouse Click** tab. If you want to activate the hyperlink by moving the mouse over the object, select the **Mouse Over** tab.

Figure 26.1

Select the location to which you want to jump.

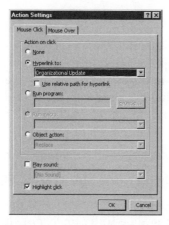

More Than One Action Per Hyperlink   One object may have more than one action assigned to it, such as assigning both a hyperlink and a sound to an object. Set up the hyperlink on the **Mouse Click** tab and the sound on the **Mouse Over** tab.

5. Select the **Hyperlink To** option. From the drop-down list, select the destination for the jump. Choose **Slide** to specify a particular slide in the same presentation (it's a good idea to add a hyperlink on that slide that returns you to the original slide, so you can go back to where you were in the presentation). Select **Use Relative Path for Hyperlink** so you can specify a relative link such as **/images/logo.gif** instead of having to use an absolute link such as **http:// www.mywebsite.com/images/logo.gif**.

6. (Optional) Select the **Highlight Click** option if you want the object or text to be highlighted when you click it or move the mouse over it.

7. Click **OK**. Run the slide show to test the link. If it doesn't work, check that you entered the information correctly (especially with URLs).

Action Buttons   Create the object and the hyperlink in one step by using an action button (see Lesson 23, "Viewing a Slide Show," to learn more about adding action buttons to your slides). When you create the action button, the Action Settings dialog box automatically appears so you can set up the hyperlink.

Hiding Slides

In your presentation you may prepare a slide that you don't want to appear during the slide show, unless you need it. For example, a graph in your presentation gives an overview of sales for the last quarter but someone in the audience wants more details. Luckily, you've anticipated the question and included a slide with the details. You hide the slide unless it's required, because you don't want to get sidetracked with the details unless asked.

To hide a slide so it does not appear during a slide show, do one of the following:

▶ When you're in the Slide view, choose **Slide Show**, **Hide Slide** from the menu.

▶ When you're in the Slide Sorter view, select the slide you want to hide and then click the **Hide Slide** button on the Slide Sorter toolbar or choose **Slide Show**, **Hide Slide** from the menu. A "no" sign (a rectangle around the slide number with a slash through it) appears over the slide number to indicate that the slide is hidden (see Figure 26.2).

Figure 26.2

A "no" sign indicates a hidden slide.

To display the hidden slide during a slide show, do one of the following:

▶ Right-click any slide in the presentation; select **Go**, **Slide Navigator** from the pop-up menu. Double-click the slide you want (numbers in parentheses indicate hidden slides), as shown in Figure 26.3.

▶ If you know the hidden slide is the next one in sequence, right-click the slide you're on and choose **Go**, **Hidden Slide** from the pop-up menu.

Figure 26.3

Numbers in parentheses indicate hidden slides in the Slide Navigator.

If you no longer want to hide the slide during future slide shows, go to the Slide Sorter, select the slide, and click the **Hide Slide** button on the Slide Sorter toolbar or choose **Slide Show**, **Hide Slide** from the menu.

Review Questions

1. How do you add a hyperlink to an object that jumps to another slide in the presentation?

2. How do you hide a slide when you're in the Slide Sorter view?

3. Explain how to display a hidden slide during a slide show.

4. How do you "unhide" a hidden slide?

Review Question Answers

1. Save the presentation. Select the object or text that you want to turn into a hyperlink. Choose **Slide Show**, **Action Settings** from the menu. Select **Hyperlink To** and choose a destination from the drop-down list. Click **OK**. For more information, refer to "Adding Links to Other Slides Within the Presentation."

2. Select the slide you want to hide. Click the **Hide Slide** button on the Slide Sorter toolbar. For more information, refer to "Hiding Slides."

3. Right-click any slide. Choose **Go**, **Slide Navigator** from the pop-up menu. Double-click the name of the slide. For more information, refer to "Hiding Slides."

4. In the Slide Sorter, select the hidden slide and choose **Slide Show**, **Hide Slide** from the menu or click the **Hide Slide** button on the Slide Sorter toolbar. For more information, refer to "Hiding Slides."

Practice Lab

The Microsoft Expert User Exam lists seven Required Tasks for the Skill Area "Customizing Presentations." Two of these tasks have been covered in this lesson. Following you will find a practice lab for these two tasks.

 Required Tasks   The Required Tasks covered in this lesson are Add Links to Other Slides Within the Presentation and Hide Slides.

Add Links to Other Slides Within the Presentation

Open the file Lesson26.ppt from the CD-ROM. Select the clip art on Slide 1 and add a hyperlink to it that jumps to Slide 5. On Slide 5, add an action button or add an action to an existing object to create a hyperlink back to the original slide.

Hide Slides

Hide Slide 7. Run the slide show and make that slide appear during the show. Save your presentation as Hide26.ppt.

To see an example of the slide show with the hyperlinks in place and with Slide 7 hidden, open the file Lesson26a.ppt on the CD-ROM.

Taking Notes During a Slide Show

This lesson covers two of the eleven Required Tasks for the "Delivering Presentations" Skill Area.

In this lesson, you learn the following Required Tasks for your exam:

▶ Generate meeting notes

▶ Incorporate meeting feedback electronically

For a complete list of Required Tasks for the Skill Area "Delivering Presentations," refer to the User Skills Roadmap.

Annotating Slides

As you are presenting your slide show, you can satisfy the urge to write on-screen by using the Pen to annotate the slides so that your audience can see your highlights and points of concern. The writing you put on the screen only lasts as long as the slide is being displayed, but it helps involve your audience in what is on-screen or point out particular facts on a slide. Figure 27.1 shows an annotated slide.

Figure 27.1

Use the Pen to circle, underline, draw arrows, or write on the slide during the slide show.

Pen ———

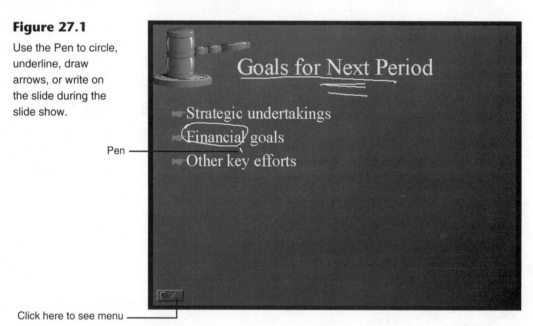

Click here to see menu ———

To annotate a slide during a slide show, do the following:

1. Move the mouse slightly across the screen to display a triangle in the lower-left corner (see Figure 27.1).

2. Click that triangle to see a pop-up menu.

3. Choose **Pen**.

4. Drag to write on-screen.

5. When you want to return to using the mouse as a pointer, click the triangle and choose **Arrow**.

Quick Switch   To quickly switch to the pen, right-click a slide and select **Pen** from the pop-up menu, or press **Ctrl+P**. Press **Ctrl+A** to return to the arrow.

The color of the pen is automatically set to complement the colors in the slide background. To change the color of the pen, do one of the following:

▶ During the slide show, right-click, choose **Pointer Options**, **Pen Color** from the pop-up menu, and then click the color you want.

▶ Before the slide show, choose **Slide Show**, **Set Up Show** from the menu. Select the color you want from the Pen Color dialog box.

Generating Meeting Notes

The Meeting Minder feature of Microsoft PowerPoint lets you take minutes during a slide show and record action items. You export the meeting minutes to Word where you compose the official minutes document. The action items become a new slide at the end of your slide show, which is helpful if you know assignments will be made during a meeting and you want to review them at the end of the meeting.

During a presentation conference, the other participants do not see the Meeting Minder. It appears only on your screen. To learn more about presentation conferencing, see Lesson 28, "Presentation Conferencing."

To take meeting minutes during a slide show, do the following:

1. Right-click the slide and select **Meeting Minder** from the pop-up menu.

2. Click in the box and type your minutes (see Figure 27.2). The minutes are all kept together; you don't have different minutes for each slide. For each slide, you add to the existing text.

Figure 27.2

Enter your notes or minutes in the Meeting Minder box.

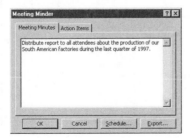

3. Click **OK**.

4. Click **Export** to export your minutes to a Microsoft Word document.

5. If you have Microsoft Outlook and want to schedule a meeting, click **Schedule**.

In some meetings you generate tasks or projects that you'd like to assign right there. You do this from the Meeting Minder:

1. Right-click on the slide and select **Meeting Minder** from the pop-up menu.

2. Select the **Action Items** tab (see Figure 27.3).

Figure 27.3

Enter a description, the name of the person responsible for the task, and a due date.

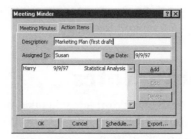

3. Type a brief description of the task in the **Description** box.

4. Enter the name of the person or department responsible for completing the task in the **Assigned To** box.

5. Enter a **Due Date**.

6. Click **Add**.

7. Click **Export** to export your action items to Microsoft Outlook.

8. Click **OK** to close the Meeting Minder. The action items appear on a new slide at the end of the slide show (see Figure 27.4).

Figure 27.4

The action items appear on a new slide at the end of the slide show.

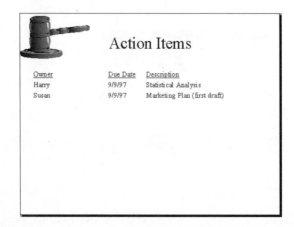

Incorporating Meeting Feedback Electronically

If you have Microsoft Outlook, the action items you create during the slide show can be posted to Outlook. Outlook then transmits these items to the people involved.

Follow these instructions to send a list of action items to Outlook:

1. During the slide show, right-click a slide and select **Meeting Minder** from the pop-up menu.

   From the Slide or Slide Sorter views, choose **Tools**, **Meeting Minder**.

2. Select the **Action Items** tab to display the items you entered (refer to Figure 27.3).

3. Click **Export**.

4. Select **Post Action Items to Microsoft Outlook**.

5. Click **Export Now**. This posts the action items to your Outlook task list. From there you can assign the tasks and follow-up dates.

 No Outlook?   When you click **Export** in the Meeting Minder, you also have the option of sending the list of action items to a Microsoft Word document. From there you can send the document to a mail recipient or route it to several recipients (choose **File**, **Send To** from the menu).

Review Questions

1. How do you activate the pen during a slide show?

2. How do you take minutes or notes during a slide show?

3. How do you send the meeting minutes to a Microsoft Word document?

4. Describe how to add action items during a slide show.

5. If you have Microsoft Outlook, how do you post the action items to the Outlook to-do list?

Review Question Answers

1. Click the triangle in the lower-left corner and choose **Pen** from the menu, right-click a slide and choose **Pen** from the pop-up menu, or press **Ctrl+P**. For more information, refer to "Annotating Slides."

2. Right-click the slide and choose **Meeting Minder** from the pop-up menu. Enter the notes in the box. Click **OK** to close the Meeting Minder. For more information, refer to "Generating Meeting Notes."

3. Click the **Export** button in the Meeting Minder window and choose the option that exports the minutes to a Word document. For more information, refer to "Generating Meeting Notes."

4. Right-click the slide and choose **Meeting Minder** from the pop-up menu. Select the **Action Items** tab. Enter a description, the name of the person assigned the task, and a due date. Click **Add**. For more information, refer to "Generating Meeting Notes."

5. Right-click the slide and choose **Meeting Minder** from the pop-up menu. Select the **Action Items** tab. Click **Export** and choose the option to post the items to Outlook. Then click **Export Now**. For more information, refer to "Incorporating Meeting Feedback Electronically."

Practice Lab

The Microsoft Expert User Exam lists eleven Required Tasks for the Skill Area "Delivering Presentations." Two of these tasks have been covered in this lesson. Following you will find a practice lab for these two tasks.

 Required Tasks The Required Tasks covered in this lesson are Generate Meeting Notes and Incorporate Meeting Feedback Electronically.

Generate Meeting Notes

Open the file Lesson27.ppt. Start the slide show. Add the following meeting minutes:

Distribute report to all attendees about the production of our South American factories during the last quarter of 1997.

Add the following action items:

Statistical Analysis, assigned to Harry, due 11/20/97

Marketing Plan (first draft), assigned to Susan, due 11/15/97

Incorporate Meeting Feedback Electronically

Post the action items to the Microsoft Outlook to-do list. Export the meeting minutes and the action items to a Microsoft Word document.

Open Lesson27a.ppt on the CD-ROM to see an example of a slide show with the meeting minutes and action items incorporated.

Presentation Conferencing

This lesson covers one of the eleven Required Tasks for the "Delivering Presentations" Skill Area.

In this lesson, you learn the following Required Task for your exam:

▶ Deliver through presentation conferencing

For a complete list of Required Tasks for the Skill Area "Delivering Presentations," refer to the User Skills Roadmap.

Delivering Through Presentation Conferencing

In these days of telecommuting and busy schedules, it's often difficult to get a group of people together for a meeting. Presentation conferencing allows you to run a presentation over a network or on the Internet.

All the participants (presenter and audience) use the Presentation Conference Wizard to participate in the meeting. The wizard supports users on a network or participants who connect directly to the Internet or who use a modem to dial in to an Internet service provider (ISP). If you have participants who connect through a proxy server or firewall, you should consult your network administrator.

Take note that there are some elements of a presentation that can't be seen or heard by all the participants during a presentation conference. Only the presenter and any members of the audience who can see his monitor or a projection of his monitor can see:

▶ Embedded objects, such as a Microsoft Graph chart.

▶ The actual editing of linked or embedded objects.

▶ Multimedia objects such as sound or video clips (if a participant has the necessary hardware, the sound effects associated with transitions and animation can be heard).

Preparing for a Presentation Conference

When you're getting ready for a presentation conference, you need to exchange some information with the participants, such as the names of the computers the audience is using or the address of the presentation (if you're using the Internet). Both the presenter and the audience use the Presentation Conference Wizard to help set up for the presentation.

Follow these instructions to set up a presentation conference:

1. Before you begin, be sure all the current slide show settings are just as you want them to be during the presentation. The wizard uses the current slide show settings as the default. Open the presentation.

2. Choose **Tools**, **Presentation Conference** from the menu.

3. The Presentation Conference Wizard appears (see Figure 28.1). Follow the instructions in the wizard: click **Next** to continue to the next step; click **Back** to return to the previous step. The first step is to get all the participants on the telephone. After you've done that, click **Next**.

Figure 28.1

Get all the participants
on the telephone and
then click Next.

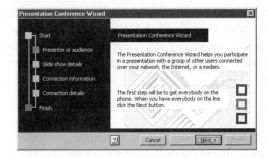

4.   Select **Presenter** if you are the person giving the presentation. Click **Next**.

5.   Remember that the wizard uses the current slide show settings to run the conference, such as Show All Slides. If you want to change the settings, you must click **Cancel**, change the settings, and then start the wizard again. If you want to accept the settings, click **Next**.

6.   If you are using the Internet for your conference, you must connect to your Internet service provider (ISP) using your modem. When you've made the connection, click **Next**.

     If you are using a network connection, click **Next**.

7.   Enter the Internet address or computer name for each participant and click **Add** after each entry (see Figure 28.2). If you plan to use the same list of participants in the future, click **Save List**. If you've already saved a list of participants, click **Open List** instead of entering each computer name or Internet address. Click **Next**.

8.   Each participant must click **Finish** before you do. After they've all confirmed that they've done so, click **Finish**.

Figure 28.2

Enter the computer
name or Internet
address for each
participant.

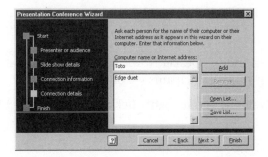

If any audience member is not ready, an error box appears noting that PowerPoint couldn't make a connection. Click OK and return to the Wizard. Check the highlighted name to see if it's correctly entered. Fix the name and continue with the Wizard if the name is correct. If the name is correct, contact your network administrator or Internet Service Provider to have the problem resolved.

Don't be alarmed if it takes some time to make all the connections. A "Please wait..." message displays to indicate that PowerPoint is working to make the connections. After the computers connect and the presentation begins, right-click to see a menu of all the tools you need to control the show, monitor your timing, review speaker notes, and record meeting minutes and action items.

Conducting a Presentation Conference

Only the presenter can use the Slide Navigator to control the show, the Slide Meter to monitor the timing of the presentation, speaker notes as a reminder of what to say about each slide, and the Meeting Minder to record meeting minutes and action items. All participants can use the annotation pen during the slide show.

To use any of these tools, all the presenter has to do is right-click on the slide during the slide show and then do one of the following:

▶ To view the speaker notes, choose **Speaker Notes** from the pop-up menu.

▶ To take notes or minutes, choose **Meeting Minder** from the pop-up menu. (See Lesson 27 for more information about Meeting Minder.)

▶ To add an action item, choose **Meeting Minder** from the pop-up menu. Select the **Action Items** tab.

▶ To view the timing of the presentation, choose **Slide Meter** from the pop-up menu. (See Lesson 25 for more information about slide timing.)

▶ To jump to a specific slide, choose **Go, Slide Navigator** from the pop-up menu.

The slide meter, Meeting Minder, Speaker Notes, or Slide Navigator appear only on the presenter's computer. The other participants see only the slide show.

Any participant can activate the pen by right-clicking the slide and choosing **Pen** from the pop-up menu.

Participating in a Presentation Conference

When you are asked to be a participant in a presentation conference, you use the Presentation Conference Wizard to connect to the presentation:

1. Choose **Tools**, **Presentation Conference** from the menu.

2. The Presentation Conference Wizard appears. Follow the instructions in the wizard: click **Next** to continue to the next step; click **Back** to return to the previous step. The first step is to get all the participants on the telephone. After you receive the phone call and are told that all the other participants are on the line, click **Next**.

3. Select **Audience** and then click **Next**.

4. Choose the option for the type of connection you'll use for the presentation: **Local Area Network** or **Dial In to Internet**. Click **Next**.

5. If you chose Local Area Network, the name of your computer appears. Tell the presenter the name of your computer and then click **Next**.

    If you chose to dial in to the Internet, connect to the Internet via your modem and then click **Next**. Your Internet address appears. Tell the presenter your Internet address as shown in the wizard and then click **Next**.

6. Click **Finish** and then wait for the presenter to begin the slide show, as indicated by a "Please Wait…" message on your screen.

If you are viewing the presentation on a network computer, you can click and then write with the pen on the slide. The other participants in the conference can see your annotations.

Review Questions

1. What items should you avoid adding to a slide show if it will be used for presentation conferencing?

2. Describe how to set up a presentation conference.

3. List the tools the presenter can use during the slide show.

4. How do you set up for participation in a presentation conference?

Review Question Answers

1. Avoid using embedded objects, sounds, and videos because they cannot be seen by the participants. For more information, refer to "Delivering Through Presentation Conferencing."

2. Open the presentation you want to use. Choose **Tools**, **Presentation Conference** to start the Presentation Conference Wizard. Place a conference call to all the participants. When they're all on the telephone, click **Next** in the wizard. Choose **Presenter** and then click **Next**. Accept the slide show settings by clicking **Next**.

   If you are using the Internet for your conference, you must connect to your Internet service provider (ISP) using your modem. When you've made the connection, click **Next**.

   If you are using a network connection, simply click **Next**. Enter the Internet address or computer name for each participant and click **Add** after each entry. Click **Next**. Each participant must click **Finish** before you do. After they've all confirmed that they've done so, click **Finish**.

   For more information, refer to "Preparing for a Presentation Conference."

3. The presenter can use the Pen, Slide Meter, and Meeting Minder for meeting minutes and action items, as well as Speaker Notes and the Slide Navigator. For more information, refer to "Conducting a Presentation Conference."

4. Choose **Tools**, **Presentation Conference** from the menu. The Presentation Conference Wizard appears. Once you receive the phone call from the presenter and are told that all the other participants are on the line, click **Next**. Select **Audience** and then click **Next**. Choose the option for the type of connection you'll use for the presentation: **Local Area Network** or **Dial In to Internet**.

Click **Next**. If you chose Local Area Network, the name of your computer appears. Tell the presenter the name of your computer and then click **Next**. If you chose to dial in to the Internet, connect to the Internet via your modem and then click **Next**. Your Internet address appears. Tell the presenter your Internet address as shown in the wizard and then click **Next**. Click **Finish**. For more information, refer to "Participating in a Presentation Conference."

Practice Lab

The Microsoft Expert User Exam lists eleven Required Tasks for the Skill Area "Delivering Presentations." One of these tasks has been covered in this lesson. Following you will find a practice lab for that task.

 Required Tasks The Required Task covered in this lesson is Delivery Through Presentation Conferencing.

Delivery Through Presentation Conferencing

This practice lab requires at least two computers that are connected in a local area network (LAN) or can connect to each other via the Internet. If you have this equipment setup, open the file Lesson28.ppt on the CD-ROM. Act as the presenter and set up a presentation conference with the other computer.

Printing Presentations, Notes, and Handouts

This lesson covers four of the eleven Required Tasks for the "Delivering Presentations" Skill Area.

In this lesson, you learn the following Required Tasks for your exam:

- ▶ Print slides in a variety of formats
- ▶ Print color presentations
- ▶ Export to overheads
- ▶ Export to 35mm slides

For a complete list of Required Tasks for the Skill Area "Delivering Presentations," refer to the User Skills Roadmap.

Printing Color Presentations

 The quickest way to print your presentation is to click the **Print** button on the Standard toolbar. This prints out one copy of each slide in landscape orientation.

 Orientation The orientation setting tells the printer which edge of the paper should be at the "top" of the printout. If the wide edge is at the top, the orientation is *landscape*. If the narrow edge is at the top, the orientation is *portrait*.

If you have a color printer, the slides automatically print in the colors shown on the screen. If you have a black-and-white printer, PowerPoint translates the colors into shades of gray. (To learn how to print a black-and-white copy of your presentation on a color printer, see the section "Printing in Black and White" later in this lesson.)

Printing Slides in a Variety of Formats

When you click the **Print** button, PowerPoint prints the presentation and you have no opportunity to set options. If you want to specify the number of copies or whether you want to print handouts or slides, you need to use the Print dialog box.

To set your print options, follow these steps:

1. Choose **File**, **Print** from the menu or press **Ctrl+P**. The Print dialog box appears (see Figure 29.1).

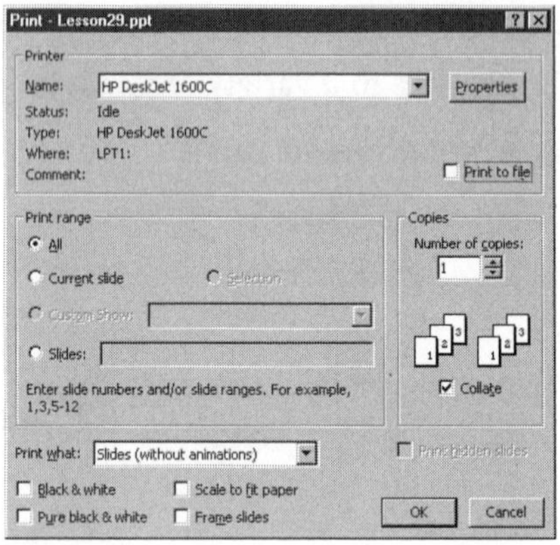

Figure 29.1

Set your printing options in the Print dialog box.

2. The name of the currently selected printer appears in the **Name** box. If you want to use a different printer for this job (you may want to use a color printer for your slides, but a black-and-white printer for handouts, speaker notes, and out-lines), select the printer you want from the drop-down list.

3. Click **Properties** to make changes to your printer setup, such as size of paper used, paper tray, graphics quality, and so on. The properties vary from printer to printer.

4. In the Print Range section, choose which slides you want to print:

    ▷ **All** prints all the slides in the presentation.

    ▷ **Current Slide** prints only the slide currently displayed on the screen.

    ▷ **Selection** prints the slides you currently have selected in the Slide Sorter view.

    ▷ **Custom Show** prints the custom slide show—the presentation within a presentation—that you select from the drop-down list. This option is un-available if you don't have any custom shows.

 Custom Show   If you want to give almost the same presentation to two separate groups, you create the slide show including the slides both groups have in common. Then you create custom shows for the parts of the presentation that are different. During the presentation you right-click a slide to see the menu, choose **Go**, **Custom Show**, and then select the name of the show you want. You create a custom show by choosing **Slide Show**, **Custom Show**, **New** from the menu.

    ▷ **Slides** prints the slides you list in the text box. Use a hyphen to indicate a range of slides (1-4 prints 1, 2, 3, and 4) and commas to indicate individual slides (1,3,7 prints slides 1, 3, and 7). You may combine ranges with lists of individual slides (1-5,9,10). The Slides option in the print box will let the user choose which slides he or she wants to print.

5. Select what you want to print from the **Print What** drop-down list: slides, handouts, notes pages, or outlines.

6. Enter a number in the **Number of Copies** text box to indicate how many cop-ies you want of each slide or page.

7. If you're printing more than one copy, select **Collate** to have the copies collated (1-2-3, 1-2-3, 1-2-3) instead of printing all the copies of each page (1-1-1, 2-2-2, 3-3-3).

8. Select the appropriate options:

> **Black & White** sets up your color slides to print crisply on a black-and-white printer, or forces your color printer to produce black-and-white output.

> **Pure Black & White** prints the entire presentation in only black-and-white, without any gray shading.

> **Scale to Fit Paper** reduces or enlarges slide images so that they fill the printed page.

> **Frame Slides** prints a border around each slide.

> **Print to File** sends the output to a file for printing elsewhere.

> **Print Hidden Slides** prints any slides you have hidden. This option is grayed out if you don't have any hidden slides.

9. Click **OK**.

Printing in Black and White

Your screen shows you the slides in color, but your printer is black and white. As explained in the previous section, PowerPoint will automatically convert the colors in your presentation to gray shading when you print on a black-and-white printer. To get a crisper copy, select the Black and White option in the Print dialog box.

When you know your output is going to be in black and white, the problem is that you don't know what effect your color choices have on your final output. The solution is to click the **Black and White** view button or choose **View**, **Black and White**. This changes the colors of the slides on your screen to shades of gray. A slide miniature appears displaying the color version of the slide, in case you also want color output (for a slide show, for example) and need to see both views. If you print while in Black and White view, PowerPoint automatically selects the Black and White option in the Print dialog box.

To return to the color view, click the **Black and White** view button again or choose **View**, **Black and White** from the menu.

Exporting to Overheads

If you want color overheads and you have a color printer, buy transparency film for your printer (buy ink jet transparency film for ink jet printers, and laser transparency film for laser printers). Print on the film as you would on paper (check your printer manual to see if there are any special requirements to print transparencies).

Before you print your transparencies, or even before you start your presentation, change the page setup for your presentation from on-screen to overhead. Here's how:

1. Open the presentation.

2. Choose **File**, **Page Setup** from the menu. The Page Setup dialog box appears (see Figure 29.2).

Figure 29.2

Set the type of output you want and the page orientation and size.

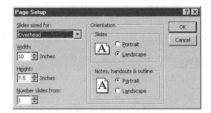

3. From the **Slides Sized For** box, select **Overhead**.

4. In the **Width** and **Height** boxes, enter the number of inches to define the printing area on the page. The default is 10 inches wide and 7.5 inches high, which is a one-inch margin all around.

5. Enter the starting number for your slides in the **Number the Slides From** box. The default setting is 1. These numbers only appear if you choose to include headers and footers, which were discussed in Lesson 19.

6. Under Orientation, set the print orientation for the slides (**Landscape** or **Portrait**) and for the notes, handouts, and outline.

7. Click **OK**. Print the overheads using the instructions in the "Printing Slides in a Variety of Formats" section earlier in this lesson.

If you don't have a color printer but you still want color transparencies, you'll have to deal with a service bureau that can create the overheads for you. These services will simply take your presentation file on disk or via modem and print it for you. When searching for the right company, here are some tips that may save you trouble:

▶ **Confirm file compatibility.** Make sure they accept PowerPoint 97 files in case you need them to make last minute changes for you. Also find out if they work with the Macintosh or PC platform. If they have to convert your files to the other platform, it might cause some problems down the line.

▶ **Confirm font compatibility.** Ask what fonts they can accept. They may not have the same set of fonts available to them as you have on your computer. You may have to send the font files along with your presentation, or you may have to limit the fonts you use to the set they have.

▶ **Decide whether to use PostScript.** Some service bureaus ask you to install a printer driver on your system and then send them PostScript files, while other services accept your PowerPoint files. Although the PostScript files produce beautiful slides, you might not want to go to this bother if another service provides equally good slides from your PowerPoint files.

▶ **Confirm color compatibility.** Not all services can produce the colors exactly as you have them on-screen (not even color printers can do that exactly), and you need to see a sample first. You might want to do a small presentation with the company first, before you commit to doing a large, important presentation.

▶ **Confirm style compatibility.** Check to see if there are any patterns, textures, or gradients that the service bureau can't produce, so you avoid including them in your presentation.

 Genigraphics   PowerPoint comes with the Genigraphics Wizard, which sets up and sends your presentation by modem to a Genigraphics service bureau. To use this wizard, choose **File**, **Send To**, **Genigraphics** from the menu and follow the instructions in the wizard.

Some service bureaus ask for a *print file* instead of the standard PowerPoint presentation file. In this case, they ask you to install a print driver that matches the printing device they use. Once you've installed the correct print driver, do the following to create the print file:

1. Open the presentation from which you want to create the print file.

2. Choose **File**, **Print** from the menu.

3. In the Print dialog box, select the **Print to File** option (refer to Figure 29.1).

4. From the **Name** box, select the printer or printer driver you want to use.

5. Click **OK**. The Print to File dialog box appears (see Figure 29.3).

Figure 29.3

Enter the name of the print file in the File Name box and click Save.

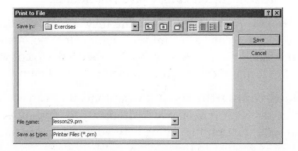

6. In the **Save In** box, select the drive and/or folder in which you want to store the file.

7. In the **File Name** box, enter the name of the print file. PowerPoint automatically stores it in a print file format with a file extension of .prn.

8. Click **Save**. Send the file via modem to the service bureau or send a disk to the service bureau.

Exporting to 35mm Slides

If you have a film recorder, you can print 35mm slides or capture your presentation on 35mm film to develop as slides. The film recorder driver appears as a choice in the Name box of the Print dialog box, if you have one. Just specify that as the print device you want to use and print.

Before you print, you should change the page setup for slides:

1. Open the presentation.

2. Choose **File**, **Page Setup** from the menu. The Page Setup dialog box appears (refer to Figure 29.2).

3. From the **Slides Sized For** box, select **35mm Slides**.

4. In the **Width** and **Height** boxes, enter the number of inches to define the printing area on the page, if you want different measurements than the default settings.

5. Enter the starting number for your slides in the **Number the Slides From** box.

6. Under Orientation, set the print orientation for the slides (**Landscape** or **Portrait**) and for the notes, handouts, and outline.

7. Click **OK**. Print the slides using the instructions in the "Printing Slides in a Variety of Formats" section earlier in this lesson.

If you don't have a film recorder, there are a number of service bureaus that will prepare the 35mm slides for you. The information about service bureaus and preparing print files for service bureaus in the "Exporting to Overheads" section also applies to 35mm slides.

Review Questions

1. What are the three methods of starting the printing process?

2. Which method doesn't allow you to set any print options?

3. How do you print only slides 5, 6, 7, 8, 12, and 15?

4. How do you set your color printer to print in shades of gray?

5. How do you add a border around your slides when they print?

6. How do you print handouts?

7. How do you create a print file?

8. How do you set up your presentation to print 35mm slides?

Review Question Answers

1. Click the **Print** button on the Standard toolbar, press **Ctrl+P**, or choose **File**, **Print** from the menu. For more information, refer to "Printing Color Presentations" and "Printing Slides in a Variety of Formats."

2. The **Print** button starts printing without allowing you to set options. For more information, refer to "Printing Slides in a Variety of Formats."

3. In the Print dialog box, select the **Slides** option under Print Range and enter **5-8,12,15** in the text box. Click **OK**. For more information, refer to "Printing Color Presentations" and "Printing Slides in a Variety of Formats."

4. In the Print dialog box, select the **Black and White** option. Or, change to the Black and White view by clicking the **Black and White** view button and then print. For more information, refer to "Printing in Black and White."

5. In the Print dialog box, select the **Frame Slides** option. For more information, refer to "Printing Slides in a Variety of Formats."

6. Open the Print dialog box, choose **Handouts** (1 per page, 2 per page, or 6 per page) from the **Print What** box, and click **OK**. For more information, refer to "Printing Slides in a Variety of Formats."

7. Open the Print dialog box, select **Print to File**, click **OK**, enter a name and location for the file, and click **Save**. For more information, refer to "Exporting to Overheads."

8. Choose **File**, **Page Setup**. From the Slides Sized For box, select **35mm Slides**. Click **OK**. For more information, refer to "Exporting to 35mm Slides."

Practice Lab

The Microsoft Expert User Exam lists eleven Required Tasks for the Skill Area "Delivering Presentations." Four of these tasks have been covered in this lesson. Following you will find a practice lab for these tasks.

 Required Tasks   The Required Tasks covered in this lesson are Print Slides in a Variety of Formats, Print Color Presentations, Export to Overheads, and Export to 35mm Slides.

Print Slides in a Variety of Formats

Open the file Lesson29.ppt from the CD-ROM. Print one copy of the handouts in the two slides per page format. Then print the outline.

Print Color Presentations

Change to the Notes Pages view and print the presentation by clicking the **Print** button.

Export to Overheads

Change the page setup to overhead and create a print file for the overhead print job. Name the file overhead.prn.

Export to 35mm Slides

Change the page setup to 35mm slides and create a print file for the 35mm slide print job. Name the file 35mm.prn.

Using PowerPoint Presentations on the Internet

This lesson covers one of the eleven Required Tasks for the "Delivering Presentations" Skill Area.

In this lesson, you learn the following Required Task for your exam:

▶ Save a presentation to deliver over the Internet

For a complete list of Required Tasks for the Skill Area "Delivering Presentations," refer to the User Skills Roadmap.

Using Web Presentation Designs

The Internet is a worldwide conglomeration of computer networks—one network of computers that can talk to another, and then in turn talk to another network of computers, and so on.

The World Wide Web (or just Web) is the graphical component of the Internet. It's a collection of documents accessible through the Internet. These documents contain a special technology called *hypertext*. When you click your mouse on hypertext, you are taken to a new document or *Web page*, maybe even to a Web page on a different computer (or *Web site*). The Web uses a type of address called a uniform resource locator (URL) to identify specific documents and locations.

What dictates how Web pages look and work is HyperText Markup Language (HTML). HTML is a collection of instructions, or *tags*, that tells a browser program how to display a document—when the text is bold, italic, and so on. A Web page has a series of tag entries, such as <B> to turn on bold and </B> to turn bold off. Unfortunately, using these tags is tedious. However, PowerPoint acts as a web-authoring tool, and automatically converts your formatting selections into HTML code for you.

To easily browse through presentations, use the Web toolbar (choose **View**, **Toolbar**, **Web** to see the toolbar) to open a start page or a search page in your Web browser. You should have a Web browser such as Internet Explorer or Netscape Navigator installed and set up for connecting to the Internet to get full use of the Web toolbar. However, you can also use it to browse HTML pages that are stored on your hard drive or a network drive. Refer to Table 30.1 to learn more about the buttons on the Web toolbar.

Table 30.1   The Web Toolbar Buttons

Button	Name	Description
⇦	Back	Go back to previous page in history list of Web pages visited.
⇨	Forward	Go to next page in history list of Web pages visited.
⊗	Stop Current Jump	Cancels a hyperlink jump that takes too long (doesn't work on jumps to other sites on your hard disk).
⟳	Refresh Current Page	Refresh the display of the current Web page to pick up any new updates.

Button	Name	Description
	Start Page	The start page is always the first page that appears in the Web browser. Click this button to open your Web browser program and to jump to that site.
	Search the Web	Click to search for other sites or documents on the Web.
Favorites ▾	Favorites	Add sites you visit often to the Favorites folder or open one of those favorite sites.
Go ▾	Go	Click to open a particular Web page, set a Start Page, or set a Search Page, go to the Start Page, or Search the Web.
	Show Only Web Toolbar	Click to see only the Web toolbar.
Document1 ▾	Address	Enter the address for the site or document you want to visit or select the address of a previously visited site from the drop-down list.

Using PowerPoint's Presentation Templates for the Web

PowerPoint includes several presentation templates designed for use on the Web. The easiest way to access them is to use the AutoContent Wizard (see Lesson 1). In addition to the Corporate Home Page and Personal Home Page templates, there are on-line versions of many of the other contents templates. If you intend to use a presentation on the Internet, choose **Internet**, **Kiosk** as the destination in the AutoContent Wizard (see Figure 30.1).

Figure 30.1

Choose Internet, Kiosk to indicate that the presentation will be given on the Internet.

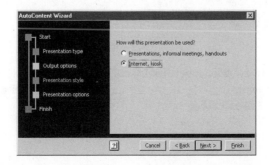

The slides in your presentation become the Web pages on the Internet. After you've completed your presentation, add hyperlinks to link the pages, and then save the presentation in HTML format, as described in the next two sections of this lesson.

Adding URL Hyperlinks

Any object on a slide—text, shapes, tables, charts, pictures—can serve as the hyperlink to other slides or presentations or an address on the Web. You attach an action to the object, and the link is activated when you click the object or move the mouse over it (depending on the option you chose) during a slide show. See Lesson 26 to learn more about adding links to a slide show.

When you want to create a link to another site on the Web, as opposed to another slide in your presentation or another presentation on your hard disk or network, you need to specify the uniform resource locator (URL) of the Web page (such as **http:// www.microsoft.com**).

Follow these steps to create a hyperlink to another Web site:

1. Save the presentation prior to adding a hyperlink.

2. Select the text or object you want to use for the hyperlink.

3. Choose **Slide Show**, **Action Settings**. The Action Settings dialog box appears (see Figure 30.2).

Figure 30.2

Select Hyperlink To and then choose URL.

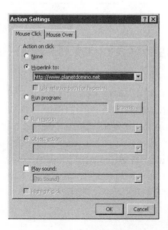

4. If you want to activate the hyperlink by clicking the object, select the **Mouse Click** tab. If you want to activate the hyperlink by moving the mouse over the object, select the **Mouse Over** tab.

5. Select the **Hyperlink To** option. From the drop-down list, select **URL**.

6. The Hyperlink To URL dialog box appears (see Figure 30.3). Enter the address of the Web site to which you want to link and then click OK.

Figure 30.3

Enter the address of the Web site.

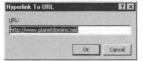

7. Click **OK** to close the Action Settings dialog box.

The quick method of adding a hyperlink to the presentation is to select an object on a slide that you want to create as the hyperlink and then click the **Insert Hyperlink** button on the Standard toolbar. The Insert Hyperlink dialog box opens (see Figure 30.4). Enter the Web site address in the **Link to File or URL** box. Enter the information you need to reach a particular location on that Web site in the Named Location in File box (optional), if there are named locations in the page. Click **OK**. It is good practice to start your browser and check that the hyperlink is working properly.

Figure 30.4

Enter the URL that is the destination for the hyperlink.

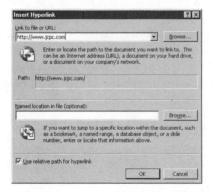

Saving a Presentation to Deliver over the Internet

Once you have your slide show set up, you need to save it in HTML format in order to publish the presentation to the Web. Part of this process involves the Internet Assistant, which comes with PowerPoint and helps you customize your presentation for the Web.

HyperText Markup Language (HTML) HTML is a collection of instructions, or *tags*, that tell a browser program how to display a page—when the text should be bold, italic, and so on. It is the markup language used on the Web.

To save your presentation in HTML format, do the following:

1. Open the presentation you want to save in HTML format.

2. Choose **File**, **Save as HTML** from the menu.

3. The Internet Assistant opens. Click **Next** to continue (click **Back** to go to a previous screen in the Internet Assistant).

4. Choose **New Layout** to create a new layout for the presentation or **Load Existing Layout** (select a layout from the list). Click **Next**.

5. When you select New Layout, you need to choose either the **Standard** or the **Browser Frames** page style (browser frames divide the window into separate panes). Click **Next**.

6. Choose the graphical format you want to use for the pictures in your presentation—**GIF**, **JPEG** (you must specify the percentage of compression; ask the administrator of your Web server which format to use and which compression setting), or **PowerPoint Animation**. If you choose the latter, your viewers will be prompted to download the Microsoft PowerPoint Animation Player add-in program if it's not installed on their systems, which is a time-consuming process. Click **Next**.

The PowerPoint Animation Player If you want your audience to see the animation in your Web presentation, choose PowerPoint Animation as your graphic type. However, your views must be running Windows 95 or Windows NT Workstation, must have Microsoft Internet Explorer 2.0 or 3.0 or Netscape Navigator 1.22 or 2.0 installed, and must have installed the Animation Player add-in. For information about installing the Microsoft Animation Player, choose **Help**, **Microsoft on the Web on the Help menu**, **Product News**.

7. Select the monitor resolution for which you want to create the graphics (if you aren't sure, choose 640 x 480 as the lowest common denominator). Set the width of the graphics by making a selection from the drop-down list (full width of screen, 1/4 width, 1/2 width, 3/4 width). Click **Next**.

8. In the appropriate boxes enter the e-mail address you want to appear on the page, the address of your home page, any other information you want on the page, and whether you want to give the viewer the option of downloading the presentation or downloading a copy of the Internet Explorer program. Click **Next**.

9. Choose whether you want to use the Browser Colors in your presentation or if you want to set Custom Colors. If you choose custom colors, click the buttons and select the colors you want to use for background, text, links, and so on. Be aware that your viewers might override your custom colors and also that many browsers or monitors might not be capable of showing all the colors. Click **Next**.

10. Select a button style (select the Next Slide option if you want to use text only), and then click **Next**.

11. If you selected the Standard Layout option at the beginning of the wizard, select a location for the buttons and then click **Next**.

12. If you want the information from your Notes Pages to appear in the presentation, select the **Include Slides Notes in Pages** option. Click **Next**.

13. Specify a location for your HTML folder. Click **Browse** to help you find a location. Click **Next**.

14. Click **Finish**.

15. If you want to save the HTML settings so you can use them again (see step 4, where you selected a layout, to see how you could apply these settings to a future Web presentation), enter a name for the settings. Click **Save**.

16. You can check the appearance and format of the presentation in your own browser by entering the name of the file into the URL box at the top of your browser. (For example, if the file is on your own machine and named HomePage, you can enter **c:\homepage.html** to view it. Be sure to enter all directories and subdirectories in the path as well.) This enables you to view the presentation without putting it on the Web.

After you have reviewed the presentation on your own browser and are satisfied with how it looks, load the HTML files on your server if you're running an intranet (ask your system administrator how to do that), or have your Internet Service Provider (ISP) load the pages on the Web server for publishing to the Internet. When the pages are available for viewing, open your Web browser (connect to the Web first if you're not dealing with an intranet) and open your pages. It may help to view your presentation using a different Web browser to see if it is still acceptable. Many any necessary changes to your presentation, save it again as HTML, and send the changed files to your ISP or store them in the proper location for use on your company's intranet.

Review Questions

1. How do you begin a new presentation for the Web?

2. What are the two methods for adding links to URLs on your slides?

3. True or False: Once you create the presentation, it's ready for use on the Web.

4. How do you save a presentation in HTML format?

Review Question Answers

1. Use the AutoContent Wizard to select one of the presentation designs for the Web and enter the information you need on Web pages. Be sure to select **Internet**, **Kiosk** as the type of delivery system you want to use for the presentation. For more information, refer to "Using Web Presentation Designs."

2. The first method is to select the object for the hyperlink, choose **Slide Show**, **Action Settings** from the menu. In the **Hyperlink To** box, select **URL**. Enter the URL address and click **OK**. Click **OK** to close the Action Settings dialog box.

The second method is to select the object for the hyperlink and then click the **Insert Hyperlink** button. Enter the URL in the dialog box and click **OK**.

For more information, refer to "Adding URL Hyperlinks."

3. False. It must first be saved in HTML format. For more information, refer to "Saving a Presentation to Deliver over the Internet."

4. Choose **File**, **Save As HTML** from the menu. Follow the steps in the Internet Assistant to save the file. For more information, refer to "Saving a Presentation to Deliver over the Internet."

Practice Lab

The Microsoft Expert User Exam lists eleven Required Tasks for the Skill Area "Delivering Presentations." One of these tasks has been covered in this lesson. Following you will find a practice lab for that task.

 Required Tasks   The Required Task covered in this lesson is Save a Presentation to Deliver over the Internet.

Save a Presentation to Deliver over the Internet

Open the file Lesson30.ppt from the CD-ROM. Select the words **Lace Curtain Lovelies** on the first page. Make that text a hyperlink to the Web site: **http:\\www.microsoft.com**. Save the file as HTML, adding your own e-mail address and home page (make one up if you don't have one) in the appropriate text boxes. Choose whatever layouts, page styles, and colors you like. Save the file as MyWeb. If you have a Web browser, view your page by specifying its path and filename (such as **C:\Data\MyWeb.html**).

APPENDIX A

Glossary

Active Cell   The currently selected cell in the Datasheet; marked by a heavy border.

Animation   In PowerPoint, the movement on-screen that acts as a transition from one object on the slide to the next.

Annotation   A note or comment added to a slide during a slide show using the annotation pen.

AutoContent Wizard   A wizard that lets you select the type of presentation you want to create, asks for basic information about how you want to present to the audience and what you want on each slide, and then produces a presentation with sample text in it. You replace the sample text with your own information to customize the presentation for your own use.

AutoLayouts   Predefined layouts of different types of slides—title, bulleted list, graph, organization chart, and so on. The AutoLayouts have placeholders for entering text, placing graphs, or holding clip art.

Axis (plural **Axes**)   A line that serves as a major reference for plotting data in a graph. Generally, the data values are plotted along the vertical axis, called the Y, or Value, axis, and the categories of data are plotted along the horizontal axis, called the X, or Category, axis. Where the two axes intersect is the zero (0) point of the Value axis.

Bitmap Image   A bitmap image is artwork created in paint programs such as Windows Paint (*.bmp), saved in a image editing program such as Adobe PhotoShop, or captured by a scanner (*.tif). These programs color each pixel of the image and map those pixels to save them.

Browser   A program that translates the HTML codes in a Web page to a layout that is viewed by the user.

Cell   One rectangle of the Datasheet in which a row and a column intersect. You enter each piece of data in a cell.

Chart   See *Graph.*

Clip Art   A collection of previously created pictures or images that is available for use without infringement of the artist's copyright.

Clipboard   See *Windows Clipboard.*

Color Scheme   Set of professionally selected complementary colors assigned to different elements in the presentation.

Control Box   The gray boxes above the row headings and to the left of the column headings. Click a control box to highlight a row or column. Double-click the control box to exclude the data in that row or column from the chart. A control box appears black when the row or column is included in the chart and dimmed when it is not.

Copy   When you copy an object, PowerPoint places a duplicate of it in the Clipboard but leaves the original on the slide.

Cut   When you cut an object, PowerPoint removes it from the slide and stores it in the Clipboard.

Data Marker   A bar (in column and bar charts), a shape (in area and pie charts), or a dot or symbol (in line and scatter charts) that marks a single data point or value. Related markers in a graph make up a data series.

Data Point   A single cell value, representing a single item in a data series. In a line chart, for example, it is one of the points that is plotted along the line.

Data Series   A row or column of data used to plot one line, one pie, or one set of bars or columns in a graph.

Datasheet. The Datasheet is set up like a spreadsheet with rows and columns. Each rectangle in the Datasheet is a cell that can hold text or numbers. Each cell has an address, which is defined by its intersecting points. Microsoft Graph converts the data you enter in the Datasheet into a graph that it displays in the Graph window.

Demote   To change the level of a paragraph from title down to bullet paragraph or from a bullet paragraph down to an indented bullet paragraph (or "sub topic").

Effect   An animated movement from one item to another, but it pertains to individual objects on the slide, such as a bulleted list or a movie, rather than to the appearance or disappearance of the entire slide.

Embedding   An object (such as a spreadsheet range or a drawing) created in one program but appearing as part of an object (such as a PowerPoint slide) created in another program. The embedded object is a copy of the original object; changing the embedded copy does not change the original; changing the original does not change the embedded copy. See also *Linking*.

Font   A family of characters that share the same design or typeface, such as Courier or Arial.

GIF   Graphic Interchange Format. A compressed bitmat file format that uses "lossless" compression—the compressed version of a file is identical to the pre-compressed version.

Gradient Fill   A background effect in which the background starts out one color on one side of the slide and gradually changes to another color. When one of the colors is white or black, the shading is called a one-color gradient. When neither color is white or black, the gradient is two-color.

Graph   The entire area inside the Chart window, including all the chart elements, such as labels, axes, and markers.

Graph Text   Text that describes data or items in a graph. Attached text is any label linked to a graph object such as an axis or data marker. Attached text moves with the item when it's repositioned, but cannot be moved independently of the graph object.

Gridlines   Optional lines that extend from the tick marks on an axis across the plot area. Gridlines make it easier to evaluate data values.

Group   A set of objects that can be moved or sized as if they were one object.

Handles   Small boxes that appear around a selected object. You drag the handles to change the size of the object.

Handouts   Printed copies of a slide presentation, used to distribute to attendees. Several formats are available for Handouts including handouts displaying Speaker Notes.

Hyperlink   A graphical object or block of colored and underlined text that you click in order to jump to a different location in the file, to a different file, an HTML page on the World Wide Web, or to an HTML page on an intranet.

HyperText Markup Language (HTML)   HTML is a collection of standard notations embedded in a string of text. When you view the text with an HTML reader (such as a Web browser), the reader interprets the HTML notations as formatting commands. Plain text becomes formatted text complete with headlines, italics, centerd paragraphs, and so forth.

Internet   A worldwide conglomeration of computer networks that can talk to each other.

Intranet   A company's computer network working with software that lets it route HTML documents. The documents can be read on the network using a browser.

JPEG   A compressed bitmap file format developed by the Joint Photographic Experts Group (hence, the name JPEG). JPEG uses "lossy" compression, which permts you to compress a file more if you are willing to give up fidelity to the original version. The more fidelity you are willing to lose, the more you can compress the file. This type of compression is good for photographs.

Legend   A key that identifies the patterns, colors, or symbols associated with the markers of a data series and shows the data series name that corresponds to each marker.

Linking   An object (such as a spreadsheet range or a drawing) created in one program but appearing as part of an object (such as a PowerPoint slide) created in another program. The embedded object includes a link or pointer to the original object; changing the linked copy actually changes the original; changing the original also changes the linked copy. See also *Embedding*.

Meeting Minder   A slide containing notes, minutes, and action items. The Meeting Minder is automatically generated and appears at the end of a presentation, listing all recorded action items.

Notes Page View   A view which displays speaker notes associated with slides.

Object   Any item on a slide, including text, graphics, and charts.

Organization Chart   An illustration of the hierarchy of an organization, showing who works for whom in the organization.

Orientation   The orientation setting tells the printer which edge of the paper should be at the "top" of the printout. If the wide edge is at the top, the orientation is *landscape*. If the narrow edge is at the top, the orientation is *portrait*.

Paste   When you paste an object, a copy of the Clipboard contents appears on your slide.

Placeholder   A box on a slide where you put text, graphs, charts, tables, clip art, or objects. The position and type of the placeholders are determined by the AutoLayout.

Plot Area   The area in which Microsoft Graph plots your data. It includes the axes and all markers that represent data points.

Promote   Moving a indented paragraph out to a bullet paragraph or a bullet paragraph to the left to become a title.

Series Name   The name that identifies each row or column of data. These names appear in the legend.

Slide Background   The colors, patterns, textures, or gradients that fill the slide and appear behind all the other slide elements.

Slide Show   The slide show is a view in which each slide fills the screen. Use this view when presenting your slides to a group using a projector or in an informal atmosphere, allowing the group to view the slides without seeing PowerPoint menus, toolbars, and so forth.

Slide Sorter View   A view in which you see a miniature of each slide in the presentation. Designed to assist you in repositioning, deleting, or copying slides.

Slide View   A view that displays one slide at a time. In this view you can edit a slide.

Speaker Notes   Comments added to a slide which are displayed only to the presenter of the slide show. Speaker Notes can also be printed on Handouts.

Template   A template is a set of related slide designs that comes with PowerPoint. When you select a template, PowerPoint applies the color scheme and general layout of the template to each slide in the presentation.

Text Box   A receptacle for the text on a slide. Text boxes often contain bulleted lists, notes, and labels (used to point to important parts of illustrations).

Tick Mark   A small line that intersects an axis and marks off a category, scale, or data series.

Tick Mark Label   The names that appear along the horizontal axis of an area, column, or line graph, and along the vertical axis of a bar graph. When data series are in rows, the tick mark labels are the column headings. When data series are in columns, the tick mark labels are the row headings.

Transition   A way of moving from one slide to the next. For example, with a vertical blinds transition, the slide takes on the look of window blinds that turn to reveal the next slide.

URL   Uniform Resource Locator, the address that you use to locate a Web site.

Web   The World Wide Web (or just Web) is the graphical component of the Internet. It's a collection of documents accessible through the Internet.

Web Page   One of the graphical documents that make up the World Wide Web.

Windows Clipboard   A temporary memory holding area for items you have cut or copied. The items remain in the Clipboard until you cut or copy another item or until you shut down your computer. They can be pasted out again and again.

Wizard   A wizard is a feature that automates an operation and helps you perform that operation. It displays a series of dialog boxes that ask you design and content questions. You select options and type text. When you are done, the wizard creates something (in this case, a presentation) according to your instructions.

WordArt   A tool for creating special text effects. In previous versions of PowerPoint (prior to version 7), WordArt was a separate program. In PowerPoint 7, WordArt is included as a tool on the Drawing toolbar and enhances features, such as textured fills and 3-D effects.

Student Preparation Guide

The purpose of this appendix is to provide you with information you'll need about the certification tests—how to register, what is covered in the tests, how the tests work, and so on.

Studying for the Tests

Although you aren't required to take a training course to pass the Certified Microsoft Office User exams, you certainly need to be sure you can successfully complete the tasks that are covered by the exams. Although a training class provides guidance, support, and practice, it may not be convenient or necessary for you.

This book provides the tutorial, review questions, and practice to help you complete your exams successfully. It can be used in a classroom situation or you can work through the lessons on your own. You don't have to work through the book from front to back, as each lesson stands on its own. Therefore, if you're familiar with an area, you may skip that lesson and go on to another. The Practice Labs at the end of each lesson give you a chance to become familiar with the tasks, and the CD-ROM that's included with the book has samples of the completed exercises.

Levels of Certification

For the Certified Microsoft Office User exam for Microsoft PowerPoint 97, there is one level of certification:

▶ **Certified Microsoft Expert User**   In addition to everyday tasks, you should be able to handle complex assignments involving advanced formatting and functionality.

Microsoft also has a special Office 97 certification, the Certified Microsoft Office Expert. To attain this level, you must be an Expert User in each of the Microsoft Office applications (Access, Excel, Word, PowerPoint, and Outlook) and have taken the Office Integration Exam to prove you can integrate these applications. This exam was scheduled to be available in Fall 1997.

The specific topics covered at each level are listed in the "Required Tasks" section of this appendix. In this book, these tasks are broken down into lessons. At the beginning of each lesson is a list of which tasks are covered in that lesson and which subject area they fall under in the tests.

Required Tasks

Each exam involves a list of Required Tasks that you may be asked to perform. The list of possible tasks is categorized by Skill Area. The tear-out card provided with this book lists the skill areas and tasks covered by the exams and gives you a roadmap of where those topics are covered in the book.

Expert User

According to Microsoft, an Expert User should be able to deliver presentations in a variety of media. The Skill Areas covered in the exam and the Required Tasks for those Skill Areas are listed in Table B.1.

Table B.1 Expert User Skills

Skill Area	Required Tasks
Creating Presentations	Create from a template
	Create from an existing presentation
	Delete slides
Adding Textual Information	Enter text in a slide and outline view
	Enter bulleted information
	Change the text alignment
Adding Visual Elements	Add formatting
	Build a graph
	Draw an object
	Rotate and fill and object
	Scale and size an object
	Add a table
	Add shapes
	Animate objects
	Add transitions
	Add an organizational chart
	Set custom options
	Check styles
Importing and Exporting Data	Add clip art
	Insert a Microsoft Excel chart
	Import text from MicrosoftWord
	Add scanned images

continues

Table B.1 Continued

Skill Area	Required Tasks
	Add sound and movies
	Export an outline to Word
Modifying Presentations	Change the sequence of a slide
	Find and replace text
	Modify the slide master
	Modify the sequence in outline mode
	Change tabs
	Change fonts
	Change the alignment of text
Editing Presentations	Using the spelling checker
	Add speaker notes
	Set automatic slide timing
Customizing Presentations	Create a custom background
	Customize a color scheme
	Customize clip art and other objects
	Recolor and edit objects
	Apply a template from another presentation
	Add links to other slides within the presentation
	Hide slides
Delivering Presentations	Start a slide show from any slide
	Use on-screen navigation tools
	Generate meeting notes
	Incorporate meeting feedback electronically
	Print slides in a variety of formats
	Print color presentations
	Export to overhead
	Export to 35mm slides

Skill Area	Required Tasks
	Deliver through presentation conferencing
	Save a presentation to use on another computer
	Save a presentation to deliver over the Internet

Registering for the Exams

Certified Microsoft Office User exams are administered by Approved Certification Testing (ACT) centers. To find out where the nearest ACT center is, call (800) 933-4493. You'll have to call the ACT center to find out what their test policies and schedules are, whether they accept walk-ins or only candidates who register in advance, how the exams are conducted, and what they are charging for the tests. The estimated retail price of each exam is $50.00 in the United States, but that can vary based on the center's sales policies. Payment for the tests must be paid in advance. There is no refund for missed exam appointments or failed tests.

Exams are currently available only in English, although Microsoft plans to offer the Office 97 exams in Japanese. The exams will be offered in other languages as soon as the course-ware in those languages becomes available.

Taking the Tests

Certified Microsoft Office User exams are not multiple choice or true/false tests. Instead, they are based on the types of tasks you might encounter in the everyday world. When you take the test you sit at a computer that uses Windows 95 or Windows NT Workstation, work with a Microsoft PowerPoint 97 document, and use the features of PowerPoint to perform the tasks outlined for you.

You can't use notes, manuals, laptops, tape recorders, or other aids during the tests.

Exams are one hour or less (some are as short as 30 minutes). Your score is based on the number of tasks you successfully perform in the allotted time. This measures your productivity and efficiency, as well as your skill and knowledge.

Each test has a minimum score. If your score meets or exceeds that minimum, you pass the test. If not, you can take the test as many times as you need until you pass. However, there is no refund if you don't pass the test.

You see your test results as soon as your test is completed. Successful candidates receive a certificate a week or two after the testing. Test scores are confidential; only you and Microsoft see them.

Exam Updates on the Web   To keep up to date on the Certified Microsoft Office User exams, check Microsoft's Web site at **http://www.microsoft.com/office/train_cert/**.

INDEX

SYMBOLS

3-D (three-dimensional) charts, 114
35mm slides, printing, 285
   service bureaus, 283-285

A

action buttons, 234-236
   choosing buttons, 234
   defining actions, 234-235
action items
   assigning, 266
   posting to Outlook, 267
Action Settings dialog box
   linking slides, 258-259
   Web presentations, 292-293
advancing slides
   action buttons, 234-236
   mouse/keyboard, 230
   on-screen navigation, 230-231
   setup options, 233
   timings, 252-254
      setting automatic timings, 252-254
      viewing during shows (Slide Meter), 254
   transitions, *see* transitions

agenda (summary) slides, 31
aligning
   bulleted paragraphs, 44-45
   objects, 164
   text
      graphs, 108
      organizational charts, 127
      text boxes, 52-53, 67
Anchor Points (AutoShapes), 152
animation, 244-247
   Animation Effects toolbar, 247
   Animation Player, 294
   custom animation, 178, 245-247
   playing media clips automatically, 177-178
   text, 244
   transitions, *see* transitions
annotating slides (Pen), 264
applying templates to existing presentations, 200-201
arrows
   drawing, 150
   mouse pointer, 232
   selecting line attributes, 168-169

aspect ratios, objects, 165
AutoContent Wizard
  (creating presentations),
  6-10
  Web presentations,
    291-292
AutoCorrect, 88-89
  abbreviations, 89
  adding words
    *AutoCorrect dialog
    box, 88*
    *Spelling dialog box,
    87*
  disabling, 89
Autofit, tables (column
  width), 142
AutoFormat, tables,
  139-140
AutoLayouts, 201-202
  new slides, 30-31
  templates, 11
Automatic Word Selection,
  24
AutoShapes, 150-152
  adding text, 151-152
  changing shapes, 151
  Curve/Scribble/Freeform
    tools, 182-183
  drawing, 150-151
  text anchors, aligning
    text, 44-45
axes (graphs), 104
  formatting, 109-111
  tick marks, 109
  titling, 106-107

B

backgrounds, 208
  customizing, 211-212
  tables, 137-138
  Web presentations, 212
  see also colors, schemes;
    shading
bitmap images, 185
  customizing, 186-187

Black and White command
  (View menu), 23, 282
black and white
  presentations, printing,
  282
blank presentations, 6, 12
borders
  graphs, 112
  tables, 137-139
    *Tables and Borders
    toolbar, 139*
Borders and Shading
  command (Format menu),
  137
building graphs, 94-95
bullets
  bulleted paragraphs
    aligning, 44-45
    *changing levels, 25,
    42-43*
    selecting, 23
  characters (symbols),
    changing, 40-41
  entering bulleted
    information, 40
  indenting bulleted
    paragraphs, 43-44
  moving bulleted items,
    40
  turning bullets on/off,
    40
buttons
  action buttons, 234-236
    choosing buttons, 234
    *defining actions,
    234-235*
  toolbar buttons, *see*
    toolbars

C

Cell Height and Width
  command (Table menu),
  141-143
cells
  graph Datasheets, *see*
    graphs, Datasheets
  tables, *see* tables, cells

certification, 306
  see also exams
characters, bullets, 40-41
charts
  importing Microsoft
    Excel charts, 192-193
  organizational charts,
    122-127
    adding, 122-124
    *formatting
    boxes/lines, 127*
    *formatting text,
    126-127*
    *moving/deleting
    boxes, 125*
    selecting boxes, 125
    selecting styles, 126
    undoing actions, 125
    zooming, 124
  see also graphs
checking styles, drawings,
  153-155
Clear command (Edit
  menu), Microsoft Graph,
  96
clip art, 174-176
  adding to slides, 175
  customizing, 185
  downloading from
    Microsoft Web site,
    174
  exporting to Clip
    Gallery, 176
  links to Clip Gallery,
    185
  recoloring, 184
Clip Gallery, 174-177
  inserting movies/sound,
    177
Clipboard, 36
Close command (File
  menu), 15
collapsing outlines, 74
color
  Color command (View
    menu), 23
  Colors and Lines
    command (Format
    menu), 184

fonts, 65
graphs, 115-116
objects
    fill color, 166-168
    line attributes, 168
    recoloring, 184
Pen, 233, 265
printing color
  presentations, 280
schemes, 208-211
    copying from slide to
    slide, 211
    customizing, 209-210
    selecting, 208-209
    see also backgrounds;
    templates
tables, 137-138
see also shading
columns
tabbed, changing tabs,
65-67
tables, *see* tables
commands
Chart menu
    3-D view, 114
    Chart Options, 106,
    116-117
    Chart Type (Microsoft
    Graph), 99-100
Data menu (Microsoft
Graph)
    Series in Columns, 98
    Series in Rows, 98
Delete menu (Microsoft
Graph), Cut, 98
Edit menu
    Chart (Microsoft
    Graph), 105
    Clear (Microsoft
    Graph), 96
    Copy, 35, 52, 163
    Copy (Microsoft
    Graph), 97
    Cut, 24, 35, 52, 163
    Cut (Microsoft
    Graph), 97
    Delete Slide, 35
    Duplicate, 163

Find, 80
Paste, 24, 36, 52,
    163, 192
Paste Link, 194
Paste Special, 192
Replace, 81
Select (Microsoft
    Organization
    Chart), 125
Undo, 35, 170
Undo (Microsoft
    Graph), 97
Undo (Microsoft
    Organization
    Chart), 125
File menu
    Close, 15
    New, 7, 11-12
    Open, 13
    Pack and Go, 237
    Page Setup, 283-285
    Print, 280
    Save, 13-14
    Save as HTML, 294
    Send To, 196
    Send To,
    Genigraphics, 284
Format menu
    Alignment, 53, 67
    Apply Design, 200
    AutoShape, 44, 151
    Background, 211
    Borders and Shading,
    137
    Bullet, 40
    Colors and Lines, 184
    Font, 62
    Line Spacing, 53
    Selected Axis (Graph),
    109
    Selected Chart Area,
    112
    Selected Data Point,
    115
    Selected Data Series,
    115
    Selected Gridlines,
    113

Selected Legend, 112
Slide Color Scheme,
    208-209
Slide Layout, 201
Text Direction, 140
Insert menu
    Cells (Microsoft
    Graph), 97
    Chart (Microsoft
    Graph), 94
    Duplicate Slide, 31
    Movies and Sounds,
    177
    New Slide, 30
    Object, 193
    Picture, 122, 175
    Picture, From File,
    176
    Picture, WordArt, 55
    Slides from Files, 31
    Slides from Outline,
    33, 195
    Text Box, 50
Paste menu (Microsoft
Graph), Cut, 97
Slide Show menu
    Action Buttons, 234
    Action Settings, 258,
    292
    Custom Animation,
    178, 245
    Custom Show, 281
    Hide Slide, 74, 260
    Record Narration, 233
    Rehearse Timings,
    253
    Set Up Show, 232,
    253
    Slide Transitions,
    242, 252
    View Show, 230
Table menu
    Cell Height and
    Width, 141-143
    context-sensitivity,
    136
    Delete Cells, 135

Distribute Columns Evenly, 142
Distribute Rows Evenly, 144
Hide Gridlines, 138
Insert Columns, 136
Insert Rows, 136
Merge Cells, 144
Show Gridlines, 138
Split Cells, 144
Table AutoFormat, 139
Tools menu
AutoCorrect, 88
Options, 24, 89
Presentation Conference, 272, 275
Spelling, 86
Style Checker, 153
View menu
Black and White, 23, 282
Color, 23
Datasheet (Microsoft Graph), 95-96
Header and Footer, 203
Master, Notes Master, 224
Master, Slide Master, 202
Notes Page, 20, 222
Outline, 20
Ruler, 43
Slide, 20
Slide Miniature, 22
Slide Show, 20, 230
Slide Sorter, 20
Speaker Notes, 223
conferences (presentation conferencing), 272
conducting, 274
participating, 275
preparing, 272-274
see also Meeting Minder

contents templates, creating, 217
see also templates
Copy command (Edit menu), 35, 52
Microsoft Graph, 97
objects, 163
copying
color schemes, 211
Datasheet cells (graphs), 97
objects, 153, 162-163
duplicating, 163
organizational chart boxes, 125
slides, 35, 72
duplicating, 31
table items, 136
text, 52
formatting (Format Painter), 65
creating presentations, 6-15
AutoContent Wizard, 7-10
blank presentations, 12
existing presentations, 13-14
practice lab, 17
review questions, 16-17
saving, 14-15
slides
deleting, 35
inserting, 30-33
selecting, 34
templates, 10-12
cropping pictures, 169-170
curved lines, drawing/editing, 182-183
Custom Animation command (Slide Show menu), 178, 245
Custom Animation dialog box, 245-247
Effects tab, 246
Play Settings tab, 178
Timing tab, 178, 245-246
custom chart types, 100

custom shows, printing, 281-282
customizing
backgrounds, 208, 211-212
Web presentations, 212
bitmap images, 186-187
clip art, 185
recoloring, 184
color schemes, 208-211
copying to other slides, 211
selecting, 208-209
custom animation, 245-247
hiding slides, 74-75, 260
linking slides within presentations, 258-259
templates
applying from other presentations, 217-218
creating, 216-217
cutting
Datasheet cells (graphs), 97
objects, 162-163
organizational chart boxes, 125
slides, 35
table items, 136
text, 24
in text boxes, 52
paragraphs, 25

D

data, graphs
Datasheets, 94-98
changing data series, 98
editing, 96-98
formatting data series, 115-116
labels, 116-117
tables, 117-118

date/time, *see* **headers/ footers**
deleting
   Datasheets (Graph)
      cell contents, 96
      rows/columns, 98
   objects, 153
   organizational chart boxes, 125
   slides, 35
   table items, 135
   text, 52
      boxes, 51
delivering presentations, 230
   action buttons, 234-236
      choosing buttons, 234
      defining actions, 234-235
   annotating slides (Pen), 264
   ending shows, 230-232
   exporting, 282-285
      35mm slides, 285
      overheads, 282-285
      service bureaus, 283-285
   generating meeting notes (Meeting Minder), 265-266
   incorporating meeting feedback electronically, 267
   on-screen navigation, 230-232
   pointer options, 232
   presentation conferencing, 272-275
      conducting, 274
      participating, 275
      preparing, 272-274
      see also Meeting Minder
   printing, 280-282
      black-and-white presentations, 282
      color presentations, 280
   custom shows, 281-282
   setting print options, 280-281
   saving Internet presentations, 293-295
   setting up shows, 232-233
   starting shows, 230
      from any slide, 230
      Pack and Go Wizard, 237
   viewing timings (Slide Meter), 254
   see also slide shows
demoting
   bulleted paragraphs, 42-43
   text (Outline view), 25
design templates, *see* **templates**
dialog boxes
   Action Settings, 234-235
      linking slides, 258-259
      Web presentations, 292-293
   Apply Design, 200-201
   AutoCorrect, 88
   AutoFormat (tables), 139-140
   Background, 211-212
   Borders and Shading (tables), 137-138
   Bullet, 40-41
   Cell Height and Width (tables), 141-142
      Column tab, 142
      Row tab, 143-144
   Chart Options
      Data Labels tab, 116-117
      Data Table tab, 117-118
      Titles tab, 106-107
   Chart Type (Microsoft Graph), 99
      Custom types tab, 100
   Clip Gallery 3.0, *see* Clip Gallery
   Color Scheme
      Custom tab, 209-210
      Standard tab, 208-209
   Custom Animation, 245-247
      Effects tab, 246
      Play Settings tab, 178
      Timing tab, 178, 245-246
   Delete Cells, 135
   Edit WordArt Text, 55-56
   Fill Effects, 167-168
   Find, 80-81
   Font, 62-63
   Format AutoShape, 151-152
      Text Box tab, 44-45
   Format Axis, 109-110
   Format Chart Area, 112
   Format Data Series, Patterns tab, 115-116
   Insert (Microsoft Graph), 97
   Insert Object (imported objects), 193-194
   Insert Outline, 33, 195
   Insert Slides from Files, 31-32
   Insert Word Table, 132-133
   Line Spacing, 53-54
   New Presentation
      General tab, 12
      Presentation Designs tab, 10
      Presentations tab, 7-8
   New Slide, 11
      AutoLayouts, 30-31

Open, 13
    Favorites lists, 33
    opening outlines, 195
Options, *see* Options
    dialog box
Page Setup
    35mm slides, 285
    printing overheads,
    283
Paste Special, 192-193
Patterned Lines, 169
PowerPoint, 6-7
Print, 280-282
Print to File, 284-285
Recolor Picture, 184
Replace, 81-82
Set Up Show, 232-233
    setting timings, 253
Slide Finder, 31-32
Slide Transition,
    242-243, 252-253
Spelling, 87
Style Checker, 153-154
Style Checker Options,
    154
WordArt Gallery, 55
Write-Up, 196
dictionary, *see* **spell check**
distributing
    objects, 164
    tables
        columns, 142
        rows, 144
downloading clip art from
  Microsoft Web site, 174
dragging/dropping
    objects, 163
    organizational chart
      boxes, 125
    paragraphs, 25
    slides between
      presentations, 73
    see also moving
drawing
    checking styles, 153-155
    Drawing toolbar
        Font Color button, 65
        Insert WordArt
          button, 55
        Text Box button, 50

lines, curves/scribbles/
  freeform, 182-183
objects, 150-153
    adding text, 151-152
    AutoShapes, 150-151
    multiple objects, 153
    see also objects
tools, 148-149
    see also AutoShapes
duplicating
    objects, 163
    slides, 31

E

Edit menu commands
    Chart (Microsoft Graph),
      105
    Clear (Microsoft Graph),
      96
    Copy, 35, 52
        Microsoft Graph, 97
        objects, 163
    Cut, 24, 35, 52
        Microsoft Graph, 97
        objects, 163
    Delete (Microsoft
      Graph), 98
    Delete Slide, 35
    Duplicate (objects), 163
    Find, 80
    Paste, 24, 36, 52, 192
        Microsoft Graph, 97
        objects, 163
    Paste Link, 194
    Paste Special, 192
    Replace, 81
    Select (Microsoft
      Organization Chart),
      125
    Undo, 35
        Microsoft Graph, 97
        Microsoft
          Organization Chart,
          125
        uncropping pictures,
          170

Edit WordArt Text dialog
  box, 55-56
editing
    freeform objects, 183
    graph Datasheets, 96-98
        data series, 98
    organizational charts,
      124-127
        chart styles, 126
        formatting boxes/
          lines, 127
        formatting text,
          126-127
        moving/deleting
          boxes, 125
        selecting boxes, 125
        undoing actions, 125
    slide timings, 252-254
    speaker's notes, *see*
      speaker's notes
    spelling checker, 86
        AutoCorrect, 88-89
        checking after typing,
          86-87
        checking while typing,
          86
    tables, 134-136, 140-144
        column width,
          141-142
        deleting items, 135
        inserting items, 136
        merging/splitting
          cells, 144
        moving/copying items,
          136
        row height, 142-144
        selecting items, 134
    text
        Automatic Word
          Selection, 24
        finding/replacing,
          80-82
        Outline view, 23-24
        Slide view, 26
        text boxes, 52
    WordArt, 55-56

effects
 animation, *see*
  animation
 transitions, *see*
  transitions
embedding imported
 objects, 193-194
ending slide shows,
 230-232
entering text
 bulleted information, 40
 Outline view, 23
 Slide view, 26
erasing Pen marks, 232
exams, 305-309
 certification, 306
 Microsoft Web site
  updates, 310
 registering, 309
 Required Tasks, 306-309
 studying, 306
 taking, 309
Excel charts, importing,
 192-193
existing presentations,
 creating new
 presentations, 13-14
expanding outlines, 74
exporting
 35mm slides, 285
 clip art to Clip Gallery,
  176
 meeting action items to
  Outlook, 267
 meeting minutes to
  Word, 266
 outlines to Microsoft
  Word, 196
 overheads, 282-285
 service bureaus, 283-285

F

Favorites lists, adding
 presentations, 33
File menu commands
 Close, 15
 New, 7, 11-12
 Open, 13
 Pack and Go, 237
 Page Setup, 283-285
 Print, 280
 Save, 13-14
 Save as HTML, 294
 Send To
  Genigraphics, 284
  Microsoft Word, 196
file size, Web
 presentations, 175
fill effects
 backgrounds, 211-212
 gradient fill, 208
 objects, 166-168
finding/replacing text
 finding, 80-81
 replacing, 81-82
fonts
 bullet characters, 40-41
 changing, 62-65
  color, Drawing
   toolbar, 65
  Font dialog box,
   62-63
  Formatting toolbar,
   63-64
 graphs, 108
 TrueType (TT), 62
footers, *see* headers/footers
Format AutoShape dialog
 box, Text Box tab, 44-45
Format menu commands
 Alignment, 53, 67
 Apply Design, 200
 AutoShape, 44, 151
 Background, 211
 Borders and Shading,
  137
 Bullet, 40

 Colors and Lines, 184
 Font, 62
 Line Spacing, 53
 Selected Axis (Graph),
  109
 Selected Chart Area
  (Graph), 112
 Selected Data Point
  (Graph), 115
 Selected Data Series
  (Graph), 115
 Selected Gridlines
  (Graph), 113
 Selected Legend (Graph),
  112
 Slide Color Scheme,
  208-209
 Slide Layout, 201
 Text Direction, 140
formatting
 bullets
  aligning bulleted
   paragraphs, 44-45
  characters (symbols),
   40-41
 copying (Format
  Painter), 65
  color schemes, 211
 fonts, *see* fonts
 Formatting toolbar, 24,
  63-64
  Borders button, 138
  Bullets button, 40
  Decrease Paragraph
   Spacing button, 55
  Increase Paragraph
   Spacing button, 55
 graphs, 104, 107
  3-D charts, 114
  axes, 109-111
  borders/shading, 112
  colors/patterns,
   115-116
  gridlines, 113-114
  legend, 112-113
  text, 107-109

organizational charts
  boxes/lines, 127
  text, 126-127
tables
  AutoFormat, 139-140
  borders/shading,
    137-139
  rotating text, 140
freeform lines/objects,
  drawing/editing, 182-183

G

generating meeting notes
  (Meeting Minder),
  265-266
Genigraphics Wizard, 284
  see also service bureaus,
    printing presentations
gradient fill, 208
graphics, *see* pictures;
  objects
graphs (Microsoft Graph),
  94-100
  axes, 104
    formatting, 109-111
    tick marks, 109
    titling, 106-107
  building, 94-95
  chart types
    changing, 98-99
    custom chart types,
      100
  data labels, 116-117
  data tables, 117-118
  Datasheets, 94-98
    changing data series,
      98
    editing, 96-98
    formatting data
      series, 115-116
  displaying charts, 105
  exploding (cutting) pie
    slices, 116

formatting, 104, 107
  3-D charts, 114
  axes, 109-111
  borders/shading, 112
  colors/patterns,
    115-116
  gridlines, 113-114
  legends, 112-113
  text, 107-109
importing Microsoft
  Excel charts, 192-193
objects, editing
  appearance, 105-106
sizing, 96
titles, 106-107
  legend placement,
    112-113
gridlines
  charts, 113-114
  tables, 138
grouping/ungrouping
  objects, 162

H

Header and Footer
  command (View menu),
  203
headers/footers
  notes masters, 225
  slide masters, 203
hiding
  mouse pointer, 232
  slides, 74-75, 260
    displaying, 74, 260
    presenting, 75
    printing, 75, 282
  table gridlines, 138
HTML (HyperText Markup
  Language), 290
  hyperlinks
    linking slides within
      presentations,
      258-259
    Web presentations,
      292-293
    see also action
      buttons

saving presentations in
  HTML, 293-295
tags, 290

I

importing
  clip art, 175
    downloading from
      Web, 174
  Clip Gallery, 175
  Microsoft Excel charts,
    192-193
  Microsoft Word text,
    193-195
    into outlines, 195
    into slides, 193-194
    Word tables, 132-133
  movies/sounds, 176-177
  scanned images, 175-176
incorporating meeting
  feedback electronically,
  267
indenting paragraphs
  (bulleted paragraphs),
  43-44
Insert menu commands
  Cells (Microsoft Graph),
    97
  Chart (Microsoft Graph),
    94
  Duplicate Slide, 31
  Movies and Sounds, 177
  New Slide, 30
  Object, 193
  Picture
    Clip Art, 175
    From File, 176
    Organization Chart,
      122
    WordArt, 55
  Slides from Files, 31
  Slides from Outline, 33,
    195
  Text Box, 50

inserting
columns, 136
imported
objects, 193-194
Word tables, 132-133
outlines, 33, 195
rows, 136
slides, 30
from document
outlines, 33
from other
presentations, 31-33
Internet
Internet Assistant,
294-295
presentation
conferencing, *see*
presentation
conferencing
Web presentations, *see*
Web presentations

J-K

justifying text, *see*
aligning, text

keyboard shortcuts
advancing slides, 230
Arrow, 265
Center Alignment,
53, 67
Copy, 35, 52
Cut, 35, 52
Demote, 25, 43
Duplicate, 163
Graph
editing Datasheets,
96
Undo, 97
Left Alignment, 53, 67
Paste, 36, 52
Pen, 265
Print, 280
Promote, 25, 43
Right Alignment, 53, 67
Save, 13-14

Select All (Microsoft
Organization Chart),
126
table navigation, 133
Undo, 35
Microsoft Organiza-
tion Chart, 125
kiosk presentations, 233
saving, 291

L

labels, data labels (graphs),
116-117
see also legends
labs, *see* **practice labs**
layering/ordering objects,
161
layouts, slides, *see*
AutoLayouts
legends, graphs, 106-107
placing, 112-113
lines
attributes, selecting,
168-169
drawing, 150
curves/scribbles/
freeform, 182-183
spacing, 53-55
links
linking imported
objects, 193-194
linking slides within
presentations, 258-259
Web presentations,
292-293
see also action buttons
lists
bulleted, 40-45
aligning paragraphs,
44-45
characters (symbols),
changing, 40-41
entering bulleted
information, 40
indenting paragraphs,
43-44
moving bulleted
items, 40

promoting/demoting
paragraphs, 42-43
turning bullets on/off,
40
numbered, 41
tabbed columns,
changing tabs, 65-67
looping
movies/sound, 178
slide shows, 233
transition sounds, 243

M

Master toolbar, 203
masters
notes masters, 224-225
slide masters
actions buttons, see
action buttons
headers/footers, 203
modifying, 202-203
media clips, *see*
multimedia
Meeting Minder, 231,
265-266
assigning action items,
266-267
posting to Outlook,
267
generating meeting
notes, 265-266
presentation
conferences, 274
merging cells, tables, 144
Microsoft
Excel charts, importing,
192-193
Graph, *see* graphs
Organization Chart
program, 122-125
exiting, 122
Icon Bar, 123-124
starting, 122
Undo command, 125
views/zooming, 124
see also
organizational
charts

Outlook, scheduling
meeting action items,
267
Word
*exporting outlines to
Word, 196*
*importing text into
outlines, 195*
*importing text into
slides, 193-194*
*importing Word
tables, 132-133*
*importing Word text,
193-195*
**modifying presentations,
62**
aligning text, 67
applying templates,
200-201
AutoLayouts, 201-202
changing fonts, 62-65
*Drawing toolbar
(color), 65*
*Font dialog box,
62-64*
copying text formatting
(Format Painter), 65
finding/replacing text,
80-82
hiding slides, 74-75, 260
slide masters, 202-203
slide sequence, 72-74
Outline view, 73-74
*Slide Sorter view,
72-73*
tabs, changing (tabbed
columns), 65-67
mouse
action button initiation,
234
advancing slides, 230
pointers,
hiding/selecting, 232
see also Pen

movies
adding to slides, 176-177
playing automatically,
177-178
playing continuously,
178
moving
bulleted items, 40
objects, 153, 162-163
organizational chart
boxes, 125
paragraphs (Outline
view), 25
slides
*between
presentations, 73*
sequence, 72-74
table items, 136
text boxes, 51
multimedia
Clip Gallery, 174
movies/sounds, adding
to slides, 176-177
playing automatically,
177-178
playing continuously,
178

N

naming
graph titles, 106-107
*legend placement,
112-113*
presentations, 14
narration options, 233
**navigating slide shows,
230-232**
*see also slide shows,
advancing slides*
**New command (File
menu), 7, 11-12**
**New Presentation dialog
box**
General tab, 12
Presentation Designs
tab, 10
Presentations tab, 7-8

**New Slide command
(Insert menu), 30**
New Slide dialog box, 11
AutoLayouts, 30-31
**next slide, *see* slide shows,
advancing slides**
notes
annotating slides during
shows (Pen), 264
generating meeting
notes (Meeting
Minder), 265-266
Notes Pages view, 20,
222
*adding speaker's
notes, 222-223*
*moving between
slides, 21-22*
*notes masters,
224-225*
*sizing slides/text
boxes, 223-224*
numbered lists, 41

O

objects, 23
adding text, 151-152
previewing, 152
aligning/distributing,
164
animation, 244-247
*Animation Effects
toolbar, 247*
*custom animation,
245-247*
text, 244
charts (graphs),
changing appearance,
105-106
checking styles, 153-155
color
fill color, 166-168
line color, 168
recoloring, 184
copying, 153, 162-163
duplicating, 163

cropping pictures,
169-170
cutting, 162-163
deleting, 153
drawing, 150-153
AutoShapes, 150-151
curves/scribbles/
freeform lines,
182-183
multiple objects, 153
tools, 148-149
filling, 166-168
grouping/ungrouping,
162
importing, *see* importing
layering/ordering, 161
line attributes, selecting,
168-169
linking, *see* links
moving, 153, 162-163
outlines, *see* objects, line
attributes, selecting
pasting, 162-163
rotating, 165-166
selecting, 153, 160
deselecting, 160
sizing, 164-165
maintaining shapes
(scaling), 153, 165
see also pictures
OLE (Object Linking and
Embedding), imported
objects, 193-194
see also links
on-screen navigation, slide
shows, 230-232
see also advancing slides
opening
existing presentations,
13
Favorites lists, 33
outlines, 195
Options dialog box
Edit tab, Automatic
Word Selection, 24
Spelling tab, disabling
AutoCorrect, 89

ordering/layering objects,
161
organizational charts,
122-127
adding, 122-124
editing, 124-127
chart styles, 126
formatting
boxes/lines, 127
formatting text,
126-127
moving/deleting
boxes, 125
selecting boxes, 125
undoing actions, 125
Icon bar, 123-124
zooming, 124
orientation, printing, 280
Outline view, 20
adding speaker's notes,
223
collapsing/expanding
outlines, 74
moving between slides,
21
outlines
creating slides from
document outlines,
33
exporting to Microsoft
Word, 196
importing Microsoft
Word text, 195
opening, 195
Outlining toolbar, 24
Collapse All button,
74
Collapse button, 74
Demote button, 25,
43
Expand button, 74
Move Down button,
25, 74
Move Up button, 25,
74
Promote button, 25,
43
Summary Slide
button, 31

promoting/demoting
bulleted paragraphs,
42-43
slide miniature window,
22
slide sequence,
changing, 73-74
text
changing outline
levels, 24-25
entering/editing,
23-24
moving paragraphs,
25
Outlook, scheduling
meeting action items, 267
ovals, drawing, 150
overheads, printing,
282-285
service bureaus, 283-285

P

Pack and Go Wizard,
236-237
page setup, printing
35mm slides, 285
printing overheads, 283
paragraphs
aligning, 52-53, 67
bulleted paragraphs
aligning, 44-45
indenting, 43-44
promoting/demoting,
42-43
line spacing, 53-55
moving (Outline view),
25
promoting/demoting
(Outline view), 24-25
pasting
Datasheet cells (graphs),
97
importing
Excel charts, 192-193
Word text, 194

objects, 162-163
organizational chart
   boxes, 125
paragraphs (Outline
   view), 25
Paste Link command
   (Edit menu), 194
Paste Special command
   (Edit menu), 192
slides, 35-36
table items, 136
text (Outline view), 24
patterns, graphs, 115-116
pausing slide shows, 232
Pen, 232, 264-265
   color, 233, 265
   erasing marks, 232
   presentation
      conferences, 274
pictures
   adding to Clip Gallery,
      176
   bitmap images, 185
      customizing, 186-187
   clip art, 174
      adding to slides, 175
      customizing, 185
      linking to Clip
         Gallery, 185
      recoloring, 184
   cropping, 169-170
   organizational charts, *see*
      organizational charts
   Picture toolbar, 186-187
   scanned images, adding
      to slides, 175-176
   WordArt, 55-57
   see also objects
**pie charts, exploding
   (cutting) pie slices, 116**
   see also graphs
**placeholders, slide
   templates, 12**
   entering text, 25-26
   font, changing, 63

pointer options, 232
   Pen, 232, 264-265
      color, 233, 265
      erasing marks, 232
      presentation
         conferences, 274
**points, freeform objects,
   183**
PowerPoint
   starting, 6-7
   Viewer, 236-237
practice labs
   aligning text, 59, 69
   animating objects, 249
   automatic slide timing,
      256
   bulleted lists, 47
   color schemes/
      backgrounds, 214
   creating presentations,
      17
   customizing clip art, 189
   deleting slides, 37-38
   delivering presentations
      generating meeting
         notes, 269
      incorporating meeting
         feedback
         electronically, 269
      on-screen navigation,
         239
      presentation
         conferencing, 277
      printing/exporting,
         287
      saving Internet
         presentations, 296
      starting shows, 239
      using on other
         computers, 239
   entering text in Slide
      and Outline views,
      27-28
   exporting outlines to
      Word, 198
   finding/replacing text,
      83

graphs, 102
   formatting, 120
hiding slides, 261-262
importing, 179-180
   Excel charts/Word
      text, 198
linking slides, 261-262
modifying slide masters,
   204-205
objects/shapes
   checking styles,
      156-157
   drawing, 156-157
   rotating/filling,
      171-172
   sizing/scaling,
      171-172
organizational charts,
   128-129
recoloring/editing
   objects, 189
slide sequences, 76-77
speaker's notes, 226-227
spelling checker, 91
tables, 146
templates,
   applying/creating, 219
transitions, 249
**presentation conferencing,
   272-275**
   conducting, 274
   participating, 275
   preparing, 272-274
   see also Meeting Minder
presentations
   applying templates to
      existing presentations,
      200-201
   creating, 6-14
      AutoContent Wizard,
         7-10
      blank presentations,
         12
      deleting slides, 35
      existing presentations,
         13-14
      inserting slides, 30-33

practice lab, 17
review questions,
16-17
selecting slides, 34
templates, 10-12
delivering, *see* delivering
presentations
modifying, *see*
modifying
presentations
naming, 14
printing, 280-285
35mm slides, 285
black-and-white
presentations, 282
color presentations,
280
custom shows,
281-282
overheads, 282-285
setting print options,
280-281
saving, 14-15
as templates,
216-217
Internet presentations,
293-295
using on other
computers, 236-237
World Wide, *see* Web
presentations
see also slide shows
previewing
animation
animated text, 244
custom animation,
246
color schemes, 209
custom schemes, 210
movies/sounds, 177
scanned images, 176
slides, slide miniature
window, 22-23
text added to objects,
152
transition effects, 242
Web presentations, 295

previous slide, *see* **slide
shows, advancing slides**
printing, 280-285
35mm slides, 285
black-and-white
presentations, 282
color presentations, 280
creating print files,
284-285
custom shows, 281-282
hidden slides, 75, 282
orientation, 280
overheads, 282-285
service bureaus, 283-285
setting print options,
280-281
**promoting text (Outline
view),** 25
bulleted paragraphs,
42-43

Q-R

questions, *see* **review
questions**
quitting slide shows,
230-232

recoloring objects, 184
recording narration, 233
rectangles, drawing, 150
registering for exams, 309
rehearsing
setting automatic
timings, 253-254
viewing rehearsed
timings during shows,
254
replacing text, 81-82
review questions
animating objects, 248
automatic slide timing,
255
bulleted lists, 46
color schemes/
backgrounds, 213

creating presentations,
16-17
customizing clip art,
188-189
deleting slides, 37
delivering, 238
exporting outlines to
Word, 197
generating meeting
notes, 268
graphs, 101
formatting, 119
hiding slides, 76, 261
importing, 179
Excel charts/Word
text, 197
incorporating meeting
feedback electronically,
268
inserting slides, 37
Internet/Web
presentations, 296
linking slides, 261
modifying slide masters,
204
objects/shapes
checking styles, 156
drawing, 156
rotating/filling, 171
scaling, 171
organizational charts,
128
Outline view, 27
presentation
conferencing, 276
printing/exporting, 286
recoloring/editing
objects, 188-189
slide sequences, 76
speaker's notes, 226
spelling checker, 90
tables, 145
tabs, changing, 69
templates,
applying/creating, 219

text
changing font, 69
finding/replacing text,
83
formatting, 68
text boxes, 58
transitions, 248
rotating
objects, 165-166
text, tables, 140
rows, tables, *see* **tables**
ruler
indenting bulleted
paragraphs, 43-44
tables, changing column
width, 141
tabbed columns, 65-67

S

sample text, 11
saving
presentations, 14-15
as templates,
216-217
Internet presentations,
293-295
using on other
computers, 236-237
scaling objects, 153, 165
scanned images, adding to
slides, 175-176
scheduling meeting action
items (Outlook), 267
scribbled lines,
drawing/editing, 182-183
scrollbars, slide show
windows, 233
searching text, 80-82
Selected
Axis command (Format
menu), Graph, 109
Chart Area command
(Format menu), Graph,
112

Data Point command
(Format menu), Graph,
115
Data Series command
(Format menu), Graph,
115
Gridlines command
(Format menu), Graph,
113
Legend command
(Format menu), Graph,
112
selecting
objects, 153, 160
deselecting, 160
organizational chart
boxes, 125
slides, 34
table items, 134
text, 23
Automatic Word
Selection, 24
Send To command (File
menu)
Genigraphics, 284
Microsoft Word, 196
series, *see* **data, graphs,**
Datasheets
service bureaus, printing
presentations, 283-285
Set Up Show dialog box,
232-233
setting timings, 253
shading
graphs, 112
tables, 137-139
Tables and Borders
toolbar, 139
shapes, drawing, 150-153
AutoShapes, 150-151
adding text, 151-152
changing shapes, 151
checking styles, 153-155
curves/scribbles/
freeform lines, 182-183
multiple objects, 153
sizing shapes (scaling),
153, 165
see also objects

Show Gridlines command
(Table menu), 138
shows, *see* **slide shows**
sizing
Notes Pages view
objects, 223-224
objects, 153, 164-165
maintaining shapes
(scaling), 153, 165
Slide Show view, 20
slide shows
advancing slides, 233
action buttons,
234-236
mouse/keyboard, 230
on-screen navigation,
230
timings, 252-254
transitions, 242-243
animation, *see*
animation
assigning tasks, 266-267
posting to Outlook,
267
conferences, *see*
presentation
conferencing
ending, 230-232
hidden slides, 74-75
looping, 233
Meeting Minder, 231
multimedia
playing
automatically,
177-178
playing continuously,
178
narration, 233
navigating, 230-232
see also slide shows,
advancing slides
pausing, 232
pointer options, 232
set up, 232-233
Slide Meter, 254
presentation
conferences, 274

Slide Navigator, 230-231
  hidden slides, 260
  presentation
    conferences, 274
  starting, 230
  from any slide, 230
  Pack and Go Wizard,
    237
  taking notes
    Meeting Minder,
      265-266
    Pen, 264
  timings, 252-254
    time measurement
      (Slide Meter), 231
  transitions, 242-243
  Web presentations, *see*
    Web presentations
Slide Sorter view, 20
  adding
    speaker's notes, 223
    transitions, 242-243
  animating text, 244
  hiding slides, 260
  moving between slides,
    22
  slide sequence,
    changing, 72-73
Slide view, 20
  adding
    buttons, 234-235
    clip art, 175
    movies/sounds,
      176-177
    scanned images,
      175-176
    speaker's notes, 223
    tables, 132
  building graphs, 94-95
  custom animation,
    245-247
  customizing clip art, 185
  displaying charts, 105
  entering/editing text, 26
  moving between slides,
    21-22

slides
  35mm slides, printing,
    285
  adding to presentations,
    30
    from document
      outlines, 33
    from other
      presentations, 31-33
  advancing, *see* slide
    shows, advancing
    slides
  AutoLayouts, 201-202
  copying, 72
    duplicating, 31
  creating from document
    outlines, 33
  deleting, 35
  finding (Slide Finder), 32
  hiding, 74-75, 260
  masters
    action buttons, see
      action buttons
    headers/footers, 203
    modifying, 202-203
  moving
    between
      presentations, 73
    between slides, 21-22
  objects, *see* objects
  placeholders, entering
    text, 25-26
  previewing, slide
    miniature window,
    22-23
  printing, *see* printing
  selecting, 34
  sequence, changing
    Outline view, 73-74
    Slide Sorter view,
      72-73
  slide miniature window,
    22-23
  shows, *see* slide shows
  summary (agenda)
    slides, 31
  text, Outline view, 23-25
  titles, changing font, 63
  transitions, 242-243

sounds
  adding to slides, 176-177
  playing automatically,
    177-178
  playing continuously,
    178
  transitions, 243
speaker's notes, 222-225
  adding to slides, 222-223
  notes masters, 224-225
  presentation
    conferences, 274
  sizing slides/text boxes,
    223-224
spelling checker, 86-89
  AutoCorrect, 88-89
    adding words
      (AutoCorrect dialog
      box), 88
    adding words
      (Spelling dialog
      box), 87
  checking after typing,
    86-87
  checking while typing,
    86
splitting cells, tables, 144
Standard toolbar, 24
  Apply Design button,
    200
  Black and White View
    button, 282
  Category Axis Gridlines
    button, 114
  Chart Type button, 95
  Color/Black and White
    button, 23
  Copy button, 52
    Microsoft Graph, 97
  Cut button, 25, 52
    Microsoft Graph, 97
  Format Painter button,
    65, 211
  Insert Chart button, 94
  Insert Clip Art button,
    175
  Insert Hyperlink button,
    293

Legend button (Graph), 113
New button, 12
New Slide button, 30, 122, 132
Open button, 13
Paste button, 25, 52
  Microsoft Graph, 97
Print button, 280
Save button, 14
Slide Layout button, 122
  tables, 132
Spelling button, 86
Tables and Borders button, 139
Undo button, 35
Value Axis Gridlines button, 114
View Datasheet button, 95-96
Zoom Control button, 223
starting
Microsoft Organization Chart program, 122
PowerPoint, 6-7
presentations, 6
slide shows, 230
  from any slide, 230
  Pack and Go Wizard, 237
stopping slide shows, 230-232
Style Checker, 153-155
summary (agenda) slides, 31
symbols, bullet characters, 40-41

T

Table menu commands
Cell Height and Width, 141-143
context-sensitivity, 136
Delete Cells, 135
Distribute Columns Evenly, 142
Distribute Rows Evenly, 144
Hide Gridlines, 138
Insert Columns, 136
Insert Rows, 136
Merge Cells, 144
Show Gridlines, 138
Split Cells, 144
Table AutoFormat, 139
tables, 132-133
adding, 132-133
AutoFormatting, 139-140
borders/shading, 137-139
  Tables and Borders toolbar, 139
cells, 132, 141-144
data tables (graphs), 117-118
editing, 134-136
  deleting items, 135
  inserting items, 136
  moving/copying items, 136
  selecting items, 134
  structure, see tables, structure
gridlines, 138
keyboard shortcuts, 133
navigating, 133
rotating text, 140
structure, 140-144
  column width, 141-142
  merging/splitting cells, 144
  row height, 142-144
tabbed columns, changing tabs, 65-67
templates, 6, 200
applying
  from other presentations, 217-218
  to existing presentations, 200-201
AutoLayouts, 11
color schemes, *see* color, schemes
creating, 13, 216-217
  creating presentations, 6, 10-12
slides, *see* slides, masters
Web presentations, 291-292
tests, *see* exams
text
adding to drawn objects, 151-152
  previewing, 152
aligning
  graphs, 108
  organizational charts, 127
  text boxes, 52-53, 67
anchors, aligning bulleted paragraphs, 44-45
animating, 244
boxes, 50-55
  aligning text, 52-53, 67
  creating, 50
  deleting, 51
  editing text, 52
  line spacing, 53-55
  moving, 51
  Notes Pages view, 223
  sizing, 51
editing
  spelling checking, see spelling checker
  text boxes, 52
finding/replacing, 80-82
fonts
  changing, 62-64
  color, Drawing toolbar, 65
  graphs, 108
formatting
  Formatting toolbar, 63-64
  graphs, 107-109
  organizational charts, 126-127

graphs, 107-109
importing from
Microsoft Word,
193-195
into outlines, 195
into slides, 193-194
Outline view
changing outline
levels, 24-25
entering/editing,
23-24
moving paragraphs,
25
sample text, 11
selecting, 23
Automatic Word
Selection, 24
Slide view,
entering/editing, 26
speaker's notes, *see*
speaker's notes
tables, rotating text, 140
WordArt, 55-57
three-dimensional (3-D)
charts, 114
tick marks, graph axes, 109
timings, 252-254
custom animation,
245-246
playing multimedia clips
automatically, 178
setting automatic
timings, 252-254
during rehearsal,
253-254
manually, 252-253
viewing during shows
(Slide Meter), 254
titles, changing font, 63
toolbars
Animation Effects, 247
Drawing, 148-149
Font Color button, 65
Insert WordArt
button, 55
Text Box button, 50

Formatting, 24, 63-64
Borders button, 138
Bullets button, 40
Decrease Paragraph
Spacing button, 55
Increase Paragraph
Spacing button, 55
Master, 203
Microsoft Organization
Chart Icon Bar,
123-124
Outlining, 24
Collapse All button,
74
Collapse button, 74
Demote button, 25,
43
Expand button, 74
Move Down button,
25, 74
Move Up button, 25,
74
Promote button, 25,
43
Summary Slide
button, 31
Picture, 186-187
Crop button, 169
Slide Sorter
animating text, 244
slide transitions,
242-243
Summary Slide
button, 31
Standard, 24
Apply Design button,
200
Black and White
View button, 282
Category Axis
Gridlines button,
114
Chart Type button,
95
Color/Black and
White button, 23

Copy button, 52
Copy button (Graph),
97
Cut button, 25, 52
Cut button (Graph),
97
Format Painter
button, 65, 211
Insert Chart button,
94
Insert Clip Art button,
175
Insert Hyperlink
button, 293
Legend button
(Graph), 113
New button, 12
New Slide button, 30,
122, 132
Open button, 13
Paste button, 25, 52
Paste button (Graph),
97
Print button, 280
Save button, 14
Slide Layout button,
122, 132
Spelling button, 86
Tables and Borders
button, 139
Undo button, 35
Value Axis Gridlines
button, 114
View Datasheet
button, 95-96
Zoom Control button,
223
Tables and Borders, 139
Web, 290-291
WordArt, 57
Tools menu commands
AutoCorrect, 88
Options, 24, 89
Presentation
Conference, 272, 275
Spelling, 86
Style Checker, 153

transitions, 242-243
transparencies, *see*
  overheads, printing
TrueType (TT) fonts, 62

U

Undo command (Edit
  menu), 35
    Microsoft Graph, 97
    Microsoft Organization
      Chart, 125
    uncropping pictures,
      170
ungrouping objects, 162
uploading Web
  presentations, 295
URLs (uniform resource
  locators), 292
    Web hyperlinks,
      292-293

V

View menu commands
    Black and White, 23,
      282
    Color, 23
    Datasheet (Microsoft
      Graph), 95-96
    Header and Footer, 203
    Master
        Notes Master, 224
        Slide Master, 202
    Notes Pages, 20, 222
    Outline, 20
    Ruler, 43

Slide, 20
Slide Miniature, 22
Slide Show, 20, 230
Slide Sorter, 20
Speaker Notes, 223
viewing presentations,
PowerPoint Viewer,
236-237
    see also delivering
      presentations
views, 20-21
    changing, 20-21
    slides
        *moving between,
          21-22*
        *previewing (slide
          miniature window),
          22-23*
    see also notes, Notes
      Pages view, Outline
      view, Slide view, Slide
      Sorter view

W-X-Y-Z

Web presentations, 290-293
    Animation Player, 294
    background colors, 212
    file size, 175
    hyperlinks, 292-293
    previewing, 295
    saving for Internet
      delivery, 293-295
    templates, 291-292
    uploading, 295
    Web toolbar, 290-291

wizards, 6
    AutoContent Wizard
      (creating
      presentations), 6-10
        *Web presentations,
          291-292*
    Genigraphics Wizard,
      284
        *see also service
          bureaus, printing
          presentations*
    Pack and Go Wizard,
      236-237
    Presentation Conference
      Wizard, 272
        participating, 275
        preparing, 272-274
Word
    exporting meeting
      minutes to Word, 266
    exporting outlines to
      Word, 196
    importing tables,
      132-133
    importing text from
      Word, 193-195
        into outlines, 195
        into slides, 193-194
        see also tables
WordArt, 55-57
    toolbar, 57
World Wide Web, *see* Web
  presentations
Write-Up dialog box, 196

zooming, organizational
  charts, 124

Check out Que® Books
on the World Wide Web
http://www.quecorp.com

As the biggest software release in computer history, Windows 95 continues to redefine the computer industry. Click here for the latest info on our Windows 95 books

Make computing quick and easy with these products designed exclusively for new and casual users

Examine the latest releases in word processing, spreadsheets, operating systems, and suites

The Internet, The World Wide Web, CompuServe®, America Online®, Prodigy® —it's a world of ever-changing information. Don't get left behind!

Find out about new additions to our site, new bestsellers and hot topics

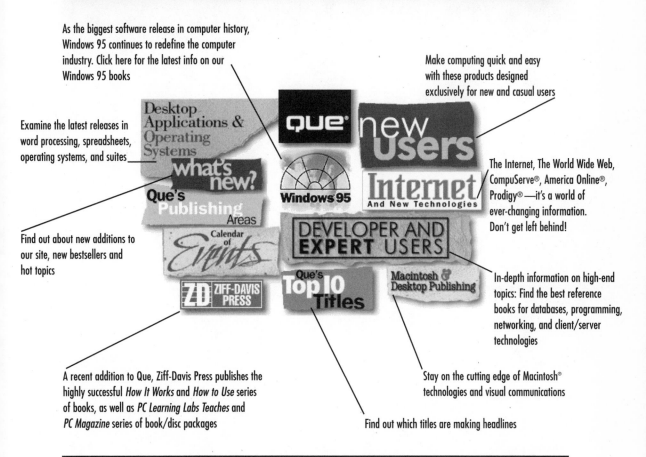

In-depth information on high-end topics: Find the best reference books for databases, programming, networking, and client/server technologies

A recent addition to Que, Ziff-Davis Press publishes the highly successful *How It Works* and *How to Use* series of books, as well as *PC Learning Labs Teaches* and *PC Magazine* series of book/disc packages

Stay on the cutting edge of Macintosh® technologies and visual communications

Find out which titles are making headlines

With six separate publishing groups, Que develops products for many specific market segments and areas of computer technology. Explore our Web site and you'll find information on best-selling titles, newly published titles, upcoming products, authors, and much more.

- Stay informed on the latest industry trends and products available

- Visit our online bookstore for the latest information and editions

- Download software from Que's library of the best shareware and freeware

Complete and Return this Card
for a *FREE* Computer Book Catalog

Thank you for purchasing this book! You have purchased a superior computer book written expressly for your needs. To continue to provide the kind of up-to-date, pertinent coverage you've come to expect from us, we need to hear from you. Please take a minute to complete and return this self-addressed, postage-paid form. In return, we'll send you a free catalog of all our computer books on topics ranging from word processing to programming and the Internet.

Mr. ☐ Mrs. ☐ Ms. ☐ Dr. ☐

Name (first) ☐☐☐☐☐☐☐☐☐☐☐☐☐☐☐☐☐☐ (M.I.) ☐ (last) ☐☐☐☐☐☐☐☐☐☐☐☐☐☐☐☐☐☐☐

Address ☐☐☐☐☐☐☐☐☐☐☐☐☐☐☐☐☐☐☐☐☐☐☐☐☐☐☐☐☐☐☐☐☐☐☐☐☐☐

☐☐☐☐☐☐☐☐☐☐☐☐☐☐☐☐☐☐☐☐☐☐☐☐☐☐☐☐☐☐☐☐☐☐☐☐☐☐

City ☐☐☐☐☐☐☐☐☐☐☐☐☐☐☐☐☐☐☐☐ State ☐☐ Zip ☐☐☐☐☐ ☐☐☐☐

Phone ☐☐☐ ☐☐☐☐☐ Fax ☐☐☐

Company Name ☐☐☐☐☐☐☐☐☐☐☐☐☐☐☐☐☐☐☐☐☐☐☐☐☐☐☐☐☐☐☐☐☐☐☐

E-mail address ☐☐☐☐☐☐☐☐☐☐☐☐☐☐☐☐☐☐☐☐☐☐☐☐☐☐☐☐☐☐☐☐☐☐☐

1. Please check at least (3) influencing factors for purchasing this book.

Front or back cover information on book .... ☐
Special approach to the content .... ☐
Completeness of content .... ☐
Author's reputation .... ☐
Publisher's reputation .... ☐
Book cover design or layout .... ☐
Index or table of contents of book .... ☐
Price of book .... ☐
Special effects, graphics, illustrations .... ☐
Other (please specify): _____ ☐

2. How did you first learn about this book?

Saw in Macmillan Computer Publishing catalog .... ☐
Recommended by store personnel .... ☐
Saw the book on bookshelf at store .... ☐
Recommended by a friend .... ☐
Received advertisement in the mail .... ☐
Saw an advertisement in: _____ ☐
Read book review in: _____ ☐
Other (please specify): _____ ☐

3. How many computer books have you purchased in the last six months?

This book only .... ☐   3 to 5 books .... ☐
books .... ☐   More than 5 .... ☐

4. Where did you purchase this book?

Bookstore .... ☐
Computer Store .... ☐
Consumer Electronics Store .... ☐
Department Store .... ☐
Office Club .... ☐
Warehouse Club .... ☐
Mail Order .... ☐
Direct from Publisher .... ☐
Internet site .... ☐
Other (please specify): _____ ☐

5. How long have you been using a computer?

☐ Less than 6 months   ☐ 6 months to a year
☐ 1 to 3 years   ☐ More than 3 years

6. What is your level of experience with personal computers and with the subject of this book?

	With PCs	With subject of book
New	☐	☐
Casual	☐	☐
Accomplished	☐	☐
Expert	☐	☐

Source Code ISBN: 0-0000-0000-0

7. Which of the following best describes your job title?

Administrative Assistant .... ☐
Coordinator .... ☐
Manager/Supervisor .... ☐
Director .... ☐
Vice President .... ☐
President/CEO/COO .... ☐
Lawyer/Doctor/Medical Professional .... ☐
Teacher/Educator/Trainer .... ☐
Engineer/Technician .... ☐
Consultant .... ☐
Not employed/Student/Retired .... ☐
Other (please specify): _____ ☐

8. Which of the following best describes the area of the company your job title falls under?

Accounting .... ☐
Engineering .... ☐
Manufacturing .... ☐
Operations .... ☐
Marketing .... ☐
Sales .... ☐
Other (please specify): _____ ☐

Comments: _____
_____
_____

9. What is your age?

Under 20 .... ☐
21-29 .... ☐
30-39 .... ☐
40-49 .... ☐
50-59 .... ☐
60-over .... ☐

10. Are you:

Male .... ☐
Female .... ☐

11. Which computer publications do you read regularly? (Please list)

_____
_____
_____
_____
_____
_____
_____
_____
_____
_____

Fold here and scotch-tape to mail

FIRST-CLASS MAIL PERMIT NO. 9918 INDIANAPOLIS IN

POSTAGE WILL BE PAID BY THE ADDRESSEE

ATTN MARKETING
MACMILLAN COMPUTER PUBLISHING
MACMILLAN PUBLISHING USA
201 W 103RD ST
INDIANAPOLIS IN 46290-9042

NO POSTAGE
NECESSARY
IF MAILED
IN THE
UNITED STATES